SAYING IT WITH SONGS

THE OXFORD MUSIC / MEDIA SERIES
Daniel Goldmark, Series Editor

oxford
music/media series

Saying It With Songs

POPULAR MUSIC AND THE COMING OF
SOUND TO HOLLYWOOD CINEMA

Katherine Spring

OXFORD
UNIVERSITY PRESS

OXFORD
UNIVERSITY PRESS

Oxford University Press is a department of the University of Oxford.
It furthers the University's objective of excellence in research, scholarship,
and education by publishing worldwide.

Oxford   New York
Auckland   Cape Town   Dar es Salaam   Hong Kong   Karachi
Kuala Lumpur   Madrid   Melbourne   Mexico City   Nairobi
New Delhi   Shanghai   Taipei   Toronto

With offices in
Argentina   Austria   Brazil   Chile   Czech Republic   France   Greece
Guatemala   Hungary   Italy   Japan   Poland   Portugal   Singapore
South Korea   Switzerland   Thailand   Turkey   Ukraine   Vietnam

Oxford is a registered trademark of Oxford University Press
in the UK and certain other countries.

Published in the United States of America by
Oxford University Press
198 Madison Avenue, New York, NY 10016

Library of Congress Cataloging-in-Publication Data
Spring, Katherine.
Saying it with songs : popular music and the coming of sound to Hollywood
cinema / Katherine Spring.
pages cm.—(The Oxford music/media series)
Includes bibliographical references and index.
ISBN 978-0-19-984221-6 (alk. paper)—ISBN 978-0-19-984222-3 (alk.
paper)   1. Motion picture music—United States—History and criticism.   2.
Popular music—United States—1921-1930—History and criticism.   I. Title.
ML2075.S74 2013
782.421640973—dc23
2013001192

This volume is published with the generous support of the AMS 75 PAYS Endowment of the American
Musicological Society, funded in part by the National Endowment for the Humanities and the Andrew W.
Mellon Foundation.

9 8 7 6 5 4 3 2 1
Printed in the United States of America
on acid-free paper

This book is dedicated to my parents,
Mary and Paul Spring,
and to the memory of Dr. Rebecca Ann Swender.

Contents

Acknowledgments

ONE INCURS INNUMERABLE debts while writing a book. My first debt is owed to my maternal grandmother, Pearl Jakobson, whose collection of 78s found their way from a basement closet to my turntable and cemented their delightful melodies in my adolescent brain. When Pearl passed away a decade later, I was a graduate student in Dr. Lea Jacobs's course on the American film industry at the University of Wisconsin-Madison. A class assignment sent me to the Wisconsin Center for Film and Theater Research, where I discovered a series of contracts and licenses pertaining to films produced by Warner Bros. and RKO during the coming of sound. Many of the song titles that were listed in those documents were instantly familiar to me, conjuring up as they did my memories of those old 78s. The roots of my doctoral dissertation, and this book, took hold.

Thinking back on the evolution of this project, I am reminded of the generosity of friends, colleagues, archivists, and other unsuspecting individuals without whom this book would not have been possible. My professors at UW-Madison were outstanding mentors whose collective influence, I hope, can be sensed throughout this work. Lea Jacobs was a brilliant advisor who asked all the right questions, offered copious suggestions for refining my argument, and persevered through multiple drafts of the thesis that became this book's manuscript. Kelley Conway, Michele Hilmes, and Susan Cook undertook careful and considerate readings of this project in its early stages, and they each helped me to sharpen my ideas. Jeff Smith's scholarship on popular music in film blazed the trail for my own study, and I am exceedingly grateful for his many valuable comments on my work. David Bordwell was a splendid "sensei" whose teachings of film history and analysis continue to serve as my guiding forces. Julie D'Acci provided critical support and buoyant spirits when both were needed badly. Still others offered advice and motivation at key moments during my undertaking of research; I think especially of Ben Brewster, Vance Kepley, Jr., J. J. Murphy, Ben Singer, and Kristin Thompson.

My peers at UW-Madison formed an exceptionally convivial and supportive community. The faithful friendship of Vincent Bohlinger has earned my enduring gratitude. He is not only a tireless correspondent with a keen editorial eye, but also a charming gardener in both Proustian and literal senses. For their especially warm friendship, as well as guidance and inspiration, I owe heartfelt thanks to Christine Becker, Maria Belodubrovskaya, Colin Burnett, Jinhee Choi, Ethan De Seife, Lisa Jasinski, Derek Johnson, Patrick Keating, James Kreul, Pearl Latteier, Charlie Michael, Caryn Murphy, Michael Newman, Liza Palmer, Tim Palmer, Paul Ramaeker, Brad Schauer, Christopher Sieving, Jim Udden, and Tom Yoshikami.

In my newer digs at Wilfrid Laurier University, I have benefited from the intellectual generosity of Sandra Annett, Jing Jing Chang, Paul Heyer, Russell Kilbourn, Madelaine Hron, Ute Lischke, Tanis MacDonald, Mariam Pirbhai, Paul Tiessen, Eleanor Ty, and Peter Urquhart. Special thanks are owed to Philippa Gates, a terrific research partner and a reliable consultant of all things Hollywood. The final stages of this project were aided by financial support received from a grant funded partly by Wilfrid Laurier University operating funds and partly by a Social Sciences and Humanities Research Council of Canada Institutional Grant awarded to Wilfrid Laurier University.

I have also benefited from gracious correspondence with many other scholars, including Rick Altman, Gillian Anderson, Lisa Coulthard, Kevin Donnelly, Charlie Keil, Ross Melnick, Jeannie Pool, and Laurel Westrup. Rob King offered expert advice on a publication that was eventually parlayed into portions of chapters 2 and 3. Rebecca Coyle, an ardent supporter of this project, passed away before she could read this book. She is sorely missed.

This book could never have been completed in the absence of film archives and their diligent staff. Maxine Ducey and Dorinda Hartmann at the Wisconsin Center for Film and Theater Research allowed me all the time that I needed to pore over licensing agreements, studio memos, and film stills. The staff of the Margaret Herrick Library, especially Barbara Hall, Linda Mehr, Jenny Romero, and Warren Sherk, made my every visit enjoyable and productive. Equally helpful were Sandra Joy Lee Aguilar and Jonathan Auxier at the Warner Bros. Archive; Mark Quigley and Todd Wiener at the UCLA Film and Television Archive; Mike Mashon and Rosemary

Hanes at the Moving Image Section of the Library of Congress Motion Picture, Broadcasting and Recorded Sound Division; and Alexandra Terziev and Caroline Yeager of George Eastman House. Mike Pogorzelski and Snowden Becker of the AMPAS Academy Film Archive and Schawn Belston of 20th Century Fox indulged me with their vast knowledge, resources, and gifts of humor. Last but certainly not least, I thank the creators and sustainers of the Media History Digital Library.

Shortly after my dissertation was completed, I had the good fortune of attracting the attention of acquisitions editor Norm Hirschy of Oxford University Press and also Oxford Music/Media Series editor Daniel Goldmark. I have profited immensely from Norm's steadfast support and faithful nurturing of this project as he ushered it gracefully toward completion. Daniel lent this project his first-rate editorial talents just as he lent me the assurance that I needed to get this book off the ground. I owe much as well to Kate Nunn, Lisbeth Redfield, and the manuscript reviewers for Oxford whose detailed comments not only helped me to clarify my ideas but also gave me the fortitude to address the questions that they brought to my attention. I doubt there are any research assistants more fastidious than Maggie Clark, whose most conspicuous—but hardly singular—contribution can be seen in chapter 2. Eric Hoyt, Katherine Quanz, Brian Real, and Darren Watt also graciously came to my aid on short notice.

I owe a personal thanks to my parents, Mary and Paul Spring, who created a childhood for me that was saturated with love and music. My eldest brother Daniel volunteered his expert cartographic skills in a pinch. My uncle John Jakobson could always be counted on for his unwavering support and reassuring spirit, not to mention his encyclopedic knowledge of studio-era Hollywood stars.

My largest debts of gratitude are owed to the family members who have lived closest to this book for several years. My partner, Leah Neumann, has redefined for me the terms of inexhaustible love and boundless patience; my gratitude and appreciation for her are equally abundant. As a result of my work, Leah and our daughter, Eliana, suffered daily impositions even while they provided a refuge for me at home. I owe at least a beach vacation.

I have dedicated this book to my parents, for their continuing encouragement in matters great and small, and the memory of Rebecca Swender, a very dear friend and colleague who passed away on June 14, 2008. In addition to being the wittiest person whom I have ever known, Becca was a brilliant and rigorous scholar whose insights into American film history and sound left an indelible impact on this book in its earliest stages. I miss her critical acuity almost as much I miss her tendency to spontaneously burst into song numbers that she drew from her encyclopedic knowledge of Broadway and Hollywood musicals. I like to imagine her with this book in hand, singing her way through some of the pages that follow.

SAYING IT WITH SONGS

(I'm) going to jazz up the story, stick in a few hot numbers, and call it "Mammy X"!
DOROTHY PARKER TO JAMES GLEASON, on her role as a dialogue writer for the
melodrama *Madame X* (1929)[1]

Introduction

FEW FILMS BETTER demonstrate how thoroughly popular music had permeated
American cinema during the transition to sound than *A Hollywood Theme Song*. The
two-reeler produced by famed comedian Mack Sennett and released in December
1930 incorporates ten music cues into its 21-minute plot about a young man who
leaves his hometown to serve in World War I. In the opening scene, Clarence (Harry
Gribbon) bids adieu by singing two numbers, one of which, titled "My Estelle," he
directs to his sweetheart of the same name. Later, Estelle inexplicably appears on
the German battlefield and delivers a message from Clarence's mother, to which the
soldier responds by executing the hallmark move of Al Jolson, dropping to one knee
and breaking into the blackface singer's signature hit, "My Mammy." Clarence is subsequently dispatched as a spy, and he encounters an enemy agent whose seductive
advances he resists while strains of "My Estelle" can be heard in the background.
Soon captured by German soldiers, Clarence escapes while singing "The Flag I Love,"
this time backed by a three-piece orchestra of a cornet player, violinist, and bass violinist that has suddenly materialized on the German landscape. The film ends with
another allusion to Jolson's blackface routine, this time thanks to mud from the
battlefield that flies up into Clarence's face as he sings again in genuflection. By this
time, the comedy of *A Hollywood Theme Song* is without doubt trading on audience
recognition of the conventions of song use in early sound cinema.[2]

The fact that audiences could be counted on to appreciate this two-reeler's musical moments of parody is not so much surprising as it is a reminder of the cultural
relevance and aesthetic significance of popular songs during Hollywood's transition
to sound, a period demarcated by the years 1927 through 1931.[3] *Saying It With Songs*
is a study of those songs and the ways in which they were used in the service of two
cornerstones of classical Hollywood cinema: commerce and storytelling. On one

hand, the conversion to synchronized sound filmmaking undertaken by the fully integrated major studios—Fox, Loew's/MGM, Paramount, RKO, and Warner Bros.—made possible the onscreen vocal performances of singing stars at a time when live presentations were key platforms for launching popular music. (As Harry Warner reportedly said on the cusp of his studio's transition to sound, "Who the hell wants to hear actors talk? The music—that's the big plus about this."[4]) Sound cinema brought new commercial appeal to the film medium by introducing new songs to mass audiences, and it rivaled radio, Broadway, and the vaudeville stage as the country's most important platform for popular music. At the same time, as composer Miklós Rózsa later recalled, the spectacle of song performances inserted into films came to be seen as a threat to the established norms of narrative linearity and coherence that had stabilized in the late silent cinema. "The first sound pictures," Rózsa complained in 1948, "were just picturized operettas and theater accompaniment by canned music. For a while, pictures even lost their aesthetic integrity of the silent era. Song 'hits' predominated, and stories and action were subordinated to those songs. Film composers degenerated into songwriters."[5]

Although the economic incentive to showcase popular songs seemed at odds with classical Hollywood cinema's drive for narrative coherence, an investigation of the aesthetic practices that arose from the tension ushered in by popular songs can shed light on a rich and formative period of film music in American cinema. Indeed, if, as the authors of a recent textbook on film music put it, "popular music was at first *the* music of the sound film," and this was true in genres other than the film musical, then what was the impact of popular songs on the narrative form of early sound cinema?[6] Conversely, what changes, if any, did the demands of narrative filmmaking effect on the composition of popular music? Riffing off the title of *Say It With Songs* (1929), a melodrama in which Al Jolson plays a radio star who sings his way through professional and familial misfortunes, we can ask: What were early American sound films "saying with songs"?

The novelty of onscreen song performances by celebrities—Donald Crafton has dubbed the practice "virtual Broadway"—might explain why, when it comes to accounting for the early sound period, many histories of film music highlight adaptations of Broadway musical comedies, revues, and operettas, in addition to the nascent genre of the backstage musical.[7] There can be no doubting the significance of musical films, which in the 1929–1930 season, performed strongly at the box office and advanced the careers of numerous stars. However, a focus on Broadway adaptations and their derivatives forecloses a study of the many other kinds of films that contained popular songs of narrative and commercial import. Songs figured prominently in genres as wide-ranging as romantic comedies, Westerns, detective dramas, prison dramas, melodramas, and action-adventure films. A survey of entries in the

American Film Institute Catalog reveals that at least one song appeared in more than a third of all sound films produced by the major studios during the 1928–1929 season, and that this proportion increased to more than half during the 1929–1930 season.[8] Although the catalog entries disclose neither the frequency nor the function of songs in any individual movie, these figures nonetheless point up the remarkable extent to which early sound films were imbued with songs.

The industry's enthusiasm for motion picture songs was equally evident in the music-related discourse that emerged in contemporaneous trade papers. The weekly paper *Hollywood Filmograph* began in 1929 to publish "Movietunes," which over the course of the next two years became "Along Music Row," "Sharps and Flats," "Tuneful Talker Tunes," "Chit-Chat an' Chatter About Song–Music–Voice–Dance," and "Lyrics and Music"—all of which covered stories about songs in films and songwriters in Hollywood. *Exhibitors Herald-World* featured Sid Berman's "Sid Says About Songs," which turned into "Up and Down the [Tin Pan] Alley," "Theme Songs," and "Hollywood Tunes." *Motion Picture News* introduced "Melody Makers" as a means of accounting for the activities of composers and lyricists who had been hired to work on studio lots. *Variety* and *Billboard*, whose readerships were broader than those of the film trade publications, continued to devote print to the subject of film music, and articles on motion picture songs occasionally graced the pages of widely circulated popular magazines, including *Time* and *Vanity Fair*.[9] The appearance of these articles and columns is symptomatic of an extraordinary period of song use in Hollywood film history.

Nonetheless, the transitional years occupy a surprisingly small proportion of the recent proliferation of scholarship on popular music in film.[10] A grievance such as Rózsa's may explain why; given the sheer quantity of songs that were present in early sound films, it may be tempting to dismiss them as gratuitous or superfluous devices endemic to a profit-driven industry that aimed solely to capitalize on the novelty of filmed star performances—a way of bringing "virtual Broadway" to mass audiences.[11] But there are two reasons why adopting such an attitude from our contemporary perspective is myopic.

The first reason has to do with the history of media convergence. The profusion of motion picture songs points to a watershed period of transformation in the corporate landscape of American mass entertainment. As Kathryn Kalinak has observed, the advent of the synchronized soundtrack shifted the burden of musical accompaniment from the theater exhibitor, who employed theater musicians and maintained libraries of copyrighted music, to the film producer, who became responsible for licensing the rights to use copyrighted songs on synchronized soundtracks.[12] In order to evade licensing fees, motion picture companies affiliated themselves with or acquired majority stock in large music publishing firms with headquarters located in

New York, which was then considered the music capital of the country. Studio executives created music departments, lured songwriters from New York, and developed
cross-promotional strategies to sell films and music. The unprecedented attention
afforded to the creation and circulation of motion picture songs, as well as the shift
of a significant segment of the song industry to Los Angeles, marked a critical turning point in the country's media landscape and permanently altered the relationship
between its film and music industries.

A second reason to examine the allegedly superfluous presence of songs in early
sound films is that doing so recasts the problems lamented by Rózsa as windows
into an exciting period of heterogeneity in film form and style. Rózsa suggested that
popular songs in early sound films posed a double-pronged threat, insofar as they
challenged norms of classical narrative integration (which emphasize the subordination of style to principles of storytelling) as well as norms of orchestral symphonic
accompaniment germane to late silent films. But these same challenges gave rise to
an inventive period of song use in which filmmakers and music directors tested the
efficacy of songs in the contexts of narrative form, marketing campaigns, and star
performances. Songs were presented in instrumental and vocal renditions. They
appeared as both diegetic and non-diegetic elements of soundtracks. They featured
prominently in studio advertisements. In short, they were integrated into motion
picture plots in various ways, sometimes satisfying the self-effacing style of classical cinema and at other times straining the norms of diegetic plausibility. While
some of these practices diminished, others would endure for decades.[13] Therefore,
rather than view the practices engendered during the transitional era as somehow
detrimental to norms of narrative coherence and musical aesthetics, or as irrelevant
except as cautionary tales paving the way for the kind of film music that would follow, it is worth investigating the extraordinary range of song use that characterized
the transitional era in and of itself.

Such an investigation pays heed to the reminder issued some 35 years ago by
Robert C. Allen, who argued that the history of American cinema cannot be isolated
from the histories of media and entertainment.[14] And yet, scholarly work on the
concentrated ownership of media tends to emphasize the late 20th century, a period
of high-profile mergers and acquisitions among entertainment corporations.[15] It is
easy to recall Walt Disney Co.'s purchase of Miramax Films and ABC in 1993 and
1995, respectively, and Time-Warner's merger with AOL to the appalling tune of
$183 billion—mergers that are distinctive insofar as they entail the convergence of
multiple technologies and massive financial sums, but perhaps there is greater historical continuity between them and the 1920s than we have acknowledged. Corey
K. Creekmur's diagnosis of the soundtrack of the 1990s as "a multidirectional marketing tool [that] serves simultaneously as a preview, tie-in, and supplement" applies

equally well to a given piece of sheet music or phonograph record that was produced in conjunction with a motion picture of the late 1920s.[16] Despite a surge of scholarly interest in the business of American popular music of the early 20th century, the influence of business practices on the form and style of early sound cinema remains largely overlooked.[17]

Three exceptions deserve special mention. The first is Jeff Smith's *The Sounds of Commerce: Marketing Popular Film Music*, a seminal history that concentrates on the institutional contexts that sustained the emergence and evolution of motion picture "pop scores" from the 1950s through the 1990s.[18] In showing how the musical features of popular songs were particular well-suited to the commercial and dramatic demands of narrative cinema, Smith has provided an invaluable model for *Saying It With Songs*, which investigates an earlier but equally influential period in the history of motion picture songs. The other two exceptions are Steve Wurtzler's superb book on the interaction of sound technologies of the 1920s and 1930s and Ross Melnick's monumental study of impresario Samuel "Roxy" Rothafel—both exhaustive and reliable accounts of media convergence in the United States of the early 20th century.[19] Like them, *Saying It With Songs* seeks to shed light on a vital period of American media convergence, although its scope is (for better or worse) tighter in that it is concerned primarily with one strain of industrial convergence— that of film and music publishing—and zeroes in on the consequences of this convergence for narrative film form and style.

NON-MUSICAL GENRES

As this book is a study of films belonging to non-musical genres, the first question that needs to be addressed is, What is meant by the label "non-musical"? Most definitions of the film musical propose what Patrick Keating has called an "alternation model" of narrative, in which linear narrative passages are interspersed with seemingly nonlinear moments of spectacle—namely, song numbers—that encourage spectators to "focus on the present" rather than to speculate about subsequent narrative events.[20] The following excerpts derive from three seminal works on the American film musical, and they reveal a common definition based on the opposition of narrative and number:

- Only within a narrative framework does the musical number become the timeless interlude, the brake, indeed the break that eventually sets up a signifying relationship between narrative flow and musical stasis.
- In variety, the essential contradiction is between comedy and music turns; in musicals, it is between the narrative and the numbers.

- Musicals are built upon a foundation of dual registers with the contrast between narrative and number defining musical comedy as a form. The dichotomous manner in which the story is told—now spoken, now sung— is a very different mode of presentation from the single thread of the usual Hollywood movie.[21]

But film musicals produced during Hollywood's transition to sound complicate the neatness of the alternation model because the musical genre, then in its nascent years, was characterized by considerable heterogeneity.[22] Indeed, the frequency with which songs appeared in early sound films muddied the distinction between musical and non-musical categories altogether. As Crafton has written, "Around 1929–1930, it was the rare movie that was *not* a musical in some sense of the term," because most films included a theme song (a song that recurs over the course of an individual narrative), and when not packaged as a theme song, popular music still often appeared in the form of incidental (one-off) performances or as background music.[23]

Despite the impossibility of establishing a Platonic ideal of the musical genre against which non-musical films may be contrasted, neither must we accept that the two categories were entirely indiscernible from one another. For one, industry discourse suggests that at least loose distinctions were made. By mid-1929, film reviews published in contemporaneous trade papers, including *Film Daily*, *Variety*, *Motion Picture News*, and *The Motion Picture Almanac*, tended to distinguish film musicals by affixing the phrase "with songs" to established genre labels (as in "comedy-drama with songs") or, in the case of Broadway adaptations and spin-offs, by applying one of three names derived from the stage: operetta, musical comedy, and revue. For example, *The Desert Song* (1929), which was based on a stage operetta that played in New York from 1926 through 1928, was labeled an operetta, and *Fox Movietone Follies* (1929), the title of which evoked contemporaneous productions of the *Ziegfeld Follies* on Broadway, was described as a "revue in celluloid form."[24] In contrast, films that included songs but were neither Broadway adaptations nor backstage musicals were rarely referred to as musicals. *Coquette*, *Thru Different Eyes*, and *Weary River* (all made in 1929) were, respectively, a "drama of the south," a "murder mystery," and an "underworld drama." Even *Say It With Songs* and *Painted Angel* (1929), each of which contained several song numbers, were described by *Film Daily* as a "comedy drama" and a "drama of night club life."[25] Films that later became known as backstage musicals—films with theatrical settings that gave plausible diegetic motivation for the presence of songs—were usually, but not always, identified with familiar labels. *Broadway Babies* (1929) was called a comedy drama in *Film Daily* but a musical comedy in an aside in *Variety*.[26] *The Broadway Melody*, endorsed by many scholars as the first bona fide film musical was, for a *Film Daily* reviewer, a "comedy drama of Broadway show life."[27] *Close Harmony* (1929) was described by one paper as a "comedy drama confined to the wings and stage of a de luxe picture and presentation theater" and by a different paper as "another in the back-stage chain." An advertisement taken out by Paramount in *Film Daily* termed the film a "revue-romance."[28]

Differences between musicals and non-musicals can also be detected at the level of film form. Film adaptations and their close derivatives seem to have justified disruptions of narrative linearity by counting on audience familiarity with the conventions of musical theater. It is reasonable to presume, for example, that audiences of *Good News*, a 1930 film rendition of the hit musical comedy that played on Broadway from September 1927 through January 1929, would have expected the characters in the film to burst into song and dance, just as attendees of a screening of *Hollywood Revue of 1929* would have anticipated a resemblance between that film's structure and that of a standard 1920s stage revue, a format known for stringing together a series of unrelated musical, comic, and dramatic sketches as a means of showcasing numerous talents.

By contrast, non-musical films contained fewer songs than musicals, and they tended to showcase, motivate, and integrate songs in ways that could not always be explained by appealing to the conventions of stage musical genres. Rather, songs in non-musicals usually appeared in accordance with the conventions of the dominating genre. For example, the plot of *Weary River* (1929), a film branded by the trades as a melodrama, gangster movie, and underworld drama (all commonplace genre descriptors of silent movies), motivates multiple song presentations through the musical talents of its protagonist, a criminal-turned-musician.[29] Throughout the film, songs serve as narrative devices that enable the protagonist to earn early parole, redeem his public reputation, and regain the trust of an old flame. In other words, the songs are incorporated as semantic elements of the early crime/gangster genre, and they are integrated in a manner consonant with the syntax of the redemptive crime plot. Moreover, although *Weary River* includes five instances of song performance, they are repeat presentations; only two distinct numbers, "It's Up to You" and "Weary River," make up the musical soundtrack. We can contrast these with the songs found in *The Broadway Melody* (1929), which follows two sisters enlisted to perform their vaudeville act in a stage revue. The film might well be described as a comedy whose songs are motivated by the syntax of that genre, just as songs in *Weary River* are said to be motivated by the syntax of the crime/gangster genre, but the quantity of songs included in *The Broadway Melody* (there are seven) in addition to the fact that they do not always function to propel the narrative but rather serve as nonlinear attractions, endows *The Broadway Melody* with the status of a musical. *Weary River* belongs to that genre only by a great stretch of the musical's practical definition in trade papers at the time of the film's release.

THE NARRATIVE INTEGRATION OF SONGS

Given that non-musical films did not necessarily appeal to audience expectations as a means of justifying the intrusion of song numbers, a variety of strategies for incorporating songs developed over the course of the transitional period. Many of the earliest synchronized sound films attempted to emulate the form of *The Jazz Singer*, a melodrama whose song performances are at once warranted by virtue of the preoccupations of the film's central characters (a cantor and his Broadway-bound son) and presented as modular attractions that flaunt the spectacle of singing stars, particularly Al Jolson. The practice of positioning songs as discrete entities within narrative contexts was inherited from Broadway stages, where musical revues, comedies, and operettas associated particular songs with celebrities and other forms of spectacle.

At the same time, filmmakers and producers aimed to harness songs to classical narrative forms. The importance of song motivation was summarized by composer Max Steiner when he recalled:

> Music for dramatic pictures was only used when it was actually required by the script. A constant fear prevailed among producers, directors, and musicians that they would be asked: Where does the music come from? Therefore they never used music unless it could be explained by the presence of a source like an orchestra, piano player, phonograph or radio, which was specified in the script.[30]

Irene Kahn Atkins—music editor, film music historian, and daughter of famed lyricist Gus Kahn—concurred, writing, "When an excuse for music was needed, someone was seen turning on a phonograph, putting the needle on the record, and listening as the appropriate song or instrumental was heard on the soundtrack."[31] Although these quotes may be overstating the case, for not every instance of music in early sound films was given an onscreen or diegetic source, they highlight the fact that the justification for the presence of songs within narrative contexts was an aesthetic priority during the onset of sound.

But Steiner's account is intriguing for another reason. Because the aural presence of music in a film demanded the onscreen disclosure of that music's diegetic source, the plot of a film had to be orchestrated around such a disclosure. Seen in this way, Steiner's recollection that studio personnel "never used music unless it could be explained by the presence of a source like an orchestra, piano player, phonograph or radio" puts the cart before the horse. There was, after all, great incentive to use music; it sold films, as well as related commodities like sheet music (from which most major companies had by then found ways to profit directly). But how could a plot supply a pretext for music that at the same time maintained norms of narrative plausibility? Even the coordination of editing around a musical moment—say, by cutting to a shot of a character turning on a phonograph for no reason other than to reveal the source of subsequent background music—could weaken the formal unity deemed central to the system of classical storytelling.

One upshot of the tension generated by competing commercial and narrative demands was that producers, directors, and screenwriters experimented with methods of incorporating songs in narratively plausible ways. Some plots centered on characters of musicians and singers, whereas others provided elaborate narrative setups for the presentation of songs. By mid-1930, however, many of the experiments were deemed failures, inasmuch as they were seen to strain the limits of narrative coherence and diegetic verisimilitude. An increasing number of reports in the trade papers and fan magazines cast motion picture songs as irritatingly conspicuous components of otherwise unified plots, and, by the end of the year, few non-musical films contained songs performed in their entire duration. In their place were soundtracks that manifested scoring practices that would come to characterize the classical Hollywood cinema of subsequent years. These practices included the diminished use of songs, the increased use of orchestral music, and, in general, sonic techniques designed to maximize spectatorial engagement with diegetic fiction. Although the scoring practices associated with classical Hollywood cinema did not stabilize until around 1933, the curtailed use of songs as isolated entities, or as overtly motivated performances, suggests that motion picture songs, like other elements of style in the classical Hollywood cinema, were ultimately deemed acceptable outside of the musical only when they were integrated in ways that maintained classical narrative norms.

In this way, the early history of the motion picture song over the course of the transitional period—from isolated attraction to integrated narrative device—is evidence of the dominant narrative drive of the classical Hollywood cinema. The "classical model," as Keating has named it in reference to Bordwell, Staiger, and Thompson, contends that character-centered causality, rather than spectacle or affect, is the "armature of the classical story."[32] Numerous scholars have criticized this model on the grounds that so-called classical films are actually less linear and unified, and more heavily driven by spectacular effects and emotional charges, than the classical model allows.[33] From this latter perspective, song performances that disturb an otherwise logical, causal sequence of narrative events in transition-era films would instead be evidence of a classical cinema that equates the value of linear narrative with that of spectacular attractions and emotional effect, or even diminishes the former in favor of the latter.[34]

Yet, the formal devices through which songs were showcased in non-musical films of the transitional era were ultimately bounded by classical norms of causality and coherence. Such an observation does not devalue the formal and stylistic heterogeneity that characterized films of the transitional period; on the contrary, it encourages our magnification of the period so that we may consider the challenges posed by songs to norms of classical narrative outside the genre of the musical. Posing the question as a matter of the degree to which songs were constrained by those norms highlights the considerable range and inventiveness in a period of film music deserving examination in its own right.

CHAPTER ORGANIZATION

The two parts that make up this book are intended to reflect a central argument: Changes to the relationship between the film and music industries in the late 1920s influenced the form of Hollywood's earliest sound films. The first part focuses on the institutional interactions between major motion picture studios and music publishing companies. Chapter 1 sets the stage for the studios' investments in music publishing by accounting for the culture and conventions of popular songs of the 1920s, a decade often described as an apex of American popular music. The efficacies of Tin Pan Alley, the name given to the mainstream music industry located in Manhattan, generated multiple song hits that were cross-promoted through sheet music, phonograph records, radio broadcasts, and live stage performances. The most successful song hits belonged to the genre of the popular ballad, the musical conventions of which suited what Rick Altman has called a "thematic approach" to musical accompaniment.[35] By the time Hollywood's major studios prepared to convert to sound, studio producers and music publishers perceived songs released in conjunction with motion pictures as vital commercial products. Although early sound films drew on multiple genres of songs, theme songs were almost invariably popular ballads.

Chapter 2 details the institutional and legal relationships between motion picture studios and music publishing firms from 1928 through early 1930, during which time Hollywood's major studios acquired or affiliated with music publishing firms and hired songwriters from the East Coast. The studios' investments in the business of song publishing were motivated by factors that can be traced to the 1910s, when the country's largest music publishing companies, located in Tin Pan Alley, organized into powerful combines with the intent of licensing the rights to perform copyrighted music. On the cusp of the conversion to sound, studio executives regarded song copyright ownership as a means of both maintaining control over soundtrack content and freeing exhibitors from a theater-seat tax imposed by the music combines. Their investments in the creation and distribution of popular songs bifurcated the mainstream song industry into two hubs located on opposite coasts: New York and Los Angeles.

The book's second part describes three strategies for song use that arose during the transitional period: *star-song attraction, strained integration*, and *plausible integration. Star-song attraction*, the primary subject of chapter 3, was typical of the earliest sound films, which tended to adapt Broadway's propensity for championing the discrete presentation of songs over norms of narrative flow and continuity. Through the 1910s and 1920s, vaudeville and Broadway shows featured star vocalists who presented songs as accentuated, discrete moments of performance even within narrative contexts; moreover, their repeated presentations across a given show resulted in the vocalists becoming associated with particular songs. Star-song identification could be found in many early sound films whose narratives were engineered in ways to highlight distinct, modular units of song performance. The success of star-song identification was also bolstered by cross-promotion, whereby motion picture songs were marketed via sheet music, phonograph records, and radio at the same time that the songs attracted consumers to theaters. Evidence of these practices, found in contemporaneous trade press reports, studio advertisements, and other sources from the period, is corroborated by the analysis of two films, *Applause* (1929) and *Weary River* (1929), each of which narrativizes and capitalizes on the cachet of its singing star.

However, even as songs disrupted narrative continuity for the sake of foregrounding star-song performances, they also served a range of narrative and thematic functions. Chapter 4 begins by differentiating the functions of theme songs and incidental songs, and goes on to show how some non-musical films motivated star-song performances in narratively cumbersome ways. Case studies of *strained integration* in Amos 'n' Andy's first feature film, *Check and Double Check* (1930), and the Joan Crawford vehicle, *Possessed* (1931), demonstrate how film plotting was taken to considerable lengths in order to justify and integrate star-song performances within plausible contexts. In the end, however, songs integrated through such narratively awkward means were ultimately disruptive of classical norms, because the ways in which they were motivated called attention to the construction of narrative.

The practice of strained integration occurred when the performances of popular songs were justified in ways that seemed improbable by the standards of classical storytelling, and thus unintentionally drew attention to narrative construction. These instances can be distinguished from *plausible integration*, which was the favored approach toward the end of the transitional era and which has endured in non-musical films up to today. Chapter 5 accounts for the development of plausible integration in tandem with the diminished use of the popular song and the rise of the orchestral background film score. After examining debates in the trade press over the perceived problem posed by the motion picture song, the chapter recounts the studios' employment of in-house composers who attempted to cultivate a musical aesthetic based on the Romantic traditions of orchestral scoring. Analyses of a Western, *In Old Arizona* (1929), and a melodrama, *Safe in Hell* (1931), illustrate some of the practices enacted for plausible song incorporation. These analyses also reveal the use of intermittent scoring that is typically associated with the classical Hollywood film score in subsequent years, as is discussed in the book's conclusion.

Hollywood's transition to sound capped a quarter century of tremendous growth among the country's industries of popular entertainment. From the late 1890s onward, cinema developed from an itinerant and ancillary amusement to a financially and aesthetically stable enterprise; national radio broadcasting networks were created out of powerful interests in electrical power and communication; and popular music was distributed to the burgeoning population by way of new forms of technology and marketing. By the time most motion picture theaters had been wired for synchronized sound films in 1929, the landscape of America's popular amusements had undergone significant changes. One would be remiss in assuming, however, that after such a period of transformation, there could be no significant changes to come in a mere few years. Rather, quite the opposite may be seen, as the form and fate of the film song throughout Hollywood's transition to sound from 1927–1931 showcases remarkable experimentation in business and narrative practices alike. The fact that narrative cohesion ultimately won out over the discrete, disruptive song number is not to suggest that the era failed aesthetically, but that it contained a remarkably exploratory impulse around the potentialities of sound—one fostered by screenwriters, songwriters, producers, and entire institutions.

PART ONE
A Context for Convergence

This great audience for Popular Music prefers its musical tastes in lighter, sentimental or dance-appealing form; Brahms and Chopin and Wagner and Rimsky-Korsakoff [*sic*] they are frank enough to disown and leave for the intellectual minority.

PAUL WHITEMAN (1927)[1]

Theme and hit songs of the pictures seem to be without exception of ballad nature. [They] are not "Hotsy, Totsy," "You Gotta See Mamma Every Night" songs. They are instead sentimental in nature.

MURIEL BABCOCK (1928)[2]

1

Singing a Song

THE CULTURE AND CONVENTIONS OF POPULAR MUSIC IN THE 1920S

THE STANDARD STORY of how popular songs entered into Hollywood sound cinema begins in the early 20th century and on the other side of the country, in New York City.[3] It is a tale as colorful as it is apocryphal, and it starts in the dingy offices of the brownstone buildings that line two blocks of Manhattan's West 28th Street. There, fledgling songwriters hammer out tunes on cheap, upright pianos under the eyes of upstart publishers who care only to transform the songs into bankable commodities for the public. Walking on the sidewalks below, where it seems impossible to evade the cacophonic noises of clanging pianos—the "tin pans"—a journalist dubs the region Tin Pan Alley, and the name sticks.[4] The Alley comes to represent the constellation of publishers, promoters, composers, and lyricists whose offices are like factories, churning out musical products—sentimental ballads, patriotic marches, lilting waltzes—that are, as one observer later puts it, "as evanescent as the encircling smoke in which they are ground out," their solitary goal being to appeal to mass taste and then to disappear and make room for the next equally ephemeral tune.⁵ But, the story goes, from this assembly line dedicated to the bottom line emerge a handful of individuals endowed with innate creativity and a gift for infusing popular songs with idioms belonging to genres considered more respectable—namely, classical music and "jazz," the latter a fluid descriptor that signals rhythmic and harmonic innovation, as well as an increasing eradication of its roots in African American music. These "Great Innovators" and "Great Craftsmen," as one music historian would later call them, rise above the commercial demands of their profession and deliver a host of songs that define the so-called Golden Age of American popular music.⁶

With its hagiographic conception of intrinsically artistic prodigies who overcame a ruthlessly commercial industry and whose works refracted some quintessential American sentiment, the standard account of Tin Pan Alley may sound historically naïve to present readers. However, its emphasis on the commercial motivations of the Alley is astute. As music historians David Suisman and Daniel Goldmark have recently shown, song hits produced by the popular music industry in the early 20th century did not reflect public demand so much as they actively *created* that demand, thanks primarily to aggressive advertising techniques.⁷ Suisman puts it succinctly: "The primary motivation for writing a song was to sell it, not to express some inherently human feeling or musical impulse."⁸ Companies along the Alley applied modern advertising strategies to their business practices, which influenced everything from job titles (including the invention of a new kind of employee, the song plugger) right down to the physical design of sheet music. And because the order of the day was factory-like standardization, most publishers aimed for lowest common denominators: songs with melodies that could easily be sung and played on the piano and that had platitudinous lyrics. Even songwriters themselves tolerated if not embraced the Alley's commercial imperative. When Irving Caesar, best known as the lyricist for "Tea for Two," was asked the tiresome question, "What comes first, the words or the music?" he retorted, "The contract comes first!"⁹ The profit motives of the industry paid off by the 1920s, a decade that is said to have generated most of the best-selling songs in the Alley's history.¹⁰

Still, we must be careful not to privilege the industry's overly formulaic approach at the expense of examining the norms of craft that would go on to shape the form and function of music in Hollywood's earliest sound films. Whether disparaged as ephemera or valorized as products of great artists who resuscitated popular music for mass culture, songs of the 1920s became bankable commodities whose musical features were exploited to suit the narrative functions of an established classical cinema. This is not to argue that the success of Tin Pan Alley in the 1920s was a necessary precursor to the emergence of Hollywood sound cinema, but rather to suggest that the commercial and aesthetic norms of an established musical landscape were proximate and concrete influences on songwriters who worked at the studios during the transition to sound. If, in any art, "form tends to follow format, and format is often shaped by business pressures," our understanding of how songs were assimilated by Hollywood cinema demands a consideration of those pressures and forms.[11]

Just as the "gravity-like pull" of popular songs stimulated their incorporation into musical accompaniment to silent cinema during the first quarter of the century, songs of the 1920s (both for their commercial value and musical attributes) appealed to producers and filmmakers of early sound films.[12] To appreciate the early convergence of Hollywood and Tin Pan Alley as a story of two mature entertainment industries that by the 1920s had balanced commercial aspirations with artistic ones, we must therefore look more closely at various aspects of the songs produced by Alley publishers: how they were distributed and promoted, what musical forms they adopted, and the extent to which they were incorporated into accompaniment practices for silent cinema. In this context, we can better understand how and why songs became constituent components of early sound cinema.

THREE-PRONGED PROMOTION: SHEET MUSIC, RECORDS, AND RADIO

Before the 1880s, most American music publishers issued catalogs that comprised a wide variety of song genres, ranging from solo piano pieces to chamber music scores. But the young, entrepreneurial publishers who established offices in Manhattan discovered that quicker profits could be made through the production and distribution of individual songs. Although they did not eschew traditional music altogether, these publishers focused on the commercial potential of the popular song, which they conceived of not just as a manufactured product but also as a commodity subject to contemporaneous norms of salesmanship, promotion, and mass marketing.

The notion of song-as-commodity resonated with turn-of-the-century business practices, which emphasized the creation of market demand by actively familiarizing consumers with products.[13] Mass demand for popular songs did not arise spontaneously; it was created through the implementation of careful marketing strategies. "Hits did not 'just happen,'" Suisman reminds us, continuing, "They were not essential, irrepressible expressions of the Zeitgeist. Hits were *made*. Indeed, in the music industry's slang, to 'make' a song referred not to songwriting but to building a song's popularity."[14] Successful publishers devised aggressive sales techniques, and they hired song pluggers to carry them out. Many pluggers were trained salespeople, but more typically they were songwriters and musicians who were capable of applying their talents to advertising and disseminating hit songs. (Jerome Kern and Irving Berlin entered the music business as adolescent pluggers in the early 1900s.) In his oft-cited and lively history of the Alley, journalist Isaac Goldberg submitted this amusing definition of the plugger:

> The Plugger is one of the darlings of Tin Pan Alley. He is a man of many aspects with the eyes of Argus and the arms of a Hindu image—a composite photograph of anybody and everybody who can help in establishing a song in the public favor.... He it is who, by all the arts of persuasion, intrigue, bribery, mayhem, malfeasance, cajolery, entreaty, threat, insinuation, persistence and whatever else he has, sees to it that his employer's music shall be heard.... The plugger extraordinary...can "make" a bad song—he has done it time and again—and without him the best of songs may remain unmade.[15]

Despite its hyperbole, Goldberg's account highlights what was considered the cardinal rule of song plugging: The greater a hit's circulation by performance, the greater its sales of sheet music and phonograph records. In order to "put over" a song, early pluggers armed themselves with stacks of printed sheet music and descended from publishers' offices to the city streets, where they arranged to have a song sung, whistled, and hummed in every space that could tolerate the sound of a human voice. They gave live demonstrations of songs inside department stores and outside theaters. They printed photographs of celebrity vocalists on sheet music covers in exchange for the promise of song performances by those vocalists in live venues. They planted singers in theater audiences to perform new material. They paid for the incorporation of popular numbers in coin-operated pianos that were installed in bars, saloons, and restaurants across the country. And, most notoriously, they arranged pay-for-play deals with singers and arrangers in order to showcase new material.[16]

This last strategy, which would later come to be known as payola, was considered the most lucrative. Songwriter Charles K. Harris, whose watershed hit "After the Ball" reportedly sold more than five million copies of sheet music in the 1890s and is often credited as the first truly national hit song, underlined the importance of selling songs to performers. "If [a song] strikes their fancy," Harris wrote in his 1926 autobiography, "they will surely sing it for the public. Common sense tells one that the bigger the reputation and ability of the performer whose assistance the author and composer enlists, the more chances of its success in catching the public's favor.... A new song must be sung, played, hummed, and drummed into the ears of the public, not in one city alone, but in every city, town, and village, before it ever becomes popular."[17] Harris's advice echoes the recollections of celebrated plugger, lyricist, and publisher Edward B. Marks, who allegedly made the rounds to 60 venues each week in order to distribute vocal arrangements to singers and instrumental arrangements to bands.[18]

Although the live performance of songs was considered the sine qua non for the promotion of music (and is discussed in greater detail in chapter 3), Alley publishers enhanced song exposure and distribution by exploiting the power of three increasingly interdependent media: sheet music, phonograph records, and radio broadcasts. Sheet music had operated as the backbone of the music industry because, until licenses for performance rights were instituted in the 1910s, compensation for publishers and composers derived solely from royalties generated by sales of the printed medium. Songwriters stood to earn either fixed or percentage-based royalties from publishers (Charles Harris's manual of songwriting, published in 1906, cites rates of 3 to 5 cents per copy, or 10 percent of sales), but once the song was in the hands of a publisher, it was the publisher's job to maximize distribution.[19] In this context, publishers and their pluggers treated sheet music as an important commodity—a product to be sold, Philip Ennis reminds us, "just like corsets, patent medicines, and real estate."[20] Casting their promotional nets beyond conventional retail music stores, publishers and pluggers placed sheet music in mail-order catalogs and department stores, the latter of which bargained down wholesale prices in order to offer a standard retail price of 10 cents per piece.[21] The successful proliferation of sheet music, bolstered no doubt by the concurrent rise in sales of household pianos, commanded the attention of the trade press, as evidenced when, on July 19, 1913, *Billboard* began compiling sales figures provided by 112 music retailers and department stores into weekly lists of best-selling songs, a practice that the magazine has retained (in modified form) to this day.[22]

Sales of sheet music declined in the 1910s as a result of the increasing availability and affordability of phonograph records and household players. The editors of *Billboard* hailed the phonograph as a champion of song promotion, and asserted that the medium "takes songs which have earned their share of popularity on the regular sheet music market and repopularizes them in a field far more far-reaching and profitable. It also takes songs which would never experience spirited counter sales and popularizes them over the instrument."[23] Such was the case with the first known song hit to derive from a recording, an unpublished number composed by George Stoddard and titled "Mary." Recorded by Joseph C. Smith's Orchestra for the Victor Talking Machine Company in July 1918 (though most histories cite a recording date of 1919), the song by one account sold 300,000 phonograph disks and earned the composer $15,000 in royalties in less than three months.[24] Two years later, the total value of commercial phonograph record sales reached the staggering quantity of $105.6 million.[25]

That figure would not be exceeded until after World War II, in large part because the rise of radio through the 1920s and the formation of national radio networks—NBC in 1926 and CBS in 1927—meant that an increasing number of consumers made home radio sets their primary source of music. To grasp the astonishing growth of radio ownership through the middle part of the decade, one need only compare figures: In 1923, radio sets could be found in 400,000 (or one out of every 67) American households. In 1928, that figure had ballooned 20 times to eight million, or the equivalent of nearly one-third of all households in the country.[26] *The New York Times* reported tremendous increase in the number of estimated radio listeners: 16 million in 1925, 40 million in 1928, and 60 million in 1930.[27] Concomitantly, sales of phonograph records suffered a precipitous drop, as did those of both mechanical and non-mechanical pianos.[28]

To the chagrin of those who saw in the broadcasting of classical music great potential to educate the masses and inspire cultural edification, popular music retained the greatest proportion—35 to 40 percent—of broadcast hours on national networks NBC and CBS, and it dominated the airwaves during prime-time hours.[29] In his vivid account of radio music, Philip K. Eberly observes that during NBC's opening season in 1926–27, some form of popular music (usually some form of jazz, a term that applied to various styles including ragtime and commercial dance music) could be heard every night of the week and, by 1930, popular music filled approximately 30 percent of broadcast schedules of both networked and unaffiliated stations.[30]

Although it is impossible to accurately determine the number of listeners who tuned into any single broadcast, a frequently cited example of the commercial potency of song broadcasts occurred on Sunday, January 1, 1925. That night, Irish star tenor John McCormack sang Irving Berlin's "All Alone" over the airwaves, allegedly inciting combined sales of nearly 2.5 million records, sheet music copies, and piano rolls.[31] Sponsored by the Victor Talking Machine Company and broadcast over NBC's flagship station WEAF and seven affiliated stations on the East Coast, McCormack's presentation, coupled with a performance by Metropolitan Opera star Lucrezia Bori, was said to have reached between six and eight million listeners and to have inspired confidence in station managers who saw economic value in transmitting "live" celebrity voices over radio. The broadcast also gave the record company occasion to promote its other products, in order to suggest that radio would not replace traditional media but rather supplement them. B. L. Aldridge, author of *The Victor Talking Machine Company*, notes that following the broadcast the company advertised its Victrola phonograph under the headline: "YOU HEARD THIS PROGRAM ON THE RADIO—NOW YOU CAN HEAR IT WHENEVER YOU PLEASE ON THE VICTROLA."[32] Less propitious, however, was the anxiety that the broadcast inspired among theater managers, who lamented the drop in attendance at their venues. Eminent Broadway producer William A. Brady called radio "the greatest menace that the theatre has ever faced," and remarked, "I am seated now in a room with a group of people, and we are enjoying, free of charge, a musical program over the radio that I can only describe as gorgeous. Why in the world should we go to the theatre and pay money?"[33]

When Brady was quoted in early 1925, at least three groups of radio stakeholders—network broadcasters, advertising agencies, and radio listeners—were eager to address the implications of his question: namely, how should radio broadcasting be funded if programs were to continue to be offered free of expense to listeners? In response to anti-advertising crusaders, who charged that selling airtime to advertisers would render listeners altogether powerless and appeal to the "lowest common denominator" of radio's listening audience, network executives launched what cultural historian Susan Smulyan has called a "campaign for broadcast advertising."[34] Key to the campaign was the implementation of contemporaneous practices of advertising that eschewed the use of direct, descriptive advertising in favor of suggestive, oblique promotion. Methods of indirect selling resulted in the replacement of brazen sales pitches with appeals to familiar, associative tropes and decidedly sincere tones of expression. In this way, a prospective slogan such as "There is a Happiness Candy Store near you" transformed into the more suggestive affirmation "Happiness is just around the corner from you."[35]

Insofar as popular music conflated entertainment and indirect product promotion, it was an ideal vehicle for broadcast advertising. Whether new hits or "old-time" favorites, songs were endowed with audience appeal, and their capacity to seize a listener's attention and capitalize on the power of association made them effective agents of indirect selling—not only of affiliated products but also of themselves.[36] This point was not lost on music publishers, who regarded network tie-ups as first-rate platforms for song promotion. In a piece published in *Billboard* in late 1928, Joe Davis, president of Triangle Music Publishing Co., noted, "Today a publisher can go to various heads of radio hours and get a song in the program and one plug will put it over for from [*sic*] 1 to 47 stations, or whatever particular tieup the hour may have."[37] Nearly all the sponsored programs cited by Davis as providing the most lucrative plugs for publishers were named for affiliated products: *The Palmolive Hour*, *The Champion Spark Plug Hour*, *The Sonora Hour* (Sonora radios), *The Ipana Troubadors* (Bristol Myers's Ipana Toothpaste), *The Clicquot Club Eskimos* (Clicquot Club Company ginger ale; see figure 1.1), *The Dutch Masters Minstrels* (Consolidated Cigar Corporation), and the most successful of the lot, *The Lucky Strike Radio Hour* (named for the eponymous cigarette company), which in 1928 broadcast every Saturday night through WEAF to NBC's 52 stations.[38]

FIGURE 1.1 The arctic setting on the cover of the sheet music for the "Clicquot Fox Trot March" reminded listeners of the cold effervescence of Clicquot Club Ginger Ale. Fifty thousand copies of the sheet music were distributed to program listeners (author's collection).

Radio also seemed to offer unprecedented opportunities for song exposure to smaller publishing companies, because, as Davis asserted, the executives in charge of radio programs "are all broadminded people and do not judge a song by the size of the music publisher."[39] Lyricist William McKenna concurred:

> There is no denying that the radio has been a boon to the small publisher. When one considers that in one evening, on a single program broadcast over a network of stations, a song may be rendered to more people than it was possible to reach in six months thru the old 'plugging' methods, it must be conceded that a small publisher has a chance to demonstrate his song or songs to the world without going through tremendous expense.[40]

But such accounts about the advantages of radio for small publishing houses are more accurately interpreted as illustrative of naïve optimism and industry boosterism. Telling pieces of evidence are the continuity scripts of *The Lucky Strike Radio Hour*, which emphasize songs that were published by the large, established firms of Tin Pan Alley. Of the 15 numbers featured in the inaugural September 1928 broadcast, for instance, only three were copyrighted by lesser known companies, while the rights of the remaining songs belonged to E. B. Marks, Leo Feist, Harms, and Remick Music. The trend to privilege songs from established firms continued at least during the program's first year of operation.[41] Furthermore, many of these tunes were already familiar to listeners, or were on the verge of becoming familiar: Some songs were proven hits ("Bambalina," a success story from 1923); some were known numbers from Broadway shows ("When My Dreams Come True," sung by Eddie Cantor in *Whoopee!* of 1928); and some were featured in early sound films ("Singin' in the Rain," introduced in MGM's *Hollywood Revue of 1929*).

The scripts also exemplify the ways in which early radio programs were designed as armature for the showcasing of popular songs. Only two sources of dialogue—an unnamed announcer and bandleader B. A. Rolfe—appear throughout the scripts; the programs are otherwise occupied by song performances. Below is a typical passage, excerpted from a script dated August 10, 1929, that shows how dialogue took a backseat to popular songs. The passage begins following the performance of a chorus from the program's theme number "This Is My Lucky Day," a song that not only fulfills the functions of indirect advertising through its reference to "lucky," but also was likely already known to listeners, as it had been launched on Broadway by the *George White Scandals of 1926* and disseminated by just about every major record label—most notably by Victor, in a recording featuring the star quintet of the Revelers. The announcer chimes in:

ANNOUNCER:

Good evening, my friends. And so begins this hour of dance music, presented for your pleasure by the manufacturers of Lucky Strike Cigarettes. B. A. Rolfe and his Lucky Strike Dance Orchestra will be heard in the tunes that made Broadway, Broadway. If you sit out a dance, it is suggested: Reach for a Lucky.

The Lucky Strike Dance Orchestra opens with "One Step to Heaven" and "Wearing Them Higher in Hawaii."

(ONE STEP TO HEAVEN and WEARING THEM HIGHER IN HAWAII—ORCHESTRA)

ANNOUNCER:

"Deep Night" and "Old Man Sunshine" by the Lucky Strike Dance Orchestra. Under Mr. Rolfe's direction we are happy to have with us again Margaret (Micky) McKee, famous whistling soloist. You will hear her in "Deep Night."

(DEEP NIGHT and OLD MAN SUNSHINE—ORCHESTRA AND MCKEE)[42]

The announcer and Rolfe continue to introduce song performances in this manner. Occasionally interjected between songs are brief plugs for Lucky Strike cigarettes, with quotations from the likes of Douglas Fairbanks and Amelia Earhart. (The latter is said to have praised the cigarettes for serving as "life-savers" that were "smoked continuously from Trepassey [Canada] to Wales" on her trans-Atlantic flight.[43]) The program concludes with a chorus and vocal refrain of its theme song, followed by a reminder from the announcer that affiliates the Lucky Strike brand with musical entertainment ("The tunes that made Broadway, Broadway"). But the core of the program is formed by popular songs plucked from repertoires of established hits, Broadway stage shows, and sound motion pictures. Perhaps the script's championing of already popular songs was an attempt on the part of the writers—employees of the Lord & Taylor advertising agency—to give the impression that product advertisement was an afterthought or mere suggestion, and thereby align the sales objectives of the program with the prevailing philosophy of indirect advertising. Whether or not this was the case, *The Lucky Strike Radio Hour*, like other programs of its ilk, exploited the allure of popular music in order to attract listeners to a show whose primary goal was unquestionably commercial.

In sum, the use of songs as on-air advertisements made radio a valuable platform for the launching of new numbers and the renewal of listener interest in older hits. Songs were essential elements of sponsored programs and arguably played an indispensable role in the acceptance of radio as a medium for mass advertising by 1928.[44] Even if, as Stan Leibowitz has argued, on-air performances of songs did not translate into hard sales of sheet music and phonograph records (and even if they had a detrimental effect on record sales), these performances nonetheless served as a forum for the cross-promotion of motion picture songs.[45]

STAR-SONG IDENTIFICATION: THE BRANDING OF PERSONALITY

The most lucrative campaigns of cross-promotion depended not only on a stable system of print, record, and radio distribution, but also on a marketing strategy that associated specific stars with specific songs. The commercial value of such "star-song identification" was apparent to publishers and vocalists as early as the turn of the century, when publishers signed music hall and vaudeville singers to exclusive contracts that resulted in their pictures being printed on the covers of sheet music. Developments in printing technologies, particularly of photographic chromolithography in the late 19th century, allowed for the mass production of color photographs and helped to broaden the public appeal of stars. By the 1890s, photographs had replaced drawings as the dominant form of illustration on Tin Pan Alley sheet music.[46] Both parties benefited from this arrangement: Attractive photographic pictures of vocalists helped move copies of sheet music off store shelves and promoted the public's familiarity with entertainers, whose images reached a consumer mass market and augmented the publishers' coffers.

An exemplar from this period is Sophie Tucker's affiliation with the song "Some of These Days," a 1910 tune written by Shelton Brooks that became Tucker's signature hit after she introduced it in a vaudeville presentation and recorded it for Edison in February 1911. Photographs of various performers appeared on initial publications of the song through 1910, but subsequent versions tended to feature only Tucker, and although other artists recorded the song in subsequent decades, David Ewen observed correctly in 1964, "Today it is inconceivable to think of the song in any rendition but Sophie Tucker's."[47] Ewen's assertion sums up the objective of star-song identification: that is, to imbue the affiliation of singer and song with capital value so that the combined product could be differentiated from the multitude of other singers and song groupings on the market. Through repeated performances—not to mention Tucker's feats of self-mythologizing—Tucker was linked indelibly to "Some of These Days," and in so doing acquired symbolic status, an essential criterion of stardom.[48] Star-song identification meant that the once discrete activities of advertising a song and performing it coalesced around the star vocalist.[49]

The practice of associating a celebrity with a commercial product in the early 20th century was by no means unique to the music industry—it was echoed, for example, by the film industry's nascent star system of the early 1910s, when production companies began issuing photographs of movie stars for display in theater lobbies, in fan magazines, and on postcards.[50] In 1914, the motion picture star system emerged, thanks not only to the mass circulation of repeated celebrity images, but also to the fan magazines, studio press materials, and general press that articulated distinct public and private spheres of an actor's life.[51] Indeed, the rise of stars in the entertainment industries of this period should be situated within what historian Warren Susman describes as a much larger cultural transformation that was occurring in the United States in the first decade of the 20th century. In his famous essay "Personality and the Making of Twentieth-Century Culture," Susman describes that period as a time in which a "culture of character," predicated on values of moral virtue and individual responsibility, shifted into a "culture of personality" consonant with a system of consumer capitalism that rewarded an individual's magnetism, assertiveness, and creative idiosyncrasies—in other words, qualities that distinguished an individual from the masses.[52] Although star systems predated the 20th century (already firmly established in the American vaudeville and theater industries of the late 1800s, when performers discovered that they could command top billing and increasing salaries), the new "culture of personality," coupled with the means of mass production and circulation, facilitated the metamorphosis of singers and actors into stars.[53]

The affiliation of distinctive performers with individual songs gave a boost to singers who were not stage luminaries. As Daniel Goldmark points out in his meticulous analysis of sheet music samples from the period, we would expect to see Al Jolson, Paul Whiteman, or Kate Smith pictured on the covers of sheet music, but for "far lesser-known names, this sheet music might have been their one and only appearance in a print venue with the possibility for national distribution."[54] Goldmark describes the various editions of Kalmar & Puck Music Co.'s 1914 publication of "California and You," which pictured more than two dozen singers on as many covers.[55] Although these editions did not always evolve into examples of signature hits, they suggest that publishers sought to promote songs to different markets across the country, and they are especially good evidence of the advantages perceived in associating a song with an image (*any* image, it seems) of a singer. Presumably for this same reason, it was common for sheet music covers to publicize stage shows, as in the example of "She Was a Dear Little Girl," a song interpolated by Marie Cahill into the 1909 show *The Boys and Betty*. The cover of that number's sheet music centered Cahill's portrait below a title that declared "Successfully Sung by Marie Cahill" and above a caption reading "In Daniel V. Arthur's Magnificent Production *The Boys and Betty*."

Even images of songwriters graced the odd sheet music cover, arguably in testament to Tin Pan Alley's creation of a new kind of celebrity: the tunesmith, a figure to be distinguished from the mostly unnamed composers who preceded the rise of the Alley. A good example is the prominent appearance of Walter Donaldson's photograph and name on the cover of "My Blue Heaven" (figure 1.2), his best-selling hit of 1927 and, according to some accounts, the decade. Although depictions of songwriters occurred far less frequently than those of vocalists, their display on sheet music covers nonetheless suggests that the cachet of their images also contributed to the mythology of Tin Pan Alley.

Not surprisingly, the record and radio industries of the 1920s sought to bolster the efficacies of star-song identification. Just as movie stars signed with film studios in the previous decade, record companies in the 1920s offered long-term contracts with singing celebrities. In 1920, Eddie Cantor accepted a five-year contract from Brunswick that paid him $220,000—allegedly the most lucrative of such contracts at that date; Al Jolson signed with Columbia and later with Brunswick (for payment of $10,000 per usable side); and, in 1925, Gene Austin agreed to a contract with Victor that, the crooner later claimed, paid him $96,000 in royalties during the first three months.[56] Similarly, radio's diffusion across the country enhanced the potential

FIGURE 1.2 This cover of "My Blue Heaven" capitalizes on the established success of songwriter Walter Donaldson (author's collection).

for star-song identification—although not as immediately as one might suspect. Fearing that the broadcast of songs would threaten record sales, Brunswick and Victor prohibited their exclusive artists from performing on the air, at least up until 1923.[57] Still, the relentless decline in phonograph sales must have encouraged record company executives to reverse course and develop radio programs with the specific intent of featuring exclusive artists. Beginning in December 1924, Brunswick artists were featured on WJZ, RCA's station in New York, which gave rise to the *Brunswick Hour* the following year, while Victor programmed the aforementioned triumphant broadcast of John McCormack in January 1925.[58]

Just as sheet music covers helped to promote the talents of otherwise unknown singers, radio publicized marginalized musicians and singers—especially because, in its formative years, the medium championed the broadcast of live music over recorded, or "canned," presentations.[59] This being the case, it is important to remember that the formation of stars by way of radio in the 1920s was mitigated by two factors. One was what amounted to the Jim Crow policies of the major networks, which translated into the showcasing of music performed by white artists and dance bands despite the reliance of these musicians on songs composed by African Americans. As William Barlow points out, only prior to the formation of national networks did a handful of African American performers enjoy a broader audience base through radio broadcasts (bandleaders Fletcher Henderson and Duke Ellington are perhaps the most prominent examples).[60] The second factor owed to proclivities among advertisers for enforcing the use of pseudonyms that would resonate with the names of sponsored programs. For this reason, "Paul Oliver" and "Olive Palmer," and not Frank Munn and Virginia Rea, were the acknowledged stars of *The Palmolive Hour*, a leading program that ran on NBC from 1927 to 1931. Considered a strategy that upheld the doctrines of indirect advertising, the use of pseudonyms prevented numerous radio talents from attaining star status under their true names.

A pronounced exception was the case of Hubert Prior Vallee (figure 1.3), who at 20 years old took on the nickname Rudy and whose subsequent rise to national stardom owed almost entirely to radio.[61] In early 1928, programmers at the marginal New York station WABC (which would become the flagship of CBS Radio Network) were seeking program filler and broadcast the concerts performed by Vallee's band at the ornate Heigh-Ho Club on East 53rd Street in Manhattan. By that summer, more than 50 thousand listeners responded to an announcer who solicited requests for an autographed photograph of the singer, and in October of that year, Vallee was offered a position on NBC's top-positioned program,

FIGURE 1.3 Rudy Vallee with his trademark saxophone (Robert S. Birchard collection).

The Fleischmann's Yeast Hour, through which he became the country's most eminent "crooner" and radio personality.[62] The variety show, penned entirely by the Walter J. Thompson advertising agency, highlighted popular songs performed by vocalists and bands that became famous as a result. Vallee's fame also influenced his success in other entertainment media. His 1929 hit "I'm Just a Vagabond Lover" inspired the production of the film *The Vagabond Lover*, the box office profits of which owed without a doubt to the crooner's established base of radio fans.[63]

Whether or not radio broadcasts actually aided the sales of sheet music and phonograph records, the emphasis accorded by advertising to the availability of print and recorded media indicates that publishers and record companies continued to view sales of their tangible products as important sources of income. As well, we might note, markets for those products endured even if they diminished with the rise of radio. It would be prudent to view the 1920s as a decade of significant technological and industrial flux where popular media were concerned, but it was also a decade in which interests in music publishing, recording, and broadcasting tested forms of marketing and star construction across various media platforms.

THE MOST POPULAR BALLAD

Up to this point, I have considered several aspects of the mainstream American song industry of the early 20th century, concentrating on its modes of distribution and dissemination through print, recorded, and broadcast media. But just what kinds of songs were disseminated and, as a result, incorporated into motion pictures? The definition of popular music as a form of music that was mass-reproduced and distributed to mass audiences does not tell us much about the diversity of styles that comprised the American musical landscape of the 1920s—styles that included blues, hillbilly, folk, country, ragtime, and the capricious, multifaceted category of jazz—nor does it reveal which types of songs were most popular in the sense that they generated the highest sales. We know that by 1925 half of the allegedly "leading music publishers" in the United States were located in the neighborhood of Tin Pan Alley, and the increasing control over music by these publishers, as well as radio networks, led to the privileging of certain genres of music at the expense of others, such as country music.[64] The question of which genres were measurably most popular is important because they would be likelier candidates for entry into Hollywood's early sound pictures.

One way to compute song popularity is to tally up sales of sheet music and phonograph records of individual songs, and then assess whether the best-selling songs share musical traits that could be grounds for identifying a coherent genre or group style.[65] But there is an obstacle: the absence of accurate sales figures. Although *Billboard* printed weekly song rankings as early as 1913, these were based on information gathered from a limited number of sources and were not necessarily a representative sample. And, as Tim Gracyk has pointed out, any claims that this-or-that tune sold so many copies in print or recordings were probably instigated by self-promoting songwriters.[66] Sources published retrospectively, such as Joel Whitburn's *Pop Memories 1890-1954* (which compiles *Billboard* rankings) and Julius Mattfield's *Variety Music Cavalcade*, are helpful guides but dependent on selective data and chosen "representative recordings" rather than hard evidence.[67]

In the absence of reliable statistical information, we could do worse than to consult manuals and guides published in the 1910s and 1920s for aspiring songwriters.[68] These reveal the musical idioms and genres (such as they were) believed to be most promising for commercial sales—namely, sentimental ballads, Irish ballads, comic songs, ragtime numbers, old-fashioned waltzes, production songs (for Broadway musical comedies, operettas, and revues), patriotic songs, and topical songs whose categories included "mother songs" or "home songs." Some of these manuals elevated the enterprise of song classification to new heights. For instance, a 1926 guide authored by the astonishingly productive songwriter Harry J. Lincoln lists eight brands of ballads (semi-high-class, march, mother, Irish, rustic, descriptive, child/juvenile, and sentimental/philosophical) and five brands of novelty songs (flirting, comic, stage, ragtime, and "blues via jazz").[69] In spite of such idiosyncratic lists, two primary genres—the ballad and the novelty song—tended to be reiterated by manuals and were highlighted in other references to musical categories. In 1919, for instance, the head of the Sam Fox Publishing Company pointed out "the heart interest ballad and the novelty song" as the genres "likely to displace jazz" in terms of commercial success.[70]

Of the ballad and the novelty song, the former was furthermore judged by contemporaneous observers to be the more successful and enduring. The author of 1925's *How to Publish Your Own Music Successfully* opined, "Years ago the best selling numbers were ballads, but lately they have had sharp competition with novelty and comedy songs. The ballad, however, will doubtless always be a better piece of merchandise than the other, for it has a much greater chance of long life."[71] Although other genres, such as comedy songs along the lines of "Yes! We Have No Bananas," attained hit status, it was obvious to music salespeople and publishers at the time that "most people prefer ballads as a steady diet and won't take to trick numbers unless one happens to be a real novelty."[72] From Paul Whiteman's 1920 rendition of "Whispering" to Gene Austin's 1927 recording of "My Blue Heaven," the ballad not only dominated the decade's music charts but also distinguished the hallmark compositions of the country's most prolific songwriters, including Irving Berlin, George

Gershwin, Jerome Kern, Cole Porter, and Richard Rodgers. As we will see, it was the ballad that also defined most of Hollywood's theme songs during the transition to sound.

In order to distinguish the 1920s ballad from other kinds of ballads published earlier in the century, it is helpful to use the term "popular ballad," as defined by musicologist Allen Forte.[73] The musical conventions of popular ballads were similar to those of the songs characteristic of Tin Pan Alley around the turn of the century. Like those earlier forms, popular ballads typically included an introduction of four or eight measures that anticipated the song's main melody; a verse-refrain structure in which the length of the refrain usually comprised 32 measures and adhered to either the AABA or ABAC forms, in which each letter represented an eight-measure unit; lyrics written in familiar, and often colloquial, language; time signatures of simple, duple, or waltz meters; basic tonal progressions; and, above all, an easily sung melody composed for an "average" vocal range, where the definition of average gradually broadened from the presumed vocal range of a woman (women were the primary consumers of sheet music around the turn of the century) to that of a man—a shift that reflected the increasing cultivation of male vocal performance in a variety of formats, including minstrelsy, song plugging, Broadway, cabaret, and radio.[74] By emphasizing simple melodic motifs, or hooks, ballads appealed to a wide range of vocal artists, as well as to untrained listeners who wished to sing either along with an audience at a live venue or in a private setting at home—an important characteristic because repetition was key to a given song's commercial success.[75]

Although the modern popular ballad retained many of the musical attributes characteristic of earlier ballads, three notable features distinguished it from its predecessors: melodic syncopation, expanded harmonic language, and, to some extent, modernized lyrics. The first of these, melodic syncopation, was a hallmark feature of the piano rags that Alley publishers had exploited in the first two decades of the century. Such rags, examples of which included "Hello! Ma Baby" in 1899 and "Under the Bamboo Tree" in 1902, had been stripped of references to the African American culture whence the style of "ragging a song" originated, including minstrel shows and "coon songs" of the late 19th century. The white-washed rags of the Alley supplanted lyrics that had previously depicted African American protagonists with verses about generic romantic affairs, and they also replaced ragtime's instrumental diversity (which once included banjo and violin) with an emphasis on the piano. Nonetheless, they maintained what had been sanctioned as the genre's definitive characteristics: a syncopated melody written in duple time, set against alternating deep bass notes with block chords.[76] Even as the term "ragtime" acquired pejorative status toward the end of the 1910s and all but disappeared in the 1920s, rag-like syncopation endured, sustained in large part by the flood of popular social dances—such as the foxtrot, turkey trot, and one-step—that combined a duple meter with syncopated rhythms.[77] The second generation of composers working in Tin Pan Alley therefore continued to incorporate melodic syncopation into their popular ballads.

Second, songs belonging to the genre of the popular ballad revised the harmonic conventions of traditional ballads by relying more heavily on chromatic notes and chords, most notably through the frequent use of "blues notes"—the flatted third and seventh of the tonic scale—and non-dominant seventh and ninth chords. Scholars have attributed these changes to two chief influences: blues music and Western European classical (usually Romantic) music. As Peter Muir has contended, Tin Pan Alley had in the early part of the century assimilated traditional forms of the blues to the standard 32-bar structure and conventions of Alley numbers, and the resulting format of "popular blues" endured through the 1910s.[78] On the other hand, European elements could be heard in numerous examples of ballads, even by songwriters who were not classically trained (as were George Gershwin and Cole Porter, for example). Charles Hamm points to Paul Whiteman's "I'm Always Chasing Rainbows" (1918), which takes its hook from Chopin's "Fantasie Impromptu Opus 66," and Charles J. Johnson's "Iola" (192), which borrows from Johann Strauss II's infamous waltz "The Blue Danube."[79] Both blues music and European classical music offered significant resources for Tin Pan Alley's second generation of composers.

Last, as shown by Philip Furia and other scholars, some lyricists sought to distinguish their work from the saccharine, puritanical, and idyllic products of their predecessors, and so they modernized their work by injecting witticisms and euphemisms (for instance, Cole Porter's 1928 "Let's Do It [Let's Fall in Love]"), verbal idioms from blues and jazz, and references to urban environments in which many of the lyricists themselves were working.[80] This is not to say that they abandoned the use of lyrics that dealt with nostalgic and romantic subjects; "My Blue Heaven" ends its refrain with the description of an idyllic setting: "You'll see a smiling face, a fireplace, a cozy room / A little nest that's nestled where the roses bloom / Just Mollie and me, and Baby makes three / We're happy in my blue heaven." The use of nostalgic, old-fashioned lyrics was also advocated by songwriting manuals. Three brief examples from the late 1920s: Al Dubin (who would partner with Harry Warren to become one of the most famous songwriting duos in Hollywood) defined ballads as "songs that deal with love of sweethearts, of mothers, of children, of home or of places" and implored his readers to write simple lyrics, "using terms such as 'LOVE NEST' and 'COZY CORNER' in preference to 'TRYSTING PLACE' or 'RENDEZVOUS.'"[81] Abel Green, the music columnist for *Variety* who soon would be crowned the paper's editor-in-chief, asserted in his guide that the most successful songs evoke the "universally appealing" concepts of home and mother.[82] And Walter

Newcomer, the specious author of *Song Requirements of Talking Pictures*, dubbed "mother Songs" and "home Songs" the two most important genres for motion picture songs—the former because "the longer we live, the more we think of our mothers," and the latter because it "voice[s] the sweetest memories, the deepest yearnings and the highest aspirations of mankind."[83] Indeed, despite occasional warnings that listeners were growing weary of maudlin musical expression, many motion picture songs seemed to privilege sentimental lyrics over less saccharine ones—the important exceptions being songs by Cole Porter, George Gershwin, and others whose work would not make an earnest impact on Hollywood cinema until the early 1930s.[84]

The use of syncopation, expanded musical language, and updated lyrics notwithstanding, the modern popular ballad form remained highly standardized, with its verse-chorus structure adhering rigorously to a pattern in which a four-to-eight-bar introduction was followed by an optional 16-bar verse, which in turn was followed by a 32-bar refrain. An illustrative example is Harry Akst and Grant Clarke's song "Am I Blue?" (figure 1.4). Published in 1929 by M. Witmark & Sons, the song reportedly sold half a million copies of sheet music and became Ethel Waters's signature

FIGURE 1.4 Characteristic of many sheet music covers designed for motion picture songs, the cover image for "Am I Blue?" foregrounds not the title of the song but rather its associated motion picture (author's collection).

song after she performed it in *On With the Show* (1929), Warner Bros.' feature-length film.[85] Written in 4/4 time, the song begins with an eight-measure introduction that states the chorus's main theme, the melodic range of which never exceeds an octave (making it an easy sing for untrained vocalists). The notes fall on off-beats (see figure 1.5), creating a syncopated rhythm:

FIGURE 1.5 Melodic excerpt from "Am I Blue?" (by Harry Akst and Grant Clarke).

In the subsequent 16-measure verse, a "lonely woman" tells of a sweetheart who has abandoned her. This is followed by the 32-measure refrain, the structure of which adheres to the typical AABA format in terms of its lyrics, melody, and harmony. With the A section alternating between F-major and its dominant seventh (C[7]), and the B section alternating between A-minor and its dominant seventh (E[7]), the refrain follows:

A: Am I blue? Am I blue? / Ain't these tears in these eyes tellin' you?
A: Am I blue? You'd be too, / if each plan with your man done fell through.
B: Was a time I was his only one, / But now I'm the sad and lonely one, "Lawdy,"
A: Was I gay? 'Til today— / Now he's gone and we're through, am I blue?

The frequency with which chromatic notes appear in the refrain betrays the influence of blues or jazz. Of particular note are the flatted third (A-flat) and seventh (E-flat, the melody's apex), as well as the interjection of "Lawdy," a mimicry of the idiosyncratic vocal breaks of "Oh Lawdy" or "Oh baby!" common in early blues songs.[86]

The conventions of the 1920s popular ballad would prove especially well-suited to the commercial demands and narrative form of early sound films. The genre's high degree of popularity helped to ensure cross-promotional success with motion pictures, and its lyrics tended to summarize or reflect the dramatic themes of romance or nostalgia that pervaded so many mainstream films. Moreover, as we see in the second part of this book, the ballad's emphasis on short, repetitive musical motifs could be deployed in the service of narrative and thematic elements of motion pictures. But such deployment was not ushered in with synchronized sound film; rather, songs figured prominently in the musical accompaniment to late silent cinema, a context in which they worked as dramatic elements, prompted sales of sheet music and phonograph records to mass consumers, and, by 1928, generated a public vogue for motion picture "theme songs" that was critical for Hollywood's integration of onscreen song performances in early sound films. Therefore, a brief consideration of film music of the silent era is in order.

POPULAR SONGS AND MUSIC FOR SILENT CINEMA:
THE THEMATIC APPROACH

The progenitors of motion picture theme songs developed by way of what Rick Altman has termed a "thematic approach" to musical accompaniment. As Altman has shown in his peerless tome *Silent Film Sound*, some of the first motion picture production companies in the United States capitalized on familiar tunes by releasing films inspired by the titles of popular songs, such as *Everybody Works But Father* (1905), *Spook Minstrels* (1905), and *Waiting at the Church* (1906).[87] Moreover, most nickelodeon owners used songs as "ballyhoo" to attract customers to their storefront theaters where audiences, once inside, could sing along to the illustrated song slides that comprised a standard part of the nickelodeon program.[88] The use of song slides dwindled in the early 1910s, when theaters installed second projectors so that films could alternate with other films rather than with slides, but by that time popular songs had become firmly ensconced in the conventions of musical accompaniment to motion pictures. For instance, songs were the dominant feature of early cue sheets, which were printed compilations of musical phrases that circulated with film prints and informed theater musicians of what to play and when to play it.[89]

The rise of the feature film in 1913 saw the advent of "special scores," which were commissioned by producers and exhibitors who wished to raise the prestige value (and ticket prices) of feature-length films. Part of the campaign for prestige entailed the suppression of audience sing-alongs, and so popular music actually diminished through the mid-1920s, as classical and "light classical" music came to rule in silent film accompaniment.[90] But popular songs did not vanish entirely. Instead, they were placed in contexts in which the audience could be counted upon to recognize their familiar lyrics. For instance, in Joseph Carl Breil's score for D. W. Griffith's *Birth of a Nation* (1915), excerpts from Bellini's *Norma* overture are juxtaposed with Stephen Foster's "Camptown Races," and portions of Wagner's *The Ride of the Valkyries* are followed by "Dixie." Martin Miller Marks observes that Breil's integration of a total of 26 borrowed songs "suggests that he counted on audience recognition of the words associated with these tunes. The songs he (and Griffith) chose were from the standard repertoire for home and community singing, and their words, though not heard, reflect on the film's action in ways that audiences could easily understand."[91] Royal S. Brown concurs, arguing that the incorporation of "Dixie" or "The Star Spangled Banner" is "one of the strongest trump cards a film composer and/or arranger can play. For even the briefest recognizable snippet of such a piece... can evoke in the listener an entire political mythology."[92]

Still, the legacy of Breil's score resided not in its use of familiar melodies but in its engendering of one of the entertainment industry's first discernable theme songs, "The Perfect Song." Also known as "The Love Theme of Elsie Stoneman and Ben Cameron," the song recurs nine times in the score, accompanying scenes that depict the blossoming romance between the title characters. Following the film's general release in March 1915, Breil's publisher, Chappell & Co., issued "The Perfect Song" in five distinct arrangements and included it in a compilation of piano pieces based on segments of the film score.[93] Presumably as a result of the success of the film, the love ballad sold nearly ten thousand copies of sheet music in 1916 alone, appeared as musical accompaniment for other films, and eventually became the theme song for the *Amos 'n' Andy* radio show.[94]

The success of "The Perfect Song" is said to have inspired a handful of motion picture theme songs throughout the rest of the decade. Some of these were incorporated into published cue sheets, while others were written as tributes to film stars. Notable examples included "Poor Pauline," issued in 1914 with a sheet music cover featuring Pearl White, the star of the popular serial *The Perils of Pauline*; "Peace Song" for *Civilization* (1916); the highly successful "Mickey" for the film of the same name, released in 1918; and "Daddy Long Legs," which was, according to the sheet music cover, both "inspired by" and "dedicated to" Mary Pickford for her performance in First National's 1919 film *Daddy Long Legs*. A year later, veteran Tin Pan Alley composer Albert Von Tilzer ("Take Me Out to the Ballgame") wrote a follow-up number, "Dear Old Daddy Long Legs," which again displayed a photograph of Pickford on its sheet music cover. An extensive bibliography of film-related sheet music suggests that these examples represent only a few of the dozens of topical motion picture songs that were inspired by individual stars, cinema as a cultural institution, and particular films of the silent era.[95]

Concurrent with the rise of inspired theme songs was a crucial development in the practice of musical accompaniment: what Altman calls the "thematic approach."[96] Theater mogul Samuel L. ("Roxy") Rothafel sought to boost the prestige value of his New York theater presentations by applying the concept of the Wagnerian leitmotif to musical accompaniment. Roxy assigned musical motifs, often lifted from light classics, to each film's main character. This use of musical motifs spread across the country in the late 1910s, when cue sheet compilers, music composers, and musical directors began to specify main themes for each film's major characters. The thematic approach was beneficial in several ways: It simplified cue sheet compilation and orchestral execution; it publicized motion picture music; and, when themes were based on preexisting music, it exploited audiences' capacity to recognize familiar tunes. However, as Altman recounts, Roxy mistranslated the principles underpinning the Wagnerian leitmotif's use for motion picture accompaniment: Whereas authentic operatic leitmotifs transform in melody and harmony over the course of a narrative, the motifs that Roxy implemented often remained identical across a score, save for changes in tempo, dynamics, and instrumentation. As a result, the public grew weary of what became overly familiar melodies. For example, in writing of the overuse of Schumann's "Träumerei," famed cue sheet compiler Ernst Luz complained, "Could we hope that the audience would enjoy its third or fourth repetition in one hour?" Another reviewer wrote that the accompaniment for *Way Down East* constituted an example of "*theme-ing* the audience to death."[97]

Musical directors who sought to avoid abusing themes and, at the same time, exploit an audience's capacity for recognizing popular tunes inserted new songs into that conventional thematic structure. Altman describes the process:

> Well applied, thematic construction of film accompaniments delivered novelty and familiarity in the same compact package. When first played, the love theme might be unknown to the audience, but spectators were used to dealing with the unknown at the outset of a narrative. By the time the film reached its climax, the young couple huddling together to keep out of harm's way, the audience needed the security provided by familiarity. By now, the repeated and varied theme had entered every spectator's subconscious and was thus available to serve as a refuge for audience emotions.[98]

Because the critical ingredient of thematic construction was a musical motif, rather than an entire theme song, the thematic approach easily accommodated the structure of the popular ballad. As described above, chief among the ballad's defining features was a brief, melodic, and repetitive musical phrase nested within the song's refrain, so as a phrase of musical accompaniment, a song hook could serve as a leitmotif: an easily recognizable musical phrase that recurred over the course of a narrative in association with characters, objects, places, or events.[99] Popular songs fit easily into the thematic approach to musical accompaniment for the silent cinema, because their refrains contained brief and highly memorable motifs.

An example can be found in the cue sheet that circulated for the musical accompaniment of Harold Lloyd's comedy *Speedy* (1928).[100] Compiled by James C. Bradford, the sheet contains 58 musical cues, each of which corresponds to a distinct narrative action. The cues include phrases written in the classical style by cue sheet compilers and composers, as well as phrases from popular songs, such as "My New York," "Ain't We Got Fun," and a piece expressly labeled a "THEME," titled "Speedy Boy." The sheet directs the musical accompanist to open with a repetition of this theme song's

32-measure refrain, which divides evenly into an AABA structure (see figure 1.6).[101]
The A motif lasts eight measures, but its exceptionally simple (and thus easily sung)
hook occupies half that duration:

FIGURE I.6   Melodic excerpt from "Speedy Boy" (by Ray Kalges and Jesse Greer).

The entire refrain of "Speedy Boy" appears during narrative actions that on the
cue sheet are numbered 1, 13, 20, and 58 (of 58 total actions), and the accompanist is
directed to perform the refrain twice during actions 1, 20, and 58. The cue sheet also
lists four repetitions of the refrain's first half (AA) during action numbers 6, 28,
37, and 45. Across the film, therefore, the hook of "Speedy Boy" is performed 29
times: thrice each time the entire refrain is played (for each "A" in AABA), and twice
with each performance of the refrain's first half (AA). The total time allotted to the
various renderings of "Speedy Boy," according to the cue sheet, is 15 minutes—nearly
one-fifth of the film's running time.[102] The tendency for the thematic approach to
appropriate song hooks and repeat them throughout a film helps to explain the proliferation and appeal of theme songs during the era of silent cinema. Indeed, by the
late 1920s, million-copy sales of sheet music for song hits affiliated with late silent
movies, like "Charmaine" (*What Price Glory*, 1926) and "Diane" (*Seventh Heaven*,
1927), were energizing the entertainment industries' faith in movie and music
cross-promotion.

MOTION PICTURE THEME SONGS: THE SOUND SAVIORS

The advantages of the thematic approach notwithstanding, it is instructive to note
that hit theme songs emerged around the time that the music industry was suffering
a brief economic slump. From mid-1927 through early 1928, columns in *Billboard*
expressed industry concerns about declining sales of sheet music and phonograph
records. The editors were uncertain of where to place blame. Radio, crossword puzzle
books, and other domestic amusements were the first candidates, but by the summer
of 1927, the journal denounced the overproduction of "mediocre numbers," noting
that "publishers... have continued to plug one dog after another until the public has
become disgusted with the entire batch of words and music."[103] Through that winter,
Billboard bemoaned the state of the song business—writing, for example, that the
industry "is in the throes of a slump—in fact, the worst drought it has ever known.

The voice of the calamity howler is heard in the land of Tin-Pan Alley, and dire days are predicted."[104]

In the midst of this business's economic adversity, films that produced best-selling theme songs could have been hailed as saviors. By May 1928, *Variety* was reporting a "picture song vogue" and extolling the value of the theme song to the film and music industries.[105] When United Artists placed an advertisement in *Variety* that gave equal publicity to the film *Ramona* and its title song, the trade paper opined:

> [United Artists' advertisement] evidences how importantly the picture people now deem their theme songs as constant advance agents. It's a great form of free advertising to be had, considering the universal appeal of popular music. The plug (Paul) Whiteman and other maestros gave and are giving "Ramona" as a song will put over *Ramona* the picture.[106]

The response in *Variety* indicates that motion pictures had become important platforms for launching popular songs. Conversely, the film industry was said to have benefited from the tremendous popularity of theme songs. *Variety* wrote in August 1928, "From the song viewpoint, a great picture will not help a poor song but it is a fact that a great popular song hit can help a mediocre picture."[107] The article proceeded to cite a "prominent publisher" who claimed that the songs "Ramona" and "Laugh, Clown, Laugh" would have been successful hits regardless of their respective tie-ups with films. Rick Altman concludes, "Had the vogue for theme music not reached its height just as Hollywood was experimenting with sound, the industry would certainly have viewed possible conversion quite differently."[108] Although many additional factors were responsible for the studios' decision to convert to sound, there can be no doubt that the entertainment landscape in the late 1920s was ripe for the convergence of film and music, and that the studios seized on theme songs as a means to exploit synchronized sound films.

CONCLUSION

From the rise of Tin Pan Alley in the 1890s through the 1920s, publishers of popular music established an effective network for song distribution. Predicated on an aggressive commodification of the song as a product, the network in turn influenced the kind of music likeliest to succeed in the changing entertainment marketplace. To this end, publishers drew on available media to exploit the identification of stars with songs, and in so doing reworked what a star could be—by utilizing formats that allowed independent publishers a greater seat at the table and forwarding different members of the creative process into glamor-shot positions atop sheet music and records. Royalties earned from sales of sheet music and phonograph records supplemented the income that publishers received in exchange for licensing performances on broadcasting stations, and as radio exploded as an entertainment medium, publishers and record companies could count on broadcasts to stimulate sales of their tangible commodities. At the same time, the prevailing practices of musical accompaniment for silent cinema emphasized both the composition of "theme songs" and the manipulation of those songs into repetitive motifs. Popular ballads, the common genre of a majority of theme songs, met the requirements of film music accompaniment just as easily as synchronized sound films would fit into the established structures for song distribution and cross-promotion with various media. By the time the major motion picture companies prepared to convert to sound, both the music and the film industries perceived motion picture theme songs as commercial products.

It is now a question as to which has absorbed which. Is the motion picture industry a subsidiary of the music publishing business—or have film producers gone into the business of making songs?

JERRY HOFFMAN (1929)[1]

[Sound films] will make Hollywood a great musical center. I look for the film capital to become the birthplace of the big song hits of the future.

JESSE LASKY (1929)[2]

2

Owning a Song

THE RESTRUCTURING OF HOLLYWOOD AND TIN PAN ALLEY

DURING THE FIRST two decades of the 20th century, Erno Rapee was the most prolific composer, arranger, and conductor of silent film music in the United States. Having migrated from Budapest to New York in 1912, Rapee was hired to direct orchestras in the city's opulent motion picture palaces owned and managed by impresario Samuel L. "Roxy" Rothafel. While under Roxy's employ, Rapee produced two sizable collections of "photoplay music" (music created for the purpose of accompanying silent films) titled *Motion Picture Moods for Pianists and Organists* (1924) and *Encyclopedia of Music for Pictures* (1925), and he arranged orchestral scores for more than a dozen silent films, including Fox Film's *A Connecticut Yankee* (1920) and MGM's *Monte Carlo* (1926). But his most memorable contributions to film music were two popular songs, "Charmaine" and "Diane," co-written with lyricist Lew Pollack and published as theme songs for musical accompaniment to Fox Film's silent movies *What Price Glory* (1926) and *Seventh Heaven* (1927), respectively. Both songs became nationwide hits and, on the cusp of the American cinema's transition to sound, reinforced the faith held by the film and music industries in the merits of product cross-promotion. In February 1930, Rapee, then in charge of musical operations at the Roxy Theatre, was lured by Warner Bros. to Hollywood with an impressive three-year contract that guaranteed a sum upward of $320,000 (nearly $4 million in today's terms when adjusted for inflation).[3]

Rapee's tenure in Hollywood turned out to be brief, because Roxy coaxed him back to New York after the composer was only nine months into his contract with Warner Bros. Nonetheless, his engagement on the West Coast points to the critical relationships that developed between the industries of motion pictures and popular music during the transition to sound.[4] By the time Rapee arrived on the Warner Bros. lot in early 1930, all of Hollywood's major studios had entered into contractual arrangements with music publishing firms. The agreements ranged from informal mergers to outright acquisitions, and they granted the studios control over the distribution of motion picture songs at the same time that they escorted the music business toward a new, profitable platform for popular songs. Galvanized by Hollywood's attention to popular music, dozens of songwriters and musicians working in the Broadway and Tin Pan Alley districts of New York migrated to the West Coast, where they found employment in newly created studio music departments. As each of the major studios integrated horizontally into the business of music writing, recording, and publishing, the core of the American popular music industry diffused into two centers located on opposite sides of the country: New York and Los Angeles, which remain to this day the dominant hubs of the industry, thus testifying to the enduring impact of Hollywood's transitional-era forays into popular music.[5]

It is tempting to explain the investments as a result of the major studios' efforts to exploit New York songwriting talent, and there can be no doubting the importance of the contributions made by Tin Pan Alley and Broadway composers and lyricists to Hollywood's earliest sound films. However, the single most important factor that motivated the studios' ventures into song publishing was the perceived value of ownership over song copyrights. At the time of the conversion to sound, matters of copyright were legislated under the Copyright Act of 1909, which updated its predecessor of 1790 by introducing two critical provisions with lasting effects when music—especially film music—was concerned. The first provision was the *mechanical right*, which allowed a copyright owner to collect 2 cents (the statutory rate) for each mechanical reproduction of his or her work.[6] The second provision was the *public performance right*, which required that individuals seeking to perform a copyrighted work obtain a license from the copyright owner. In the two decades following the Act's inauguration, the economic potential of the second provision became especially apparent to publishers and songwriters, who discovered that handsome sums could be earned by licensing performing rights to venue proprietors.

Such proprietors included motion picture exhibitors whose "wiring" of theaters during the transition to sound all but eliminated the use of live musicians in theaters yet did little to prevent publishers from seeking license fees. The conversion to sound absolved exhibitors of having to supply live entertainment, but they were still required to take out licenses for the public performance of songs included on synchronized soundtracks. Even more propitious for music publishers was the fact that the two new copyright provisions were coupled: Movie producers could distribute films for which they had obtained synchronization licenses *only* to exhibitors who had obtained performing rights licenses. It is easy to understand, therefore, why the film companies were eager to acquire control over the production and distribution of songs. Doing so, as Russell Sanjek has explained, would enable them to award performing rights to exhibitors without charge and, even better, "force competitors to pay whatever the traffic would bear for synchronization licenses."[7] As further padding for their coffers, the studios would profit from sales of ancillary products—sheet music and phonograph records—at a time when songs written expressly for motion pictures were considered increasingly valuable commodities.

In addition to securing control over song copyrights, Hollywood's majors were invested in attracting New York songwriters and composers to studio music departments. The financial benefits of owning song copyrights may have been the chief factor in motivating the studios' investments in song publishing, but, as I discuss later in this chapter, equally important was the migration of songwriting talent to the West Coast and the consequent emergence of studio music departments. The presence of musical talent on studio lots, and the lucrative nature of the contracts with which such talent was rewarded, were revealing of Hollywood's widening control over the production and circulation of popular songs. However, none of these transformations to the film and music industries would have occurred in the absence of two organizations intent on enforcing the laws set out in the Copyright Act.

THE FORMATION OF ASCAP AND MPPA, 1909–1927

The Copyright Act reflected changes in the ways that the music industry produced and distributed songs around the turn of the century. The economic disaster following the Civil War left most Southern publishers bankrupt and the country's remaining major publishing firms scattered across urban centers in the North, including New York, Boston, Philadelphia, and Chicago. Drawn to the extraordinary and ever-increasing opportunity for song exposure on New York's musical stages, a new generation of publishers established their central offices around Union Square, at East 14th St. near Broadway. Just a few blocks away stood Tony Pastor's music hall, a venue for the city's most famous entertainers; the surrounding neighborhood boasted dozens of other theaters, dance halls, restaurants, and saloons where popular music was regularly performed. In the 1890s, as more theaters began to open

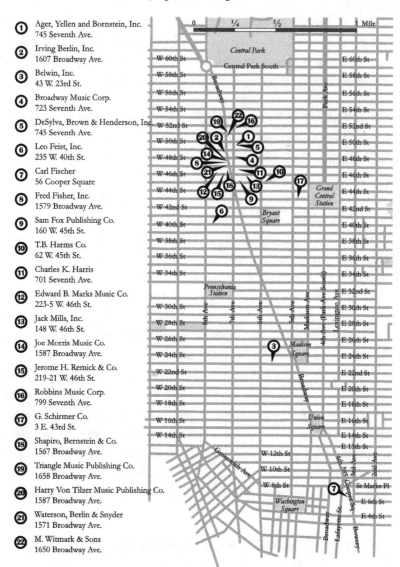

1. Ager, Yellen and Bornstein, Inc.
745 Seventh Ave.

2. Irving Berlin, Inc.
1607 Broadway Ave.

3. Belwin, Inc.
43 W. 23rd St.

4. Broadway Music Corp.
723 Seventh Ave.

5. DeSylva, Brown & Henderson, Inc.
745 Seventh Ave.

6. Leo Feist, Inc.
235 W. 40th St.

7. Carl Fischer
56 Cooper Square

8. Fred Fisher, Inc.
1579 Broadway Ave.

9. Sam Fox Publishing Co.
160 W. 45th St.

10. T.B. Harms Co.
62 W. 45th St.

11. Charles K. Harris
701 Seventh Ave.

12. Edward B. Marks Music Co.
223-5 W. 46th St.

13. Jack Mills, Inc.
148 W. 46th St.

14. Joe Morris Music Co.
1587 Broadway Ave.

15. Jerome H. Remick & Co.
219-21 W. 46th St.

16. Robbins Music Corp.
799 Seventh Ave.

17. G. Schirmer Co.
3 E. 43rd St.

18. Shapiro, Bernstein & Co.
1567 Broadway Ave.

19. Triangle Music Publishing Co.
1658 Broadway Ave.

20. Harry Von Tilzer Music Publishing Co.
1587 Broadway Ave.

21. Waterson, Berlin & Snyder
1571 Broadway Ave.

22. M. Witmark & Sons
1650 Broadway Ave.

Addresses of Music Publishing Companies in New York City, 1927

FIGURE 2.1 Sources: Abel Green, *Inside Stuff on How to Write Popular Songs* (New York: Paul Whiteman, 1927), 69–70; William B. McCourtie, *Where and How to Sell Manuscripts: A Directory for Writers*, 4th ed. (Springfield, MA: Home Correspondence School, 1927), 166–169. Credit: Daniel Spring.

uptown, the publishing entrepreneurs migrated about a dozen blocks north, to West 28th St. between 5th Ave. and Broadway.[8] Through the 1910s and 1920s, publishers would continue to move uptown, settling around Broadway between 42nd St. and 52nd St.; see figure 2.1. A locus for songwriters, musicians, and music advertisers, the region soon acquired the label "Tin Pan Alley," allegedly in tribute to the clanging sounds of its prodigious musical output.[9] Songs created in Tin Pan Alley were introduced on New York stages, neighborhood venues, and, thanks to a new national railway system, across the country as part of road show tours. In this context, the Copyright Act's provision for performing rights proved vital.[10]

Nevertheless, although the Act was designed to accommodate new modes of song publication and distribution, it failed to mandate a system of enforcement. Live performances may have attracted patrons, but songwriters received no recompense. In response, members of the music industry joined forces and created two organizations for the express purpose of regulating the use of copyrighted music. The smaller of these was the Music Publishers Protective Association (MPPA), formed in May 1917. At its helm was Edwin Claude Mills, a former vaudeville house manager (not to mention teenage runaway, trainmaster, and account examiner), and the heads of prominent music publishing firms.[11] The MPPA initially sought to curb payola—the practice of paying performers to incorporate designated numbers into their routines—but the organization soon became a trust that oversaw royalty payments to publishers from manufacturers of mechanically reproduced commodities, namely piano rolls and records. Mills and the MPPA would come to play a critical role during the transition to sound, but in order to understand that role, it is necessary to outline the development of the second and larger organization, the American Society of Composers, Authors and Publishers (ASCAP).

The MPPA tracked payments to publishers for mechanical reproductions, but the music industry lacked a systematic method for administering licenses for performing rights. ASCAP sought to remedy the problem. Conventional histories of ASCAP, including those propagated in later years by agents of the organization itself, claim that composer Victor Herbert spearheaded the organization after he heard the house band at Shanley's Restaurant in New York playing music from his current Broadway show *Sweethearts*.[12] Following that night in early 1914, it is said, Herbert sued the restaurant proprietor in the case of *Herbert v. Shanley Co.* But a more careful history supplied by Bennie L. DeWhitt shows that as early as October 1913 a group of 35 publishers, composers, and lyricists, including Herbert, began to formulate a plan to halt the unauthorized use of copyrighted music. On February 13, 1914, nine of the original group formed an official coalition, and ASCAP ("the Society") was born. Modeled on France's Société des auteurs, compositeurs et editeurs de musique, ASCAP was an unincorporated membership organization designed to function as a clearinghouse for the licensing of commercial uses of music. Its members, whether they were composers, lyricists ("authors"), or publishers, would assign to the Society the exclusive performing rights to their musical works, which the Society would assemble into a catalog of song titles. Performing rights to the entire catalog would be issued as a blanket license to venue owners and other commercial users in exchange for a fee that ranged from $10 to $15 according to an establishment's size and gross receipts. Proceeds from license fees would be distributed equally across the organization's tripartite constituency.[13]

Almost immediately after ASCAP began regulating the public performance of music, a series of lawsuits sprouted up, and it was not until January 1917 that the Society obtained legal authority to enforce venue licensing. That month, the Supreme Court overturned the lower court rulings of *Herbert v. Shanley Co.*, and Associate Justice Oliver Wendell Holmes stated that, although Shanley's did not charge its patrons an admission fee, the performance of music served to attract diners, from whom the proprietor profited. Holmes concluded the court's opinion with what became a famous assertion: "If music did not pay, it would be given up. If it pays, it pays out of the public's pocket. Whether it pays or not, the purpose of employing it is profit, and that is enough."[14] The owner of Shanley's was forced to obtain a performing rights license, and ASCAP, thus empowered by the Supreme Court, began policing and licensing venues for the public performance of music.

Through the 1910s and 1920s, the two main targets of ASCAP were radio broadcasters and motion picture theater owners. Broadcasters were especially vulnerable to litigation because their program content depended so heavily on copyrighted music. It was considered a boon to them when ASCAP provided licenses to broadcasters in their formative years for nominal fees or for free. But as radio attained commercial success, ASCAP no longer needed to nurture their potential clients, and the Society began to sponsor suits against broadcasters, ultimately extracting from them upward of $250 per infringement. Several of the cases brought against radio stations ruled that music broadcast from both station and non-station locations, like dance halls and hotel lobbies, constituted public performances for profit.[15]

ASCAP seemed to have been less efficient at regulating the activities of motion picture exhibitors, but its efforts were ultimately successful. The Society regarded motion picture exhibition venues as critical sites for the distribution of popular songs because musical accompanists frequently incorporated songs into their performances.[16] As E. C. Mills, then president and general manager of the MPPA, declared in 1922: "The exhibition value of the picture as part of the evening's entertainment was [60] percent and that of the music [40] percent, but there was no compensation for the service rendered by the men who contributed this [40] percent of entertaining value."[17] Such apocryphal statistics notwithstanding, Mills's proclamation reflects the perspective of a typical music publisher: Exhibitors profited unfairly from live performances of popular songs.

On May 2, 1917, ASCAP set rates for theater licenses between 10¢ and 14¢ per seat, with the highest rates directed at proprietors of the country's largest theaters. Almost immediately, the Motion Picture Exhibitors League of America formed a defense fund by collecting $3 from each of its members and seeking an injunction on the grounds that ASCAP constituted a monopoly in restraint of trade. The injunction was denied within a year, and another suit was brought against ASCAP by the League's successor, the Motion Picture Theater Owners of America. At that point, ASCAP launched a publicity campaign to justify its position. An advertisement taken out in *Variety* defended the seat tax, calling it "fair and reasonable," while another printed in *Film Daily* (figure 2.2) assumed the stance of an exhibitor in order to promote the benefits of taking out an ASCAP license. Under the headline "Why Pay License Fees for the Privilege of Playing Copyrighted Music?" the ad copy reads:

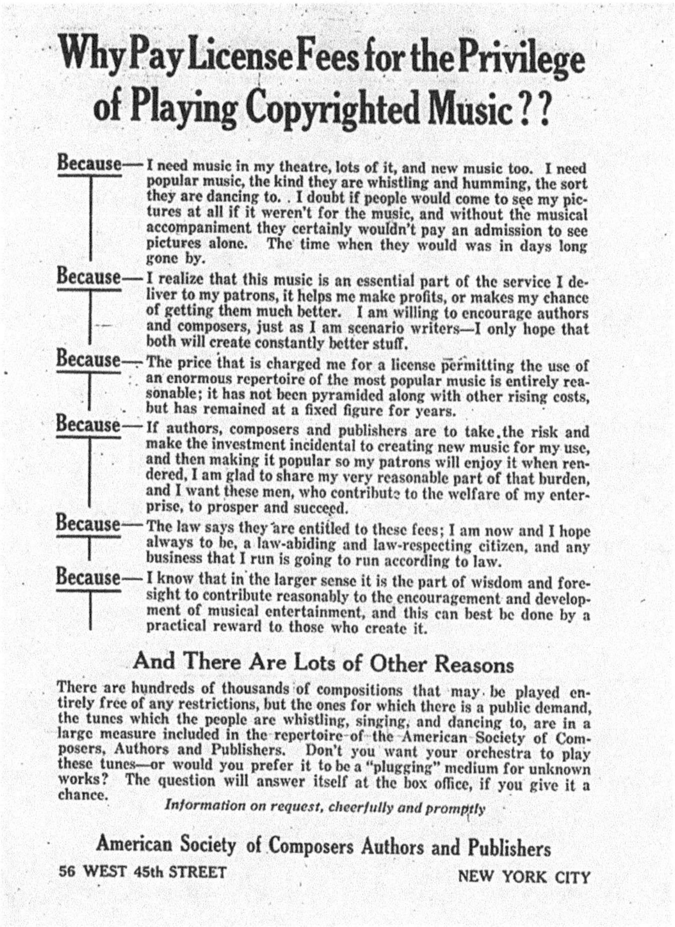

FIGURE 2.2 *Film Daily*, August 6, 1922, 70.

Because—I need music in my theatre, lots of it, and new music too. I need popular music, the kind they are whistling and humming, the sort they are dancing
to. I doubt if people would come see my pictures at all if it weren't for the music,
and without the musical accompaniment they certainly wouldn't pay an admission to see pictures alone. The time when they would was in days long gone by.[18]

April 1921 brought reports in *Variety* that executives of five large theater circuits had
"bowed" to the pressures of ASCAP by signing an agreement that granted performance rights to the circuits' eight hundred theaters in exchange for an annual fee
of 10¢ per seat.[19] By the end of the following year, ASCAP had sold similar licenses
to 5,212 additional theater owners. Individual exhibitors who brought suit against
ASCAP usually lost, and in May and July 1924, two federal courts issued their support for the Society's attempt to license every one of the country's motion picture
theaters.[20] By the start of 1927, ASCAP had licensed more than 11 thousand exhibitors and, throughout the year, collected more than half a million dollars from them.[21]

Owners of smaller and unaffiliated theaters continued to resist ASCAP. In *M.
Witmark & Sons v. Calloway*, for example, owners of the venerable publishing firm
accused the proprietor of a small theater of permitting the performance of a copyrighted work, "Smilin' Through," on a mechanical pianola. The court decided that,
whether or not the performance was incidental, the theater owner was guilty and hence
obliged to pay $250 for the infringement.[22] Similar litigation following the "Smilin'
Through" case incited protests in trade papers, as exemplified by this letter to the editor of *Billboard* from an individual residing in Schuyler, Nebraska. The author wrote:

An old gentleman, who is manager of a moving picture theater in this town—a
good old-timer, who has been manager of the same house for over 10 years and
is well liked—received notice that he was to be prosecuted for using a certain
piece of copyrighted music on his roller organ. You will note the inclosed [*sic*]
newspaper clipping states that the manager of the theater is guilty in case he
doesn't belong to the American Society of Composers, Authors and Publishers,
and pay them $15 a year. He is supposed to know all the tunes that are exempt
from the tax. He must also know, if he books acts, just what tune they use for
their acts, or be "milked" by some outfit for $250 for his ignorance. The whole
thing looks like an attempt to scare the surrounding small-town manager into
either joining the league or coughing up for playing some tune that can't be
distinguished many times from a cat fight.[23]

Some exhibitors tried to evade dealing with ASCAP by seeking tax-free music
from the public domain or from non-ASCAP publishers, such as Carl Fischer and
G. Schirmer, who printed tax-free classical music for theater use.[24] But, as more

songwriters and publishers recognized the benefits of Society membership and signed up, the number of tax-free catalogs diminished, and the selection of copyright-free songs grew increasingly limited. In addition, as ASCAP-backed publishers and songwriters prevailed in lawsuits against theater owners, membership in the organization nearly quintupled: The 116 publishers and 18 composers who constituted the Society in its inaugural year swelled to 590 publishers and 80 composers in 1929.[25] Membership came to encompass nearly every one of the country's most prominent publishing firms, including Irving Berlin, Inc., Sam Fox Publishing Co., Robbins Music Corp., Remick Music Corp., and Shapiro, Bernstein & Co. (The conspicuous absentee was Harms, Inc., for reasons that, as we will see, made a significant impact on the film industry.) The organization also changed its methods of royalty distribution in order to benefit publishers, who took in half of the royalties derived from mechanical reproductions while the creators of music—composers and lyricists—split the remainder. This inequitable system of payout would come to play an important role in the future relationship between songwriters and Hollywood producers.

THE MILLS AGREEMENT, SEPTEMBER 1927–MAY 1928

It was highly auspicious of ASCAP and the MPPA to secure control over performing and mechanical rights just as the motion picture industry was preparing to convert to synchronized sound film, because the operation of sound film depended upon both mechanically reproduced discs (and later, celluloid), as well as public performances of prerecorded music in theaters. At the same time, based on the success of theme songs produced for late silent cinema (like Rapee's "Charmaine" and "Diane"), producers at Hollywood's major studios saw the commercial value of incorporating popular songs into early sound films—and yet, under the terms of copyright law, the large, centralized majors could not evade prosecution brought about by ASCAP. Producers had two options: commission composers unaffiliated with ASCAP to write original song material for sound films, or negotiate a deal with music publishers and in so doing gain access to songwriters already under contract in addition to extant song catalogs. They opted for the latter, and, perhaps in order to evade the threat of legal action in any form, studio executives turned not to ASCAP, which had revealed its legal clout through the 1920s, but instead to the MPPA, which by that time comprised more than 50 publishers. The fact that the MPPA had only publishers as members would have implications for composers and lyricists a couple of years later, but until then, the studios handled music matters through Mills and his publishing cabal.

Warner Bros. prompted the first of two agreements forged between Hollywood executives and the MPPA. In 1925, the studio created a subsidiary, the Vitaphone Corporation, which served to license the sound-on-disc system developed by Western Electric for the production and exhibition of synchronized sound films. The following year, Vitaphone released two feature-length films—*Don Juan* and *The Better 'Ole*—and a number of sound shorts. Warner Bros. claimed that Vitaphone discs were mechanical reproductions akin to phonograph records, and therefore, under the terms of the Copyright Act's mechanical clause, they were subject to a royalty of a mere 2¢ per disc. The MPPA objected. Mills pointed out that whereas phonograph records were distributed for home use, Vitaphone discs were distributed to theaters for the purpose of public performance for profit and therefore fell under the performing rights provision of the Copyright Act. When lawyers for Warner Bros. retorted by insinuating that the studio would bypass the MPPA, Mills threatened to withdraw all of the combine's music from ASCAP's catalog. Such action would pose a grave threat to Warner Bros., because thousands of exhibitors had taken out performance rights licenses with ASCAP. If the 63 publishing companies that at the time comprised the MPPA pulled out of ASCAP, as Sanjek has written, "every theater showing a Warner product would violate the law, and Vitaphone might be strangled in its cradle."[26] On these terms, Warner Bros. was coerced into signing an agreement with the MPPA and, in October 1926, agreed to pay $104,000 in exchange for the right to record and synchronize songs published by MPPA members.[27] At the same time, exhibitors continued to pay a 10¢-per-seat tax to ASCAP in exchange for the rights to perform copyrighted music in their theaters, whether the music was performed by live musical accompanists or transmitted from prerecorded Vitaphone discs.

The prospect of an industry-wide conversion to sound precipitated a second, more far-reaching agreement with the MPPA. In December 1926, Western Electric formed a subsidiary, Electrical Research Products, Inc. (ERPI), the immediate goal of which was to persuade the motion picture majors to take out licenses on equipment distributed by Western Electric's Vitaphone rather than on equipment developed by its competitor, the Radio Corporation of America (RCA). The chairman of ERPI, John E. Otterson, knew that he would have a better chance of convincing the majors to sign if he could add a provision concerning the use of songs. So, on September 5, 1927, Otterson entered into a five-year contract with Mills that granted all prospective ERPI licensees the right to record and reproduce copyrighted music belonging to ASCAP members.[28] Later known as the Mills Agreement, the contract stipulated:

Licensor [MPPA] hereby grants to Licensee [ERPI]...the right and license: (a) To record said musical compositions or any of them in any manner, medium or form, to make copies of such recordings, and to produce and reproduce said musical compositions publicly, but only by means of apparatus for the reproduction of sound operated or controlled through the agency of said recordings (or copies thereof), in, on or as a part of such apparatus, which apparatus has been or shall be furnished by Licensee or its sublicensees to producers, distributors or exhibitors of motion pictures only; and to use, lease and sell such recordings and copies thereof, but only for the purpose of reproduction by said apparatus.[29]

Any studio that took out a license from ERPI to use Vitaphone equipment would obtain synchronization licenses to an enormous collection of copyrighted music. In exchange, the MPPA would receive guaranteed minimum payments based on the number of seats in theaters where ERPI products (i.e., Vitaphone films) were projected. The specific payment amounts seemed impressive: 2.5¢ per seat in the contract's first year, 3.5¢ in the second and third years, and 5¢ in the final two years, with guaranteed minimum payments of $100,000 in the first year and $125,000 in the second year. By the end of May 1928, all of the majors had signed on as ERPI licensees, and the Mills Agreement was ratified.[30] Subsequently, when a studio sought to use a piece of copyrighted music, it provided written notice to ERPI's newly formed music department. Upon receipt, ERPI submitted a notice to the MPPA, which in turn returned to ERPI and the studio a confirmatory license on behalf of the publisher whose song was requested (appendix 1).

Almost immediately after it was signed, the Mills Agreement proved to be onerous for music publishers, songwriters, and motion picture producers. In fixing the sliding-scale seat tax at a maximum rate of 5¢ per seat, Mills had underestimated the potential commercial power of the motion picture song. Even more distressing to songwriters and publishers, he had also failed to negotiate a guaranteed minimum payment beyond the first two years under contract. Headlines in *Variety* opined, "Music Business Sold Film Talking Rights Too Cheaply" and "Music Men Disgruntled on Sound Film's $100,000 Bargaining for Terms." In the latter article, a reporter noted, "With their music so essential to sound pictures they could have obtained much better terms had they, or their spokesman, visualized the great possibilities of the talker's development."[31] The most significant problem, however, was that even though Mills represented only the MPPA, he had implicated ASCAP in the Mills Agreement by allowing ERPI licensees to use songs from ASCAP's catalog. The Mills Agreement promised payment only to the MPPA; composers and lyricists were blocked from the guaranteed compensation. Why had Mills done this? Perhaps, as suggested by some commentators of the period, he assumed that songwriters would receive their fair share of the ERPI monies by way of separate agreements with publishers. But such an assumption was a flagrant error on Mills's part, because by 1928, ASCAP was directing a greater proportion of royalties to venerable publishing firms with a diversified portfolio (e.g., Feist, Berlin, and Harms) than to younger firms that specialized in motion picture music (e.g., Robbins Music, Sam Fox, and DeSylva, Brown & Henderson).[32] Songwriters of motion picture songs were losing out, and through the spring and summer of 1928, they protested the Mills Agreement. Indeed, their complaints were so clamorous that when ERPI's major competitor, RCA, approached Mills with a deal resembling the Mills Agreement, Mills at first refused to sign.[33]

The Mills Agreement also disappointed motion picture producers, whose chief grievance was that an ERPI license granted performing rights for venues in the United States and Canada only. Producers seeking to satisfy a growing foreign market for sound films had to obtain separate, and often costly, licenses in each foreign country.[34] Making matters worse was the fact that the Mills Agreement did not compensate producers whose films allegedly augmented the sales of sheet music and phonograph records; rather, it extended rights to record songs for the sole purpose of playback in ERPI-licensed theaters on ERPI-licensed equipment. Because film companies did not own song copyrights, they were prohibited from copying and selling phonograph records of motion picture songs to the public. Even as songs written specially for motion pictures were regarded as increasingly valuable commodities, the studios were unable to profit from prospective sales.

A brief example illustrates the potential loss of sales faced by studios in the wake of the Mills Agreement. According to *Variety*, in December 1927 Paramount signed an agreement with the Cleveland-based Sam Fox Publishing Co., whose longstanding music director, John Stepan ("J. S.") Zamecnik (figure 2.3), had gained respect as a composer and arranger thanks to his compilation of two multivolume folios of "mood" music for silent film accompaniment: *Sam Fox Moving Picture Music* (1913) and *Sam Fox Photoplay Edition* (1919–1922).[35]

FIGURE 2.3 John Stepan Zamecnik (Robert S. Birchard collection).

FIGURE 2.4 The theme song of *Redskin* (1929) was composed by J. S. Zamecnik, with lyrics by Harry D. Kerr. This advertisement placed by the Sam Fox Publishing Co. in *Variety* cites "Zamecnik's remarkable picture score" (*Variety*, January 30, 1929, 23).

Having moved from his hometown of Cleveland to Los Angeles in 1924, Zamecnik was engaged via Sam Fox to compose scores, and some songs, for *Old Ironsides* (1926), *The Rough Riders* (1927), *Wings* (1927), *Abie's Irish Rose* (1928), *The Wedding March* (1928), *Redskin* (1929), and *Betrayal* (1929). Paramount recorded the scores of the latter five films and distributed them for playback in theaters wired for sound. But even when the initially instrumental theme songs associated with the films—"Redskin" from *Redskin* and "Paradise" from *The Wedding March*—became moderate hits when they were published with lyrics (figure 2.4), it is unlikely that Paramount earned a cent from sales of sheet music and phonograph recordings; the song copyrights, after all, belonged to Sam Fox. A scenario like this surely compelled film producers to find an alternative to the Mills Agreement and obtain control over song copyrights.

THE MOTION PICTURE COMPANIES INVEST: AUGUST
1928–NOVEMBER 1929

Hollywood's first systematic investment in the business of music publishing constituted the origins of media convergence in the United States as we understand it today. Certainly tie-ups among motion picture exhibitors, music publishers, retail outlets, radio broadcasters, and other agents of entertainment existed before the coming of sound, but those earlier arrangements were erratic more often than not and tended to satisfy the immediate interests of the relevant parties rather than any long-term forecasts. In contrast, beginning in November 1928, the studios entered into a methodical and demarcated period of investment that executives saw as a means of ensuring the long-term health of their companies.

The 15-month period divided into two phases of deals. In the first phase, a number of majors affiliated with music publishing firms to create or designate subsidiary companies expressly for the purpose of publishing motion picture songs. Paramount, Fox, Warner Bros., and Loew's/MGM (hereafter referred to as MGM) were all involved in these ventures. In the second phase, Warner Bros. and RCA undertook more extensive deals by acquiring the majority or entire stock of massive publishing firms. A detailed history of this period, constructed from trade press reports and studio legal files, and represented by figure 2.5, reveals a hallmark characteristic of media convergence: the increasing concentration of corporate power.

Paramount was the first production company to attempt, albeit unsuccessfully, the acquisition of song catalogs. In the summer of 1928, executives bid on the collected song copyrights belonging to two of the country's largest music publishing firms, Harms and Robbins Music.[36] Harms was presided over by industry magnate Max Dreyfus, who had spent the earlier part of the century revitalizing an established publishing company, T. B. Harms, by signing the most distinguished musical songwriters in New York, including Richard Rodgers, Vincent Youmans, Cole

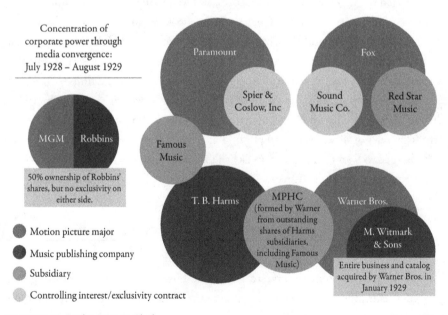

FIGURE 2.5 Credit: Maggie Clark.

Porter, Jerome Kern, and George Gershwin. By the time the firm's name changed to Harms in 1920, Dreyfus had built a publishing empire that also owned the British publisher Chappell & Company, as well as 20 percent stock in DeSylva, Brown & Henderson, home of the eponymous Broadway trio, and 50 percent stock in Remick Music, which was distributing tunes by writers who would soon become Hollywood mainstays: Al Dubin, Harry Warren, Gus Kahn, and Richard A. Whiting.[37] Notably, Harms was also the only major publishing firm that had opted out of the Mills Agreement. The other company with which Paramount sought affiliation was Robbins Music, led by former song plugger Jack Robbins, who would later be credited for the success of bandleaders Vincent Lopez, George Olsen, and (partial company stakeholder) Paul Whiteman. Robbins was no foreigner to the field of film music, because his company had also published photoplay scores composed by Erno Rapee, Hugo Reisenfeld, and Nathaniel Shilkret.

Both Robbins and Dreyfus rejected the bid from Paramount, a move that prompted studio executives to advance a proposal more modest than outright acquisition. On August 27, Paramount struck a deal with Harms that resulted in the creation of the Famous Music Corp. with 100 shares of common stock split evenly between the studio and the publishing firm.[38] The shared ownership of Famous Music, which was intended to remain in effect until January 1, 1930, entailed an even distribution of royalties earned from sales of sheet music and licenses for mechanical recordings. Almost immediately, Paramount began to encourage exhibitors to make tie-ups between film and music products, and the first entries into the Famous Music catalog included the motion picture theme songs "My Varsity Girl I'll Cling to You," from *Varsity* (1928), and "Another Kiss," Victor Schertzinger's contribution to *Manhattan Cocktail* (1928).[39]

Paramount's strategies were echoed by MGM executives, who in September 1928 attempted to secure the majority of stock in Robbins Music, but having been denied by shareholders, bought 50 percent of the company. Motion picture songs written for MGM sound films were entered into the Robbins catalog.[40] The deal with MGM shaped corporate structure at Robbins: Jack Robbins stepped down as the president and became vice president and general manager, and was replaced by MGM's former treasurer, David Bernstein, at the top of the company. But unlike Famous Music, Robbins Music had pre-existed its tie-up with MGM, so as a nonexclusive publisher, Robbins continued to release songs unrelated to motion pictures, including contemporary arrangements of Gilbert and Sullivan numbers and songs for stage musical revues.

MGM was likewise nonexclusive in its dealing with Robbins, although the studio's dabbling with songs published by firms other than Robbins quickly proved to be problematic. For instance, most of the original numbers featured in *The*

Broadway Melody (1929) were penned by studio songwriters Nacio Herb Brown and Arthur Freed and entered into the Robbins Music catalog. However, prior to signing with MGM, Brown had composed what became the film's most successful song, "The Wedding of the Painted Doll," and had published it with Sherman, Clay & Co. When Jack Robbins realized that "The Wedding of the Painted Doll," sung onscreen by James Burrows, was the film's greatest hit, he insisted on selecting all of the music for MGM's subsequent releases, presumably so that he could enter the titles into the Robbins song catalogue.[41]

In November, Fox entered into a formal arrangement with DeSylva, Brown & Henderson (hereafter referred to as DBH), a firm that had been created in February 1927 by composer Ray Henderson and lyricists Buddy (George Gard) DeSylva and Lew Brown. The triumvirate was much celebrated, though they were younger constituents of Tin Pan Alley and Broadway. Each member had written hit songs popularized by Al Jolson (who claimed to have discovered DeSylva), and together they had scored the 1925 edition of George White's *Scandals*, a Broadway musical revue, followed by a series of hit musical comedies for the stage, including *Good News* (1927) and *Hold Everything* (1928). For Hollywood, their company had published several successful songs, including "Angela Mia" for Fox's *The Street Angel* (1928) and "Sonny Boy" for Warner Bros.' *The Singing Fool* (1928). The firm's agreement with Fox in late 1928 formalized the relationship between the two companies by making DBH, which had grown to employ over 100 staff members under the direction of Robert Crawford, former sales manager for Irving Berlin's publishing company, the exclusive publisher of all of Fox's new motion picture songs.[42] Fox and DBH quickly formed a film music publishing subsidiary, Sound Music Corp., which eventually became the Crawford Music Corp. Erno Rapee, still working at the Roxy Theatre in New York, was placed in charge of all "musical activity."[43]

In December, *Variety* reported a tie-up between Warner Bros. and Irving Berlin's publishing firm. Berlin agreed to collaborate with Al Jolson on the writing and publishing of songs for Warner Bros. sound films. The studio, composer, and star resolved to split resulting royalties.[44] Jolson had already plugged two of Berlin's songs in Warner Bros. films: *The Jazz Singer*'s "Blue Skies" (originally written by Berlin for the 1926 Rodgers and Hart musical *Betsy*) and *The Singing Fool*'s "There's a Rainbow 'Round My Shoulder" (for which Jolson was given a co-author credit along with Dave Dreyer and Billy Rose). Engaged with Warner Bros., Berlin composed numerous songs for Jolson's subsequent star vehicle *Mammy* (1929), including "Let Me Sing and I'm Happy" and "Across the Breakfast Table Looking at You."[45] Like the deal between MGM and Robbins Music, the one between Warner Bros. and Berlin was not exclusive; Warner Bros. published motion picture songs under other companies, and Berlin negotiated deals with at least one other company, United Artists.[46]

Nonetheless, although the informal arrangement between Warner Bros., Berlin, and Jolson ostensibly allowed studio, composer/publisher, and star to profit from the pronounced success of motion picture songs, problems with the deal grew increasingly clear to Warner Bros. For one, while the three parties benefited from "There's a Rainbow 'Round My Shoulder," the triumphant song hit of *The Singing Fool* was "Sonny Boy," allegedly the first synchronized song of the transitional era to incite sales upward of one million records in the United States.[47] Unfortunately for Warner Bros., "Sonny Boy" was written and published by DBH prior to their tie-up with Fox. As a result, Warner Bros. earned no royalties from the sales of "Sonny Boy" sheet music and mechanical rights licenses.[48] Of even greater concern to the studio would have been the pending expiration of the Mills Agreement, slated for September 1932, which would cast the studios upon the mercy of music publishers who could charge whatever they pleased for synchronization licenses. *Variety* had anticipated as much when it noted that whether or not Mills had undersold the value of music copyrights, there was "no doubt in the film people's minds that at the expiration of [the Mills Agreement] they will have to pay considerably more for the same privileges."[49] Eager to penetrate the lucrative business of song publishing, Warner Bros. opened negotiations with the country's most prized and prodigious publishing firms: M. Witmark & Sons and Harms.

M. Witmark & Sons was an esteemed business managed by brothers Isidore, Julius, and Jay Witmark under the legal ownership of their father Marcus.[50] Since the company's inception in 1886, the Witmarks had amassed a collection of song copyrights by signing dozens of composers and lyricists whose work represented a wide range of styles, from operettas by Victor Herbert to novelty songs by Gus Edwards. In anticipation of the film industry's demand for music, Isidore prepared a catalog of more than 2,000 of the company's songs, ranging from instrumental music to period hits to vocal ballads, all of which he expected would appeal to movie producers. Isidore's intention was not to sell the firm's catalogs, but rather to loan them to the studios that had signed with ERPI. An October 1928 issue of *Billboard* quoted him as declaring, "The needs of the motion picture scorer are incalculable," and remarking on the potential for recycling "old-time numbers...for which the popular demand expired years ago."[51] Isidore anticipated that motion pictures would breathe new life into old songs.

A scarce three months later, however, Isidore's plans were trumped by a generous sum offered by Warner Bros. He later recounted that the Witmarks sold the entire publishing business and catalogs to the studio in exchange for a "large sum of cash" and the right to retain their positions as managers.[52] The amount, according to *Variety*, was $900,000, a figure that prompted *Motion Picture News* to alert its readers that this was "the first time a producing company has definitely decided to enter the music field as a publishing concern."[53]

With the Witmark deal consummated, Warner Bros. set into motion a second, even more expansive arrangement. In April 1929, the studio bid nearly $10 million to purchase Harms outright in its entirety. The trade papers jumped on the news. *Variety* trumpeted in a headline, "POP MUSIC REVOLUTION," while *Billboard* declared, "Music Publishers Find Talkies Boon," and a reporter for *Hollywood Filmograph* mused, " 'Merger, Merger, Merger' is Tin Pan Alley's theme song now. The publishers along Broadway are all sitting back and waiting for some film producer to come along with a million kopeks for their catalogues, and a ticket for Hollywood."[54]

On August 15, three weeks after an initial agreement had been signed, Max Dreyfus sold outstanding stock in Harms and its subsidiaries to Warner Bros.[55] *Variety* explained in plain terms the reasoning behind Dreyfus's decision: "He perceived that an independent publisher without a definite picture affiliation cannot exist."[56] Brokered by Goldman Sachs, the deal delivered 140,364 shares of Warner Bros. common stock, worth close to $8 million, to stakeholders in Harms, Inc., and its subsidiaries. In exchange, Warner Bros. obtained all of the issued and outstanding capital stock of the newly formed Music Publishers Holding Corporation (MPHC), a holding company that assumed all of the outstanding shares in Harms, Chappell-Harms, DBH, Remick Music, Edward A. Stege, and T. B. Harms; 50 percent of outstanding shares in Famous Music and Campbell-Connelly; and two-thirds of outstanding shares in Atlas Music and New World Music. With the acquisition and formation of the MPHC, Warner Bros. owned the lion's share of the American music publishing industry and song copyrights.[57]

Variety speculated that the purchase of the Harms empire benefited Warner Bros. in at least two ways.[58] The first derived from the fact that, as president of Harms, Dreyfus had excluded his company from the Mills Agreement, opting instead to issue synchronization licenses directly to motion picture producers.[59] Dreyfus's decision yielded impressive returns: An audit conducted in 1929 indicated that over the course of that year alone, Harms's direct licensing earned the company five times its ASCAP income.[60] By owning the copyrights to all of the songs published by Harms and its subsidiaries, Warner Bros. could bypass the Mills Agreement entirely and prosper from the direct licensing of Harms songs to the studio's competitors. This much was illustrated when Warner Bros. received $50,000 for selling a license to use George Gershwin's "Rhapsody in Blue" (from the Paul Whiteman variety picture *King of Jazz*) to Universal.[61]

Second, by obtaining song copyrights that belonged to the entire Harms publishing family, Warner Bros. was protecting itself from the anticipated effects of a prospective merger between RCA and six leading music publishers. A few months prior to the Warner Bros./Harms transaction, RCA had offered $20 million in exchange for song copyrights to the six firms.[62] The publishers declined, but the magnitude of RCA's offer signaled to Warner Bros. the importance of obtaining song copyrights as corporate assets, especially because, as *Variety* pointed out, RCA's operations extended to the radio, phonograph, and motion picture industries.[63] With Harms and nine other firms under the MPHC umbrella, Warner Bros. could easily compete with other conglomerates in the making.

In late August 1929, *Variety* published a list of the relationships between Hollywood's majors and music publishing firms (transcribed in appendix 2), showing that Warner Bros. prevailed "in complete dominance of the pick of America's musical creators for exclusive use of their work in the studio's pictures."[64] The paper further observed:

> The importance of musical copyrights to pictures and sound recordings has upset the industry so that within a very few months it is believed none of the more important music firms will remain independent in view of the value of a tie-up with either the picture companies or the electrics.[65]

As shown by the timeline in appendix 3, the magnitude of the Warner Bros./Harms deal prompted other motion picture companies to augment their music holdings as a means of avoiding having to publish under the MPHC and therefore retain prospective royalties from song licensing. In October 1929, Fox announced its creation of a new publishing entity, Red Star Music Co., which planned to be in full operation by the beginning of 1930. Under the Red Star label, the studio published its own film songs, arranged music licenses with foreign branches of Fox Film, and offered to farm out its songwriters to other studios.[66] In November 1929, RCA, which already owned interests in communications (RCA Communications, Inc.), motion picture technology (RCA Photophone Co.), motion picture exhibition (Radio-Keith Orpheum Corp., or RKO), radio broadcasting (National Broadcasting Corp.), and radio sets and talking machine manufacturing (RCA Victor Corp.), acquired Leo Feist, Inc., and Carl Fischer, Inc., both of which were distinguished Tin Pan Alley publishing companies, and created the Radio Music Corporation.[67] Also in November, Paramount, aware that its contract with Harms (which had created Famous Music) was set to expire in less than three months, purchased 80 percent stock in a young but promising firm, Spier & Coslow, Inc., home of songwriting duo Larry Spier and Sam Coslow.[68] In so doing, Paramount ensured its affiliation with at least one publishing company that was autonomous from the MPHC.

Such activities signal just how important it was for studios to obviate the expenses associated with song licensing. By owning song copyrights, the majors protected themselves from synchronization fees that could be levied upon them, and at the same time allowed them to exonerate exhibitors from having to pay licensing fees to ASCAP (and therefore avoid having to raise the price of film rentals). By 1929, monies earned from licensing synchronization rights came to outnumber those earned from sales of sheet music and mechanical licenses for recordings.[69] While the affiliations and acquisitions that transpired between August 1928 and November 1929 altered the corporate structure of film and music businesses by creating powerfully concentrated, horizontally integrated companies, they also effected lasting changes on a more modest entity: the movie studio music department.

THE INFLUX OF SONGWRITERS AND THE CREATION OF MUSIC DEPARTMENTS

Hollywood's demand for songs in films produced during the 1928–1929 season resulted in new employment opportunities for composers and lyricists, and many songwriters who were considered the best in the country migrated from New York to Los Angeles. The significance of their arrival was articulated by the reports and columns that cropped up in trade publications.[70] *Variety* inaugurated a new column titled "Along the Coast" that was exclusively devoted to news and gossip of the music scene in Hollywood; similar columns appeared in *Billboard* and *Hollywood Filmograph*. Feature articles also appeared. The August 1929 issue of *Hollywood Filmograph* included an amusing piece titled "Song Writers Desert Gotham for Filmland," in which author Fanya Graham observed:

> The deserted buildings that flank New York's famous Tin Pan Alley are only song material now, and the title of the song that they suggest might well be "The Exodus." For the inmates of Tin Pan Alley are now in Southern California. What is more, they seem to have come out on one-way tickets. Or perhaps they already sold the return tickets they had at first.[71]

In the *Motion Picture Almanac of 1930*, James Little reviewed the Hollywood industry's musical activity in during 1929 and noted:

The new "tin pan alley" of Hollywood far surpasses that of any heretofore heard of. A veritable galaxy of songwriters, composers, musical directors, popular singers, everything pertaining to music, is centered right there, doing nothing but putting into form those sweet strains that are carried to us from behind the screen.[72]

Often with tongue in cheek, reporters celebrated newfound prosperity enjoyed by songwriters. A columnist writing for the magazine *Talking Screen* joked, "Composers hitherto unable to afford much-needed barbering are leaving hair in vast quantities on the cutting-room floor,"[73] while another quipped in the May 1929 issue of *Hollywood Filmograph*, "We saw [12] song pluggers in Henry's [Café] at 4 a.m. the other morning. They refused to leave and one told why with these words, 'Believe it or not we're waiting for a theme song.'"[74]

Many accounts of the migration of Broadway talent to Hollywood during the coming of sound focus on the arrival of eminent composers, lyricists, and librettists, such as Irving Berlin, Richard Rodgers, and the Gershwin brothers. However, these highest-ranking songwriters did not arrive in Los Angeles until at least mid-1930. The majority of the first "small army of lyric writers and composers," as *Billboard* termed them, were staff employees of Tin Pan Alley publishing firms, and they found themselves on trains to California as a result of the corporate mergers that had taken place between their employers and the major studios.[75] In addition, it is worth noting that although the presence of New York songwriters influenced the soundtracks and even film form of the transitional era, the conventions of popular songs themselves did not radically change as a result of Hollywood's song vogue. To be sure, as Thomas S. Hischak recounts, numerous differences existed between the treatment of songs in Hollywood musicals and those found in their stage counterparts, but by and large, the popular song form that was characteristic of the 1920s Tin Pan Alley and Broadway productions continued to dominate the output of songwriters who were writing for both stage and film.[76]

The versatility of the new Hollywood songwriters is evidenced by the events that transpired when Fox signed with DBH in October 1928. At the time, the songwriting team was engrossed with productions in New York and Atlantic City; three of their musical comedies (*Good News*, *Three Cheers*, and *Hold Everything*), as well as a musical revue, *George White's Scandals*, were running simultaneously, and *Follow Thru* was in production and scheduled for a premiere that January. Unable to travel to Los Angeles, the triumvirate instead dispatched composer Archie Gottler and lyricists Sidney D. Mitchell and Con Conrad to the Fox lot in order to write "on behalf" of their employers.[77] Gottler, Mitchell, and Conrad were not unknown songwriters—each had penned song hits in the 1910s and early 1920s—but they

were not the household names of their employers. Once engaged as staff songwriters on the Fox lot, they wrote Alley-type tunes (such as the ballad "Christina" for the
film of the same name) for more than ten films in 1929 alone, effectively launching
their illustrious careers in Los Angeles.

Telling signs of shifting allegiances between studios and music publishers were
the studio-songwriter contracts, which carried only six- or twelve-month terms in
order to accommodate the flow of songwriters around studio lots. For example, one
of the consequences of the Warner Bros./Harms deal was that songwriters in Fox's
music department were ordered to sign contracts with Warner Bros. The impetus
came from Max Dreyfus, who had managed to secure a disproportionate amount
of corporate voting power on the board of Fox's publishing partner, DBH. Dreyfus
wielded his influence in order to send songwriters to the Warner Bros. lot; the sudden withdrawal of writers from Fox prompted the studio to create a publishing subsidiary, Red Star Music, and fill the void with lesser-known but respectable talent
from New York.[78]

A more detailed and illustrative example of the transience of songwriters at any
individual studio during this period is that of Al Dubin, the songwriter best known
in the late 1920s for writing lyrics to "Tiptoe Through the Tulips" and "A Cup of
Coffee, a Sandwich and You." In December 1928, Dubin was hired as a staff lyricist
for Gene Austin's publishing firm. The two-year contract guaranteed Dubin a weekly
salary of $100 against royalties for sheet music and sales of phonograph records; in
exchange, Austin's company would retain all rights to Dubin's work.[79] But a month
later, in January 1929, Austin forged a deal with M. Witmark & Sons, which in turn
was acquired by Warner Bros. The result was a new contract for Dubin that released
his services to Witmark and Warner Bros., but that otherwise retained the terms of
his original agreement with Austin. All works written or composed by Dubin and
published by Witmark bore the statement "Published by Witmark by Arrangement
with Gene Austin, Inc." A year later, as shown in appendix 4, Dubin's contract was
sold by Austin to the MPHC for a sum of $25,000, and a new agreement was cre-
ated. The one-year term stipulated a salary and advance totaling $500 per week
against royalties that promised much higher rates than those Austin had supplied.
In just over one year, then, Dubin's weekly salary had quintupled and his royalty
advance had tripled. The cost of such rewards, as Donald Crafton has observed, was
stringent restrictions on copyright ownership; each of Dubin's co-signers secured
the exclusive right to print, reprint, publish, copy, and sell the artist's creations. But
this seems to have been a price that Dubin and other songwriters were willing to pay
in exchange for otherwise profitable contracts with Hollywood's majors.[80]

Although contracts like the one described above helped to ensure the studios'
control over the means of song distribution, their employment of songwriters also

facilitated their control over actual song production. In order to align production practices with the ethos of efficiency that characterized the film industry at the time, the studios formed music departments, which they populated with songwriters, conductors, orchestrators, and arrangers.[81] A "snapshot" of studio activity with regard to music departments can be gleaned from a brief account of salient developments at three of the majors.

Paramount launched an embryonic music department in June 1928 when studio executives hired Nathaniel Finston, then a theater orchestra conductor in New York, to serve as musical director of what *Variety* hyped as "the greatest musical organization of the show business, comprising approximately 45 nationally known composers and over 20 orchestrators, with an executive salary list of $10,000 weekly for the 75 men who will direct the activities of the department."[82] The studio then hired a series of Tin Pan Alley success stories: Gus Kahn, Richard Whiting, Leo Robin, Sam Coslow, Fred Ahlert, Roy Turk, and, perhaps most notably, Walter Donaldson, whose number "My Blue Heaven" was the top hit of the 1920s.[83]

Meanwhile, Warner Bros. set to work constructing a music department as soon as the company had acquired the rights to the entire Witmark catalog. Ray Perkins, who was hired by Warner Bros. in January (under the terms of the contract laid out in appendix 5), was promoted to head of the new department; he was joined by roughly a dozen songwriters, nearly all of whom had worked as musicians and/ or pluggers in Tin Pan Alley. They included Herman Ruby, Harry Akst, Joe Burke, Alfred Bryan, Grant Clarke, and Al Dubin.[84] At the Burbank studio lot, a building previously designated for screenwriters was allocated to songwriters and musicians.[85]

MGM, after affiliating with Robbins Music, signed William Axt and David Mendoza, famed composers and conductors of the Capitol Theater Orchestra in New York.[86] But the importance of having a department dedicated to the creation and synchronization of music became obvious to MGM executives. Arthur Lange, best known for his 1919 arrangement of the song "Dardanella," had catapulted to success thanks to a recording of that song by Ben Selvin and his Novelty Orchestra, and was selected to head up the new unit. He arrived in February 1929, duly appointed to conduct, arrange, and supervise all musical recordings at the studio. Joining him on the MGM songwriting roster were Nacio Herb Brown, Arthur Freed, Gus Edwards, Billy Rose, Fred Fisher, Jack Yellen, and Milton Ager, as well as Jesse Greer, Ray Klages, Lou Alter, and Hugo Frent; staff songwriters from Robbins Music. Many years later, Lange's colleague Ernst Klapholz would describe their earliest days at MGM as ones in which they "had no music and...had to make a Music Department. (In 1929), it was still just bungalows. It was terrible. It was one little room with a piano in it."[87]

In addition to staff composers and lyricists, the flourishing music departments employed orchestra conductors, singing choruses, staff musicians, freelance musicians, arrangers, librarians, copyists, proofreaders to detect musical plagiarism, legal executives to handle copyright matters, and miscellaneous office staff.[88] If statistics in *Variety* are to believed, then by the end of 1929, music departments had grown into large entities with sizable numbers of employees: 180 at Warner Bros. and its subsidiary, First National, 144 at MGM, 138 at Paramount, and 46 at RKO.[89] The relative magnitude of the music departments reflected Hollywood's increasingly concentrated power over film and music, two formerly distinct forms of entertainment.

THE SONG INDUSTRY: BIFURCATED OR DIFFUSED?

Writing in 1964, music historian David Ewen recounted a common attitude toward Hollywood's involvement in song publishing: specifically, that it marked the beginning of the end of Tin Pan Alley. In his aptly named book *The Life and Death of Tin Pan Alley*, Ewen provides a before-and-after snapshot of the publishing business:

> In [New York's Tin Pan Alley], the publisher had been the central force around which everything connected with songs gravitated—the writers, performers, salesmen, pluggers. It was the publisher who selected what songs were to be printed, and he picked them because he liked them and felt that the public would like them. Then he set about the necessary business of getting songs performed and popularized.... But now, in the new scheme of things created by the movie industry, the publisher was dictated *to*. He resigned not only his basic function of selecting songs for publication but also of determining the best ways of making them popular.[90]

Ewen's account diverges from reports authored during the transitional era. Commentators of the period tended to regard the studios' entry into song publishing not as a curse on the music industry but rather as a stroke of fortune to both the film and music industries, with a possible favoring of the latter. For example, in *Variety*'s annual review issue of 1929, chief music critic Abel Green weighed in on the merits of cross-promotion and concluded that films were more effective at plugging songs than songs were at plugging films.[91] Two months later, a report in *Variety* explained, "The picture business is bigger than the music industry at large. A song theme from the screen can reach more people and penetrate more virgin territory than the music exploiters themselves could, counting radio or not."[92] Another *Variety* writer declared that summer: "As talkers remade the picture industry, so did the talkers remake, through pictures, the music industry."[93] When popular music was concerned, Hollywood was thought to have the Midas touch.

Of course, these optimistic reports published in the noted trade paper must be read with a grain of salt. The very novelty of music publishing on the West Coast surely inspired exaggerated statements and boosterism in the trades, and it would be more accurate to say that Hollywood's investments helped to *diffuse* the geographic concentration of the music business. Although branch offices and staff songwriters resided in or near Hollywood, it is crucial to remember that not only did the headquarters of most publishing firms remain on Broadway, but also, as Richard Koszarski explains in *Hollywood on the Hudson*, several studios retained music departments in New York.[94] Even while the quantity of original Broadway productions dwindled through the late 1920s, songwriters and stars of the stage and other musical entertainments remained in New York, where they continued to introduce hit songs. Many of the country's top vocalists and bandleaders, including Paul Whiteman, Ben Selvin, Ruth Etting, and Ted Lewis, continued to broadcast from and cut records of popular songs on the East Coast.[95] Moreover, such songs were, in terms of structure and style, quite similar to the motion picture tunes fashioned on the other side of the country; there is little evidence that a distinctly new song form arose as a result of the assimilation of popular music by sound films. The motion picture studios' investments inspired the migration of Tin Pan Alley personnel to the West Coast and had lasting effects on the concentrated ownership of the entertainment industries, but the wholesale shift of the music industry to Hollywood was tempered by the prominence of other media located on the East Coast and elsewhere in the country. As the next chapter shows, Hollywood executives sought to tap into those media too.

PART TWO
Models of Song Use

It's obvious that once a song is spotted in a picture, there's no such thing as influencing anyone with a song-plugger's ballyhoo or a pair of fight tickets or a swell feed to induce him to take a song out in favor of a rival publication.

ABEL GREEN (1929)[1]

3

Plugging a Song

THE DISCRETE CHARM OF THE POPULAR SONG,

FROM BROADWAY TO HOLLYWOOD

MARCH 29, 1928, was a fateful date for Hollywood and American radio. That evening, six movie stars from United Artists—John Barrymore, Charlie Chaplin, Dolores del Río, Douglas Fairbanks, D. W. Griffith, and Norma Talmadge—gathered at an NBC radio station and performed on *The Dodge Brothers Hour*, a radio program sponsored by the Detroit car company. NBC broadcast the program not only over its Red Network, which had 17 stations in Eastern and Northeastern states, but also, for what was deemed an extraordinary presentation, to the loudspeakers of 55 movie theaters located across the country, so that the stars could demonstrate to millions of Americans that they "possessed one thing which had never been regarded as remotely necessary to [the film] industry's prosperity or their own celebrity, namely *a voice*."[2] The public's reaction to the evening's broadcast was, to quote *Variety*, "brutal" and proved that "movie stars should be seen and not heard."[3] Stormy weather made for crackly reception in most theaters; audiences and exhibitors were irked by the delay of feature-length film presentations that were scheduled to follow the broadcast; and, perhaps worst of all, Talmadge and del Río were accused of using voice doubles. Despite these shortcomings, Hollywood studios during 1928 and 1929 expanded their operations in the radio industry by opening new stations in Los Angeles that could capitalize on the presence of local film talent.

The story of the first United Artists broadcast is a parable in histories of the collusion between Hollywood and radio—a signpost of the film industry's increasing receptiveness to radio as a cross-promotional vehicle in spite of the technical troubles that plagued the broadcast medium in its formative years.[4] Indeed, one of the primary objectives of the evening's program was the plugging of "Ramona," a popular song composed by Mabel Wayne and L. Wolfe Gilbert for United Artists' motion picture of the same name, slated for a premiere six weeks from the broadcast date. Though the program failed to glamorize the voices of the studio's stars, del Río's presentation of "Ramona" was part of a coordinated and successful publicity campaign that included trade paper advertisements, the star's recording of the popular waltz number for RCA Victor, and regular live performances at the film's openings in major theaters. With *Ramona* playing in theaters, as Richard Barrios has quipped, "one would have had to live on Neptune not to know that song.... By general acknowledgement, it made a sure-fire hit out of a so-so movie."[5] Published by Leo Feist, Inc., the song reportedly sold 1,750,000 copies of sheet music, while the film reportedly took in $1,500,000, four times the usual gross of a feature film.[6] Record companies benefited too; Gene Austin's recording for Victor remained at the top of *Billboard*'s charts for 17 weeks.[7] The United Artists broadcast over the NBC network was one unfortunate piece of an otherwise effective cross-marketing media campaign.

Such campaigns dovetailed with Hollywood's increasing involvement with music publishing companies, as discussed in the previous chapter. Through late 1928 and early 1929, as the studios merged with or acquired majority stock in publishing firms, trade papers extolled the capacity for songs to popularize mediocre films and vice versa. Articles in *Variety* and *Billboard* especially praised the advantage that sound films possessed over other ways to distribute music—namely that they guaranteed the identical presentation of singing stars in every theater wired for sound when other platforms for music distribution could not make this same promise. Radio offered an impression of "liveness" but lacked the visual spectacle of the star. Broadway shows were accessible to a limited audience, unless on occasion original casts embarked on road tours. Silent film accompaniment incorporated theme songs, but these songs were not vocalized and their presentation varied widely according to theater size, musicians, and instrumentation. The film industry's capacity to standardize musical accompaniment across the country and synchronize that music with images of celebrity vocalists meant that music publishers would receive an endorsement with every film booking—a significant benefit to studios that were increasingly absorbing the interests of publishing firms. At the same time, as the trades noted, studios would profit from the readily marketable and highly successful genre of popular music.[8] Shortly after Warner Bros. released *The Singing Fool* (1928), an article in *Variety* announced that one of the film's songs, "Sonny Boy," was outselling all other numbers in the United States by a ratio of two to one, and continued, "The picture companies should realize the importance of the value of such exploitation. With hundreds of thousands of copies of the sheet music and the records going into households, its value for the screen's box office is apparent."[9] Several months later, a headline declared, "'Picture songs' now most important to publishers—big hits among them," and an article observed:

> The picture song, from the music men's viewpoint, is the millennium. It's the quickest, easiest and least expensive means of song hit making ever known.... From the picture producer's standpoint, the song hook-up is invaluable. It gives their celluloid product a new form of plugging and exploitation over the radio, on the records and in the streets, through mass whistling and harmonizing, which no amount of paid advertising could accomplish.[10]

The hyperbolic tone that often characterized the style of writing in *Variety*, along with the fact that the paper relied upon generous advertising revenue supplied by film and music companies, might well arouse two suspicions: First, were the paper's claims about the triumphs of motion picture songs entirely accurate? Perhaps the editors had succumbed to industry boosterism. Second, cross-promotion was a novel rather than time-tested strategy created by the film and music industries. Both suspicions can be laid to rest.

First, other evidence corroborates the claims made by *Variety*. Motion picture songs began topping the weekly best-seller lists in the trade papers by late 1928 and through 1929; they became regular fare for recordings by various artists and for different record labels; and, according to reports submitted by regional exhibitors, they stimulated sales of sheet music and phonograph records in theater lobbies. On this count, *Variety* seemed not to be overstating the case. The second point of suspicion—on the novelty of cross-promotion—deserves more attention, because Hollywood producers, directors, and publicity agents most certainly did not fashion song hits by creating original strategies of marketing. Rather, they exploited the pre-existing strategies of cross-promotion and star-song identification (the latter being the association of a star with a particular song, as discussed in chapter 1). Both strategies aimed to advertise songs as material items available for purchase as sheet music and phonograph records, and both had evolved in the context of one of the most salient influences on early American sound cinema, the Broadway stage of the 1920s. Although studies of Broadway that consider how songs were interpolated into narrative frameworks are scarce, musical productions of the 1920s stage were important models for Hollywood's assimilation of songs into classical films—especially films belonging to non-musical, narratively integrated genres.[11] Filmmakers of the transitional era inherited conventions of song plugging from Broadway, and they adopted these conventions to highlight songs in print publicity, radio advertising, and the films themselves. The effect on film form was an aesthetic that privileged repeated units of performance, or star-song attractions, within a narrative framework.

STAR-SONG IDENTIFICATION ON BROADWAY: REPETITION,
RECYCLING, AND STEPPING OUT OF CHARACTER

The function of the star-song attraction in early sound cinema is best understood as a descendant of the Broadway stage, from which the most successful popular songs of the 1920s sprung. From the 66 theatres that New York's Broadway district had by the end of the decade, stars launched show tunes to audiences who paid to attend shows featuring their favorite celebrities.[12] During this period, the identification of stars with songs was considered such a lucrative strategy that many productions were developed as star vehicles with seemingly little regard for narrative coherence. *Sunny* (1925), penned by Jerome Kern, Otto Harbach, and Oscar Hammerstein II expressly for "queen of musical comedy" Marilyn Miller, consisted of a feeble narrative that functioned mainly to highlight Miller's song performances.[13] Similarly, *Betsy* (1926) was conceived by theater impresario Flo Ziegfeld primarily as a vehicle for vaudevillian star Belle Baker, whose incorporation of Irving Berlin's "Blue Skies" launched the song to hit status despite the musical running a slight 39 performances. Star-song identification was central to the flourishing of Broadway and the songs introduced there.

Two forms of musical theater, the revue (or "follies" show) and the musical comedy, were especially effective in advertising songs. The revue derived from vaudeville, burlesque, and minstrelsy formats of the early 1900s and was defined largely by its staging of a series of unrelated acts or "turns," such as comic routines, song-and-dance numbers, magician shows, animal routines, and dramatic skits. As music historian Charles Hamm has illustrated, the revue's episodic format encouraged the practice of song interpolation, in which entertainers performed songs "as stars" rather than as characters singing from within a narrative context.[14] Song interpolations married music with spectacle, for they were enhanced by lavish displays of sets, costumes, and massive choruses. Such extravagance frequently entailed high expense. *Ziegfeld Follies of 1919*, for example, cost $170,000, more than four times the production cost of the musical comedy *Irene* in that same year.[15] Consider the staging of Irving Berlin's song "An Orange Grove in California," part of the composer's score for the 1924 stage production of *Music Box Revue*. According to Broadway historian Gerald Bordman, when stars John Steel and Grace Moore sang the number, they were "walking together in an orange grove. Slowly the grove melted away into a kalei-doscope of shimmering orange lights and the audience found itself sprayed with orange perfume."[16] With their performances inextricably linked to such a sensational engagement of the senses, Steel and Moore helped popularize Berlin's song.[17]

Sometimes the mere presence of singing celebrities usurped the need for massive sets and choruses. In 1924, Winnie Lightner introduced Gershwin's "Somebody Loves Me" on a modest set, and the ballad became the year's second most popular song.[18] Eddie Cantor's interpolation of "My Blue Heaven" into the *Ziegfeld Follies of 1927* helped the song become one of the top hits of the entire decade. Throughout the 1920s, revues cast celebrity vocalists as song pluggers by positioning their performances as self-contained moments of spectacle. And, unlike their predecessors of the early 1900s, revues of the 1920s tended to feature the same cast, thereby facilitating the showcasing of any individual star within a sustained format.

Not all Broadway shows were as episodic as musical revues. The other major format, the musical comedy, employed narrative structures with song interludes.[19] Although stars usually remained in character throughout these productions, they nevertheless plugged songs by repeating them over the course of individual shows and across different productions. Central to this practice was the show finale, but the first-act finale, or finaletto, was equally important. The finaletto of *Sally* (1920), for instance, included musical phrases extracted from three songs introduced in the show's first act: "On with the Dance," "You Can't Keep a Good Girl Down," and "Look for the Silver Lining." Similarly, the finaletto of the original production of *Lady, Be Good!* (1924) interspersed dialogue with musical motifs from the song "Oh, Lady Be Good." When Fred Astaire's character gripes, "Why is it, every time we are having a good fight, somebody has to *play that tune*?" the chorus reprises "Fascinating Rhythm."[20] *Good News* (1927), a musical comedy written by Buddy DeSylva, Lew Brown, and Ray Henderson that registered 557 performances, introduces the song "Lucky in Love" in the first act and then, during the finaletto, uses a line of dialogue to prompt an abridged version of the song to close the first act.[21] Both an advertisement for songs and a means of reiterating important narrative events, the finaletto of musical comedies functioned as preemptory finales, enabling stars to repeat song material. In these ways, the finaletto furthered star-song identification and the audience's familiarity with new tunes.

Musical comedies and revues also positioned songs as purchasable items by recycling them across different shows. Both "Whip-poor-will" and "Look for the Silver Lining" derived from *Zip Goes a Million* (1919) but also appeared in *Sally* (1920).[22] From *Mary Jane McKane* (1923), Vincent Youmans took the music of "My Boy and I" and "Come On and Pet Me" and recycled them with new lyrics for *No, No, Nanette* (1925) and *Hit the Deck!* (1927) respectively. *No, No, Nanette* also included "Take a

Little One-Step," which Youmans had composed for *Lollipop* (1924). Although the repetition of songs across different shows would have limited the possibility of a particular star becoming identified with a specific song, these examples suggest that songs were treated as modular units that could be transferred among shows. This point is likewise suggested by Ethan Mordden when he reminds us that the essential elements of Broadway shows were the stars and the scores, not the stories.[23]

Although the repetition and recycling of song numbers were effective ways of promoting songs as entities that could be purchased and enjoyed independently of the stage shows, a third and even more intriguing method of promotion was that of song interpolation, the interjection of a song presented by a star "as a star" rather than as a character. As noted above, musical revues could incorporate song interpolations quite seamlessly because that genre of stage production lacked character-driven narratives. In contrast, interpolations in musical comedies required that a star momentarily abandon his or her character's narrative environment. An early example occurred in the 1909 production of *The Boys and Betty*, which featured Marie Cahill stepping out of character to interpolate the song "She Was a Dear Little Girl." Charles Hamm recounts: "The song's protagonist, Betsy Brown, is not even a character in the show. The piece served as a set piece for Cahill, who stepped out of her role as Betty Barbeau to deliver a comic monologue directly to the audience—as Marie Cahill, whom the audience had come to the theatre to see and to hear.... It was a song for a specific performer, not a specific show."[24] The following year, when Emma Carus interpolated Berlin's "If The Managers Only Thought the Same As Mother" into *The Jolly Bachelors* (1910), Carus stepped "out of her role in the show to address an audience that had come to the theater at least in part to see and hear her, an audience aware that she had taken dramatic as well as musical roles."[25] Early in the history of the Broadway musical, an entertainer could disrupt a show's narrative continuity to offer an interpolation as a star-song attraction. In this way, entertainers highlighted their own stage presence and packaged their performances as song plugs.

The quintessential singer-plugger during the first two decades of the 20th century was Al Jolson. Early in his career, he conflated the acts of performing and plugging, as was particularly demonstrated by the billing he received in 1903 for his first vaudeville trio, "Introducers and Promoters of High-Class Ballads and Popular Songs," which suggests little of the team's vocal talents. Jolson developed an enduring model for promoting songs within the format of sustained shows, like musical comedies and revues, by extracting a song from its narrative context and performing it by way of direct address to the audience. Most historical accounts state that he initiated this practice on the third night of *La Belle Paree*, a revue that opened at the Winter Garden Theatre in March 1911. David Ewen recounts the pivotal event that occurred on the third night:

[Jolson] stepped out of character, went to the edge of the footlights, and began to talk flippantly and informally to the few spectators scattered throughout the theatre. "Lots of brave folk out there," he remarked, peering through half-closed eyelids into the dark auditorium. "Come to think of it," he added, "after the reviews we got, there's a lot of brave folk right up here on the stage!" The audience started to chuckle. "That's better, folks! What do you say we get a bit better acquainted?" The audience applauded. "Tell you what I'm gonna do. I'm gonna sing some songs for you, if you'll listen." The applause grew louder. Then, for the following half-hour, the performer sang his heart out.[26]

One of those songs, "Paris Is a Paradise for Coons," became an instant hit, and following that evening, *La Belle Paree* drew sold-out crowds.

Jolson became renowned for creating an intimate rapport with his audiences by implementing direct address in nearly every one of his subsequent shows at the Winter Garden. These included *Honeymoon Express* ("You Made Me Love You"), *Robinson Crusoe, Jr.* ("Yacka Hula Hickey Dula"), *Bombo* ("April Showers"), *Sinbad* ("My Mammy" and "Swanee"), and *Big Boy* ("Keep Smiling at Trouble").[27] At some point in each show, Jolson performed as Jolson-the-star and not as his prescribed character. Even in *Big Boy*, a musical with a relatively compelling narrative about a stable boy, Jolson "repeated his old trick of dismissing the cast midway through the performance and singing for the audience the rest of the evening."[28] By stepping out of character, Jolson called attention to songs, isolating them from the fiction on stage and linking them to the spectacle of his own stardom—a phenomenon I refer to later in this chapter as the "Jolson effect." Indeed, as Bordman has suggested, the power of Jolson's stardom transcended genre; *Big Boy* could have been defined as a musical comedy, a revue, or "simply a unique Jolson vehicle."[29] As the case of Jolson demonstrates, the strategy of star-song identification occurred despite the narrative cohesion that otherwise grounded the theatrical genre of musical comedy. The fact that such interpolations appeared in musical comedies attests to the power of the isolatable song, and at the same time anticipates Hollywood's use of songs in early sound films.

THE STAR-SONG ATTRACTION IN STUDIO PUBLICITY: PRINT ADVERTISEMENTS, PRESSBOOKS, AND RADIO

The recruitment of Broadway performers by Hollywood studios during the conversion to sound is by now a well-established history. But discussions of the subject usually focus on the stories of Jolson, Eddie Cantor, Sophie Tucker, and other performers who starred in the nascent genre of the film musical.[30] Far more revealing of the power of the star-song attraction is the way in which films belonging to *non-musical* genres adopted conventions of the Broadway stage, both in publicity and in the films themselves. Beginning with print and radio publicity, we find ample evidence of Hollywood's attempts to capitalize on the singing celebrity by using cross-promotion and star-song identification.

In fact, early in the transitional era, the very presence of synchronized music (rather than music performed as live accompaniment) was fodder for studio publicity. Paramount's *Special Introductory Press Book* of the 1928–1929 season, aimed at theater exhibitors, begins with a promotional article about synchronized music scores. Titled "Exceptional Music Scores Great Sound Selling Aid," the text proclaims, "Exploiting sound means exploiting music and Paramount's excellent musical accompaniments, its catchy theme songs and masterful orchestrations makes exploiting Paramount Quality Sound Pictures an easy and profitable undertaking for all exhibitors."[31] On a subsequent page, the text asks, "Like music with your meals?" and supplies an answer: "You'll want SOUND with your pictures." Studio publicity used the promise of synchronized music to persuade exhibitors to "wire" their theaters for sound and thereby compete with the country's opulent motion picture palaces that housed large orchestras. As an ad for Vitaphone, subsidiary of Warner Bros., declared, "The invention (of synchronous sound) will make it possible for every performance in a motion picture theater to have a full orchestral accompaniment to the picture regardless of the size of the house."[32]

But as the novelty value of synchronized music faded, advertisements in the trade papers referred increasingly to songs associated with motion pictures. In the spirit of cross-promotion, these ads usually listed the names of both the relevant studio and its affiliated publishing firm. For example, in an early 1929 issue of *Variety*, Fox announced in large cursive font, "They'll Score—these Fox Movietone productions to be released during 1929; and so will The Remarkable Song Themes that they inspired. All of these songs are published by DeSylva, Brown & Henderson, Inc." On the bottom half of the page, four stills appear from as many films next to captions bearing each film's title and its associated theme song: *True Heaven* ("True Heaven"), *In Old Arizona* ("My Tonia"), *Four Devils* ("Marion"), and *The River* ("I Found Happiness").[33] Likewise, soon after Warner Bros. acquired the song catalog of M. Witmark & Sons in January 1929, the production company took out ads in *Variety* to publicize Witmark's motion picture theme songs.[34] These full-page ads displayed excerpts of sheet music, the title of each associated film, and banners bearing the studio's new catchphrases: "Witmarks are Hit Marks," "Sing a Song of Witmark," and "Keep Going with Witmark Winners." An ad for First National/ Warner Bros. pictures depicted a cascade of phonograph records above a promotional caption, showing that trade ads often referred to purchasable sheet music and phonograph records, as well as to radio programs and other tie-ins.[35]

Trade papers were one source for exhibitors to glean information about potential cross-promotional tactics; pressbooks, produced by studio publicity departments, were another. But unlike the trades, pressbooks emphasized the value of *localized* campaigns, and they often noted that tie-ups could be accomplished with the help of neighborhood retailers like sheet music dealers, record stores, radio broadcasters, and establishments for live music. Indeed, all but three of the Paramount pressbooks of the 1928–1929 season proffered ideas for the use of songs in local campaigns.[36] The pressbook for *Loves of an Actress* (1928) includes lyrics to the film's theme song, information about the song's publisher (Shapiro, Bernstein & Co.), and a promise: "Get the people of your city singing this song, humming these lyrics and you have your picture sold."[37] *Redskin's* (1929) book asserts that "[the theme song's] tender melody enhances the beauty of the romantic story. Songs and records are available to be sold by music dealers in your town; orchestras will be glad to feature the catchy tune."[38] The book also identifies the Paramount-affiliated publisher Sam Fox Publishing Co. as a source of sheet music and advertising material. Later, the book reminds us that the film's eponymous theme song, written by J. S. Zamecnik, "has already won universal acceptance from radio and dance orchestra audiences."[39] The book for *The Wild Party* (1929) is devoted primarily to star Clara Bow, but nevertheless reserves one-third of a page for the promotion of the theme song "My Wild Party Girl." The title is accompanied by a logo bearing the names of Paramount's other publishing affiliates, Harms and Famous Music, along with copy that reads, "The song is something with which to boost the sale of your attraction."[40]

Pressbooks designed by other studios used similar advertising techniques. For instance, MGM's books frequently noted the studio's connection with its publishing arm Robbins Music. The book for the crime film *Alias Jimmy Valentine* (1929) announces, "Important Cooperative Theme Song Tie-Up" (figure 3.1), and explains:

The theme song of this picture is "Love Dreams," published by the Robbins Music Corporation, 709 Seventh Avenue, New York City. Make a note of this additional exploitation angle so that when the time comes to exploit "Alias Jimmy Valentine" you will have every music dealer in your city lined up. The publishers assure complete 100% cooperation. They have also prepared special advertising accessories to help you put it over. If you should need any additional assistance, write or wire them direct.[41]

In connection with the Buster Keaton comedy *Doughboys* (1930), the pressbook offers a sample script for radio broadcasters so that exhibitors could coordinate programs with local radio stations. The script alternates between a plot synopsis and the titles of the film's military marches and theme song "Sing—A Happy Little Thing."

FIGURE 3.1 Pressbook for *Alias Jimmy Valentine* (1929). (Margaret Herrick Library, Academy of Motion Picture Arts and Sciences).

On the same page we find the theme song's sheet music cover and the name and address of its publisher Robbins Music.[42]

The most standardized approach to marketing theme songs appeared in the press-books of the Fox studio. These discussed songs in terms of four methods of song distribution: sheet music, phonograph records, radio, and live venues. An excerpt from the book for the drama *Romance of the Underworld* (1928), which starred Mary Astor, offers a good example:

The song cover, printed in brilliantly contrasting blue and red, makes an excellent advertisement for the picture you are running. All music dealers will be pleased to work with you on a window display. If you can get several music dealers to come in for a cooperative newspaper ad, the result will be equally advantageous to picture and song.... This song is being recorded by most of the large phonograph companies. Dealers who handle these records will be pleased to work with you. Phonographs can be used for lobbies and in special prologues. Radio stations will cooperate, announcing the name of the production whenever the song is used.... Where it is found profitable to tie up with dance halls, a special evening may be named "Mary Astor Night." The song should be sung and broadcast during the evening with an announcement about the film.[43]

Near-identical copy appears in the books for other Fox films released through the following year, including *Mother Knows Best* (1928), *Four Devils* (1929), *Frozen Justice* (1929), *Big Time* (1929), and *They Had to See Paris* (1929). As expected, in each case we find adjacent to the text the name and address of the songs' publishing companies (usually Fox's affiliate DeSylva, Brown & Henderson).

The Warner Bros. pressbooks made frequent reference to M. Witmark & Sons, the publishing company acquired by the studio in January 1929. One example concerns the soundtrack for *The Great Divide* (1929), a Western melodrama about a mine owner who falls in love with and reforms his dead partner's daughter. The film includes two songs: "At the End of the Lonesome Trail" and "Si, Si Señor," both written by Herman Ruby and Ray Perkins. The pressbook's "Exploitation" page reminds exhibitors of the affiliation between Warner Bros. and Witmark, and offers several of the usual suggestions for employing the theme song as a means to attract audiences. The book also contains a musical cue sheet, included presumably for those exhibitors whose theaters had not yet been wired for sound and would consider booking the silent version that was released one month after the sound release.[44]

While trade journal advertisements and studio pressbooks emphasized the commercial value of cross-media campaigns, regular columns published in *Film Daily*, *Billboard*, and *Motion Picture News* provided space for exhibitors to share their plugging techniques with other readers. These techniques varied, but they seemed to reproduce the initiatives recommended by the pressbooks. Examples included securing a deal with music recording companies whereby the company would provide a free phonograph player and records to the exhibitor; placing the sheet music of the songs in the windows of phonograph record dealers; holding contests for aspiring songwriters; distributing records of a movie theme song to audience members who subscribed to a local newspaper; and playing theme songs on the radio for a week in advance of a film's release. These tactics positioned motion picture songs as commodities that could be consumed independently of the movie-going experience.

At the same time, theater lobbies were seen as important spaces for selling film songs in material forms; they often displayed sheet music and phonograph records of motion picture songs, and they occasionally featured live performances by musical artists. *Billboard* described one of the lobbies of a Paramount-affiliated theater that was "being used for purposes that result in obtaining much do-re-mi for the coffers."[45] The article continues:

Attractive music stands have been erected in lobbies, with a prominent display of sheet music, records, etc. Along with it there are song pluggers to help boost sales.... A young lad, well possessed of salesmanship knowledge, is at the counter. Alongside of the stand last week was Roy Evans, recording artiste, who warbled the displayed songs while accompanying himself on a baby upright. He attracted good-sized audiences.[46]

Another example of such "do-re-mi" occurred in July 1929, when 1,500 copies of sheet music for "The Pagan Love Song," the theme song from MGM's Ramón Novarro vehicle *The Pagan* (1929), were sold in four days out of the studio's Capitol Theater in New York. *Variety* noted that the sales transpired "without undue exploitation effort whereas formerly it would take a number of acts and much painstaking plugging to attain a turnover of any one song like that."[47]

Exhibitors adopted other techniques of cross-promotion suggested by studio publicity. In advance of the opening of the part-talkie *Lilac Time* (1928) at the Central Theatre in New York, the film's theme song, "Jeannine, I Dream of Lilac Time," was broadcast over local stations and advertised through the placement of three-sheet posters in dealers' stores.[48] An exhibitor at the State Theatre in Youngstown, Ohio, arranged the advertisement of songs from *Alias Jimmy Valentine* with two local music stores. A theatre in Tulsa, Oklahoma, had loudspeakers wired from the theater lobby to the streets as an orchestra in the lobby played the theme song for the Joan Crawford star vehicle *Our Modern Maidens*.[49] These are just a few of many examples that emerged in *Billboard*'s weekly "Exploitation" column and other similar sections in the trades of 1928 and 1929.

Cross-promotion of motion picture songs thus involved a range of mass media and outlets: sheet music, newspapers, phonograph records, radio broadcasts, music retail shops, music halls, department stores, and theater lobbies. What about star-song identification? Again, studio pressbooks offer plenty of evidence for the industry's attempt to associate entertainers with songs. In Fox's pressbook for *Frozen Justice* (1929), a banner reads, "Hear Lenore Ulric sing 'The Right Kind of Man,'" and a small-scale reproduction of a sheet music cover is accompanied by the text: "Lenore Ulric sings the theme song of the William Fox Movietone *Frozen Justice*." Adjacent to this image runs a headline, "Put Theme Song To Work for You," and a recommendation: "Since all your advertising and publicity is hinged on drawing power of the star, Lenore Ulric, you will derive direct advantage from the widespread display of this song in dealers' windows."[50] In similar ways, Fox's pressbooks highlight singing appearances by Madge Bellamy and Barry Norton in *Mother Knows Best*; Will Rogers and Lenore Ulric in *They Had to See Paris*; and Louise Dresser, typed as "The Golden Blonde with the Golden Voice," in *Not Quite Decent*.[51] Warner Bros.

advertised *Lilac Time* by appealing to the reader's familiarity with the names of three stars of film and music—Colleen Moore, Gene Austin, and Nathaniel Shilkret—while MGM's publicity for *Way Out West* drew readers' attention to the appearance of celebrity Cliff Edwards ("Ukulele Ike") and his performance of the film's theme song "Singing a Song to the Stars" with the following copy:

> This is the only song in the picture and it is sung by Cliff Edwards (Ukulele Ike) to the accompaniment of his inseparable ukulele. This popular Columbia Record artist whose flair for comedy has won over all classes of motion picture audiences should be featured in all window displays in conjunction with William Haines. Copies are in the hands of most dealers. It probably has been recorded by the major disc companies. Check up on this also so that you will not overlook another helpful exploitation factor.[52]

Notably, studio pressbooks associated songs not only with film stars but also with songwriters who had already earned name recognition. On the second page of *Paramount's Special Introductory Press Book*, an eye-catching headline declares, "Sound Film Theme Song Captures Popular Fancy," and the ensuing article focuses on songwriter Walter Donaldson's composition "Out of the Dawn," the "love theme" for Paramount's first sound picture *Warming Up* (1928). The copy claims that "crowds left the theatre whistling 'Out of the Dawn' and the air is catching on all over the country."[53] Although this description reflects the overstated tone typical of studio publicity ("Out of the Dawn" failed to appear on any lists of best-selling songs through the season), it signals an intention on the part of the studio to capitalize on the public's recognition of Donaldson, the famed songwriter behind the decade's preeminent number "My Blue Heaven." On the subsequent page, readers would discover the sheet music and lyrics to "Sunbeams," another one of Donaldson's contributions to *Warming Up*.

Arranger and composer J. S. Zamecnik was accorded similar treatment, which is perhaps remarkable because, as noted in the previous chapter, Paramount would not profit from the sales of sheet music or phonograph recordings of the artist's motion picture songs; those were copyrighted by Zamecnik's long-term employer, the Sam Fox Publishing Co. But Paramount executives had good reason to try to bank on the appeal of the composer's name to boost box office receipts. Zamecnik had arisen to prominence among theater musicians in the 1910s while working as director and lead composer at Sam Fox and creating two folios of original photoplay music, but it was his subsequent work for Paramount that likely made his name known to film exhibitors. With Hugo Riesenfeld, a New York-based conductor and composer, Zamecnik wrote original scores for the silent productions of *Old Ironsides* (1926) and *The Rough Riders*

(1927), and his synchronized score for *Wings* (1927) garnered positive attention in the press (though the film's theme song, also published by Sam Fox, was written by Ballard Macdonald).[54] Encouraged by this success, Zamecnik was commissioned to compose scores for *The Wedding March* (1928), *Abie's Irish Rose* (1928), *Betrayal* (1929), and *Redskin* (1929), all of which were shot silently and retrofitted with a score for theaters wired for sound. By the time Paramount press agents assembled *Redskin*'s pressbook material, Zamecnik's name likely connoted musical accompaniment of a superior quality. Most telling of the studio's attention to theme songs, however, is the fact that the pressbook for *Redskin* does not discuss Zamecnik's original score for the film, but rather notes his composition of motion picture songs and *Redskin*'s titular theme.[55]

The director of *Redskin*, Victor Schertzinger, was another important figure in song promotion. Schertzinger's role in Hollywood was unusual in that he was also a songwriter. In the pressbook for the romantic drama *The Wheel of Life* (1929), a headline reads, "Victor Schertzinger's Tuneful Melody Hit Ready for Theatre Cooperative Plans," and goes on to note that the studio's "famous composer-director" has "contributed a melody of popular appeal" (titled "Broken Melody"). It continues, "Songs and records are available for music store dealers, orchestras, and broadcasting stations."[56] For the comedy *Fashions in Love* (1929), an article provides a report of Schertzinger's piano performance on the film's set. It then continues in typical manner: "Publishers are more than anxious to work hand-in-hand with theaters and music dealers in arranging lobby and window displays. The Paramount Theatre, New York City, 'Ace' house of the giant Publix Circuit, sells sheet music and records of all the numbers heard on its programs in the lobby. Why not you?"[57] The reputation of songwriters became a vital selling point for studio films.[58]

Cross-promotion and star-song identification are accounted above as isolated strategies, but they frequently converged in the same medium. Paramount's book for Josef von Sternberg's prison drama *Thunderbolt* (1929) refers both to the potential tie-up with sheet music, as well as to the stars associated with the film:

"Daddy, Won't You Please Come Home?," a sentimental ballad by the composer of "Memory Lane" and "Some Day" and others, is featured in a cabaret scene in "Thunderbolt." Spier and Coslow, of 745 7th Ave., N.Y.C., are the publishers. The colored [sheet music] cover carries heads of Bancroft, Fay Wray and Richard Arlen and prominent mention of the fact that it is from the Paramount Picture *Thunderbolt*. The usual window display with local music shops should stir up some unusual business.[59]

Radio broadcasts were other sites for the coexistence of cross-promotion and star-song identification. In addition to one-off events like the United Artists broadcast discussed at the beginning of this chapter, feature radio programs developed by the major studios advertised their film and music products. MGM presented "tele-shorts," aural versions of newsreels that included a narrator and music, and eventually adapted *Anna Karenina* to radio in the form of a "telemovie," which Michele Hilmes describes as "a blow-by-blow account of the film, along with music and sound effects."[60] Paramount devised the two-hour broadcast of the *Paramount Picture Hour*, and Warner Bros. created the *Warner Bros.' Vitaphone Jubilee Hour*, the latter of which boasted 28 stations and a mass of stars. A *Variety* advertisement for the show (figure 3.2) claims:

NOTHING LIKE IT IN MOVIE HISTORY! NOTHING LIKE it in the world. Every Monday night, at 9:30 p.m. It all draws people to your house to see Warner Bros. Pictures. It all contributes to the startling grosses established by "The Singing Fool," "The Home Towners," "The Terror," "On Trial," "Lights of New York"—to mention only a handful of the more remarkable box office line-up on the industry! Tie to Warner Bros. Pictures—Silent or with Vitaphone—and sit on top of the world.[61]

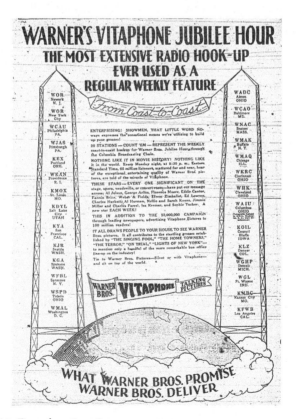

FIGURE 3.2 *Variety*, December 16, 1928, 15.

It is worth noting, finally, that stars were not always used in the service of radio cross-promotion. In advertising Warner Bros.' *Under a Texas Moon* (1930), Remick Music (purchased by Warner Bros. in 1929 as part of the massive buyout of Harms) arranged a weekly radio broadcast that presented parts of the film's plot along with individual songs from the production. *Billboard* reported, "The playlet serves as a background for the song. Remick plans to continue this idea of selling the songs and production each week with a 15-minute session over the Columbia broadcasting system."[62] Like print publicity in pressbooks and trade papers, radio broadcasts plugged motion picture songs as isolatable commodities.

THE STAR-SONG ATTRACTION IN FILM

The star-song attraction that developed on Broadway stages prior to the coming of sound furnished Hollywood filmmakers with a model for using songs in narrative films, musical and non-musical alike. But while the nature of musical films accommodated song interludes that more often than not suspended narrative flow, star-song attractions in films belonging to non-musical genres disrupted their otherwise coherent narratives. Although certain devices of visual style, like editing and shot composition, could help to anchor song performances to the fictional worlds of non-musical films, numerous other techniques isolated songs from their narrative fictions and highlighted them as discrete attractions. These techniques included the insertion of vocalized performances in otherwise instrumental soundtracks; the association of songs with overt and spectacular devices of visual style; the repetition of a song over the course of a single film; the use of flagrant references in dialogue to song titles; and the exploitation of star-song identification.

Effective song plugging in films was enhanced by vocalized rather than instrumental presentations, though vocalized renditions did not require synchronous sound (i.e., sound that matches the movement of the image, such as dialogue that matches the movement of an actor's lips). It sufficed for a voice to be heard singing lyrics from somewhere offscreen. For instance, the majority of the soundtrack of MGM's adventure drama *White Shadows in the South Seas* (1928) consists of sound effects and instrumental scoring, including several motifs from the theme song. With its non-synchronous soundtrack, the film conveys dialogue through intertitles. But when it comes time to depict a romantic tryst between the two stars (Monte Blue and Raquel Torres), a male voice can be heard singing "Flower of Love" on the soundtrack. The source of the voice is never identified, nor is it acknowledged by the film's characters. It merely accompanies the spectacle of Blue and Torres depicted in a series of alternating medium close-ups. As it seems to serve little narrative function other than supplying banal lyrics to a romantic scene, the song's conspicuous appearance on the soundtrack might well have been motivated by MGM's commercial incentive to advertise a theme song.

In the way that tight shot scales in *White Shadows* focus audience attention on the stars while a song plays on the soundtrack, other kinds of visual spectacle likewise accentuated vocal presentations in other films. During a quartet performance of "Boyfriend Blues" in MGM's *Their Own Desire* (1929), the film cuts abruptly to a startling shot of fireworks. In Fox's military drama *Salute* (1929), a striking tracking shot and pronounced composition depict a young woman (played by Helen Chandler) singing "Anchors Aweigh" through a first-story window. A Western from Warner Bros. titled *Under a Texas Moon* (1930) uses an extraordinary tracking shot to introduce three women who are drawn outside their home by the sound of a caballero's song emanating from the soundtrack. In each of these examples, popular songs are married to visual spectacle much as they were in Broadway revues of the 1920s.

Because repetition helped to cement song titles (and often their melodies) in the memories of audiences, presumably inciting them to purchase the sheet music or phonograph recordings, the reiteration of songs during a single film was another common technique of song plugging. A similar effect was attained through another strategy that came from the Broadway stage: the working of a song title into a line of dialogue. A particularly flagrant example appears in *Loose Ankles*, a flapper comedy released in February 1930 by First National, the production subsidiary of Warner Bros. *Loose Ankles* was an adaptation of a three-act play that contained three scant uses of music: a quiet performance of Tchaikovsky's version of the Goethe poem "Nur wer die Sehnsucht Kennt" ("None But the Lonely Heart"); a funeral march; and an unidentified piece played on the piano when a lead character announces that she will donate her grandmother's estate "to the cat and dog hospital."[63] For the film, the First National screenwriters replaced Goethe's poem with a peppy two-step number written by Tin Pan Alley composer Pete Wendling and lyricist Jack Meskill.[64] The song first plays in the opening credit sequence at a moderately rapid tempo, with the strings carrying the melody. The piece ends on a leading note that bleeds into a piano rendition of "Loose Ankles" as we see a new image of lower legs and feet lightly swaying in rhythm to the song. The legs belong to Ann (Loretta Young), who is enjoying a pedicure and tapping her available foot to the music while her friend Betty (Inez Courtney) sings at a piano placed in the background. The lyrics to the first stanza and refrain describe an unfettered style of dancing (and, we learn later, Betty's social behaviors): "When the music's good and hot / I start to sway a lot / And all because I've got / Loose Ankles." As she sings, a visual joke results from our assumption that the source of the piano's sound is Betty. The scene cuts to a shot of Betty holding a cigarette in her left hand and playing the piano with her right hand, although the song heard on the soundtrack clearly employs both the bass and the treble registers of the piano. To extend the joke, Betty rises from the piano bench and picks up a stack of piano rolls—and suddenly it becomes clear that Betty had been seated at a mechanical player piano, hamming up a performance for herself and her friend. In the foreground, Ann remarks, "That's an awful cute number, Betty," and asks, "What's the name of it?" Betty replies, "Oh, it's a little thing called 'Loose Ankles.'" The comical faux presentation of "Loose Ankles" calls attention to the song while at the same time the blatant reference to its title reminds audiences of the availability of "Loose Ankles" in material formats, perhaps like the piano rolls depicted onscreen.[65]

But of all the techniques that studios used to publicize songs in films of the transitional era, the most intriguing one was the thematization of star-song identification, in which the very practice of star-song identification was made a central motif of the film and as such served to advance the narrative and provide unity across different scenes. Although songs used in this way often fulfilled narrative functions (a subject addressed in the next chapter), their dominant purpose was to call attention to themselves as discrete attractions.

GLORIFYING HELEN MORGAN IN *APPLAUSE* (1929)

An exemplar of the potency of the star-song attraction is Paramount's *Applause*, directed by Rouben Mamoulian and released in 1929. Though it has been labeled a backstage musical, *Applause* was described at the time of its release as a drama, an apt classification for a story about an aging burlesque queen who is renounced by her convent-educated daughter April (Joan Peers) and disparaged by a lecherous, abusive boyfriend, Hitch (Fuller Mellis Jr.).[66] In the lead role of Kitty Darling, Paramount cast Helen Morgan, whom audiences of 1929 would have recognized as the star of the Jerome Kern and Oscar Hammerstein II production of *Show Boat* (1927), wherein Morgan sang "Bill" and "Can't Help Lovin' Dat Man." Morgan had also attained considerable fame by performing in George White's *Scandals of 1925* and by launching her signature torch songs from atop a piano at the Backstage Club in New York.

Songs in *Applause* capitalize on Morgan's established persona as a torch singer, a character suffering from unrequited love. The number "What Wouldn't I Do For That Man?" comes to serve as a theme song for Kitty's narrative situation as she is blackmailed by Hitch into steering April into a career in burlesque (and, Hitch hopes, into his bed). Despite Hitch's ignoble intentions, Kitty capitulates to his demands at the expense of April's needs for maternal affection and care. Her blind devotion to Hitch is insinuated by the song's lyrics: "I'll never leave him alone, / I'll make his troubles my own, / With all his faults, I know we'll get by, / I'm just no good when his arms are about me; / What wouldn't I do for that man?"

The first appearance of "What Wouldn't I Do For That Man?" in *Applause* embodies a characteristic tension between narrative and the star-song attraction. On the one hand, devices of editing and camerawork situate the performance firmly in the diegesis, or narrative space. As we hear Morgan's voice fade up on the soundtrack, the scene opens to reveal the star lying on the floor of Kitty's living room and singing as she leafs through letters and photographs (figure 3.3). Two insert shots (figures 3.4 and 3.5) disclose important pieces of narrative information. The first reveals a letter from April indicating that three years have elapsed since she and Kitty saw each other; the second, a photograph of Hitch addressed to "My Golden Baby" and signed "from her Big Boy, Hitch," suggests a romantic relationship between him and Kitty. The camerawork and editing deployed in this scene avoid framing Morgan in a frontal presentational style. Instead, these techniques work to anchor the song performance to its diegetic context.

At the same time, it is impossible to dismiss the potent impact of Helen Morgan's star status on our perception of the scene. When Kitty sings, she is Helen Morgan, the torch singer. Such an impression for audiences of 1929 was likely augmented by the affiliation between Morgan and the song that extended beyond *Applause* into other performances and publicity materials. In an earlier Warner Bros. sound film, *Glorifying the American Girl* (1929), Morgan sang the entire number while perched atop a piano. Sheet music for the song displayed Morgan's photograph on its cover, and on the day following the film's October 7 premiere in New York, Morgan recorded the song

FIGURES 3.3 *Applause* (Paramount, 1929).

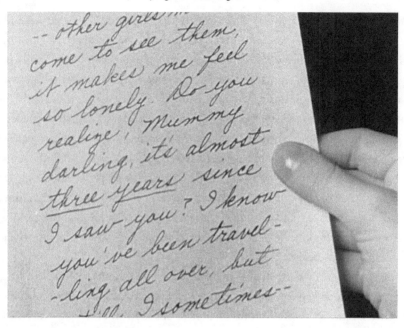

FIGURES 3.4 *Applause* (Paramount, 1929).

FIGURES 3.5 *Applause* (Paramount, 1929).

for the Victor label.[68] These strategies augmented the identification of Morgan with "What Wouldn't I Do For That Man?" much as Broadway stars like Al Jolson had been associated with specific tunes. Although the case of "What Wouldn't I Do For

That Man?" is in some ways exemplary—the majority of motion picture songs were not subjected to such intensive extra-textual marketing campaigns—it demonstrates nonetheless the extent to which a studio was able to exploit star-song identification.

The film's second theme song "Give Your Little Baby Lots of Lovin'" (written by Joe Burke and Dolly Morse) serves as Kitty's signature song on the burlesque stage. We first hear the song about one-third of the way through the film, when April returns from the convent at the behest of Hitch, who has forbidden Kitty from spending money on her daughter's education. Eager to surprise her mother, April ventures to the theater and takes a seat in the audience. A hula dance act concludes on the stage, and Kitty emerges from the wings, shaking her body to the rhythm of her signature tune.[69] April's humiliation at the sight of her mother's sexually charged performance is exacerbated by the derogatory comments she hears uttered by the men around her in the audience. One of them jokes, "Yeah, she's all wiped out by now, look at that," and the others burst into laughter. Meanwhile, on stage, the burlesque chorus line joins Kitty to complete the song. During the reprisal of the song, close-up shots of dancing girls' faces and leering men alternate in an increasingly frenzied pace, matching the escalating beat and texture of the music. April lowers her head.

Once it is identified as Kitty's signature song, "Give Your Little Baby Lots of Lovin'" figures prominently in the climax of *Applause* when April assumes the place of her mother on the burlesque stage. At last realizing that her convent education was possible only because Kitty was willing to degrade herself, April usurps her mother's role and performs "Give Your Little Baby Lots of Lovin'" for the lewd crowd. Now the song functions as a vehicle through which April reverses the act of self-sacrifice, for by singing on the disreputable burlesque stage, she fulfills her mother's wishes but forfeits her chance for marriage to a kindhearted suitor.

In this way, *Applause* makes the subject of star-song identification a key narrative concern. "Give Your Little Baby Lots of Lovin'" is identified first with Kitty, but the film gradually associates it with April as a means of conveying her self-sacrifice and intensifying the emotional force of the film's climax. Moreover, although the song is motivated by and worked into the narrative fiction, its repetition across the film belies an impression of complete integration. As with "What Wouldn't I Do For That Man?," when Kitty performs "Give Your Little Baby Lots of Lovin'" onstage, she is both Kitty performing a signature song as a burlesque star *and* Helen Morgan putting over a song to motion picture audiences.

THE DUPLICITOUS VOICE OF *WEARY RIVER*

A similar use of songs is evident in First National's production of *Weary River* (1929). Described by contemporaneous reviewers as a melodrama, a "gangster movie," and an "underworld drama," *Weary River* was the heavily publicized debut sound film

of silent film star Richard Barthelmess, who plays bootlegger-turned-musician Jerry
Larabee.[70] Jerry's penchant for music motivates the appearance of two original theme
songs, "It's Up to You" and "Weary River," both of which were penned by Warner
Bros. staff songwriters Grant Clarke and Louis Silvers. The songs were published
by Irving Berlin's firm, which, as noted in the previous chapter, had agreed to share
with Warner Bros. any profit from sheet music and record sales.[71] The studio sought
to exploit the arrangement by highlighting the songs both in advertising campaigns
and on the film's soundtrack.

Over the course of the film, devices of editing and mise-en-scène position Jerry's
performances of the songs as discrete, self-contained moments in the narrative trajectory. "It's Up to You" first appears during the film's initial dialogue sequence.
At the apartment of his girlfriend Alice (Betty Compson), Jerry sits at the piano
and begins plunking out the opening notes of the decidedly old-fashioned number "Frankie and Johnny," the famous ballad about a woman who murders her
lover after discovering his infidelity.[72] Alice interrupts Jerry, insisting that he play
a more contemporary song. Jerry launches into a modern ballad, "It's Up to You."
Alice's reaction to Jerry's voice is excessive: She swoons and collapses in rapture on
the bed. A striking tracking shot toward Alice invites us to focus on her orgasmic
facial expressions and body gestures. As Jerry starts in on the chorus, we cut to his
medium close-up, where we remain for the rest of the song, save for two relatively
brief returns to Alice's close-up. Jerry finishes the song, ending on a perfect cadence,
and the non-diegetic orchestral score returns. Alice rises to kiss Jerry, and the couple
concludes the scene by dancing to what is, diegetically speaking, imaginary music.
Throughout this scene, patterns of editing and shot scale function to guide and sustain our attention toward Barthelmess.

The appearance of *Weary River*'s eponymous theme song similarly glues our
attention to the soundtrack and Jerry's performance. We first hear strains of its
melody accompanying images of Jerry composing music in his prison cell, where
he has been sent for a murder he did not commit. The next sequence intercuts two
locations: the prison's radio broadcast room and the dance club, where Alice sits
with Jerry's former gang, listening to the broadcast on a radio wheeled in by the
club manager. As Jerry performs the entirety of "Weary River," a series of alternating, closely scaled shots shuttle us back and forth across two discontiguous
spaces: the prison and the club. However, similar to the film's depiction of "It's Up
to You," the camera and editing during this sequence linger on Jerry's medium close-
up (figure 3.6). When the song concludes, the radio station is so inundated with
telephone calls from adoring fans that the prison warden asks Jerry for an encore.
Jerry performs the song a second time in its entirety, and the editing and shot composition again emphasize Barthelmess in closely scaled, long, static takes. Over the

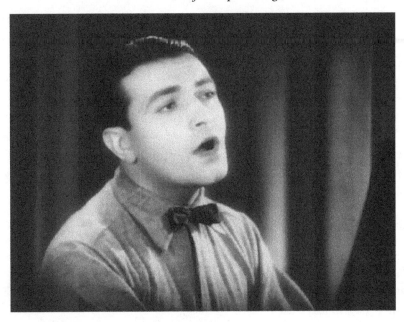

FIGURE 3.6 *Weary River* (First National/Warner Bros., 1929).

course of the film, we hear "Weary River" twice more: once when Jerry makes an attempt at a vaudeville career, and, finally, when he sings over the radio with hopes of convincing Alice that he has abandoned his criminal lifestyle. In both instances, the entire song is presented as a complete, self-contained performance.

Weary River's theme songs fulfill two commercial functions. First, because their performances are depicted via long takes and medium close-ups, they solicit and sustain audience attention to the image of Barthelmess in association with each song. These devices of visual style show Barthelmess in the act of star-song identification and encourage audiences to associate the celebrity with the songs he sings onscreen. Film advertisements designed by the studio enhanced the star-song attraction by emphasizing the mere presence of Barthelmess's voice. One advertisement printed in *Film Daily* situates the stern face of Barthelmess alongside the caption "You always knew he was the screen's greatest fighting lover.... You always knew he was the greatest male star in pictures...but YOU DON'T KNOW NOTHIN' YET," an obvious allusion to Al Jolson's legendary phrase from *The Jazz Singer*.[73] To the left of the star's face, another caption reads, "All these years the wealth of Richard Barthelmess's rich voice has been concealed.... You and millions of others have gone just to see him act. Now you can HEAR him TALK and play the piano."[74] In the film's preview trailer, Barthelmess tells costar William Holden that if the audience comes to the picture, they will hear him sing.[75] Further bolstering the song's commercial potential was the radio play it received even outside the United States: After being featured across the CBS network via the Warner Bros.-sponsored program *Vitaphone Jubilee Hour*, it was broadcast on stations in London, Berlin, and Paris.[76]

The press campaign's emphasis on the voice of Barthelmess is in fact startling, given that the theme songs were sung not by the actor but by a voice double. An exposé published in *Photoplay* in July 1929 disclosed that, as Barthelmess struck piano keys that had been deadened with felt, double Johnny Murray and pianist Frank Churchill performed just out of the camera's view.[77] Nevertheless, the reporter conceded, "[Barthlemess] merely faked the singing and playing, but he did it so beautifully that the results were convincing beyond doubt."[78] Similarly, following the film's release, *Variety* commented on the sound of Barthelmess's voice:

> A catalog of [the film's] merits includes a revealment [*sic*] by Barthelmess of a melodious, vibrant tenor with which he sings the song "Weary River," *if he sings it*, and which, take odds, will cause heavy chattering among the femme fans.... His singing is not only a climax to his performance but a new and interesting phase in his career.[79]

As I have argued elsewhere, the use of a voice double did not undermine audiences' impression of fidelity and, more important to Warner Bros., the profitability of star-song identification.[80] At the same time that the association between Barthelmess and the film's theme songs presumably attracted audiences to theaters, the songs functioned as isolated units, commercial entities that were available for sale in the material formats of sheet music and phonograph records. For instance, "Weary River" was recorded by several artists in 1929, including Rudy Vallee (for Victor), Gene Austin (for Victor), and Bob Haring & His Orchestra (for Brunswick). The presentation of the song as a discrete, self-contained entity was enhanced further by the film's pressbook, which portrays "Weary River" as a concrete product to behold and be held: A photograph depicts Barthelmess, director Frank Lloyd, and composer Louis Silvers gathering around a piece of sheet music that is, according to a caption, the first copy of the song.[81] A *Variety* review rewarded the studio's various attempts to cross-promote *Weary River* and its theme songs, noting, "The theme song(s) by Silvers and Clarke listen like big royalties which will help the picture, as the picture will make the song."[82] Indeed, both Austin's and Vallee's recordings of "Weary River" attained positions on the best-selling song lists printed in *Billboard*, a success story that likely motivated Warner Bros. to feature songs in studio publicity for Barthelmess's subsequent film *Drag* (1929) (figure 3.7), despite the star's use of a voice double in *Weary River*. An advertisement for that film stated, "Witmark theme songs, 'My Song of the Nile' and 'I'm Too Young to Be Careful,' are sure-fire follow-ups to 'Weary River.'"[83] The potent star-song attraction created by Barthelmess, his

FIGURE 3.7 A page from the pressbook for *Drag* (1929). (Margaret Herrick Library, Academy of Motion Picture Arts and Sciences.)

voice double, and techniques of visual style had at least a short-term influence on future press campaigns.

CONCLUSION: TEMPERING THE JOLSON EFFECT

In his analysis of the role of Al Jolson's musical performances in *The Jazz Singer* (1927), Charles Wolfe writes that a particular visual aesthetic involving long takes and close-ups was best suited for the association of a star and a song during the coming of sound. Jolson, hired by Warner Bros. in 1926, clearly transported the strategy of star-song identification to the studio's first synchronized sound features with little effort. In *The Jazz Singer*, his performance as Jackie Rabinowitz evokes a contradiction reminiscent of the Broadway convention of stepping out of character. The film's use of editing and mise-en-scène tie Jolson's song presentations to the film's diegetic world, but, as Wolfe has noted, when Jolson sings as Jackie, he "exceeds (his) fictional role."[84] Critics writing at the time of the film's release also observed this trait of Jolson's performance. A reviewer for *Variety* remarked, "Jolson, when singing, is

Jolson," and another argued that performance in the *Jazz Singer* "is a question not of characters but of actors."[85] These observations reflect the tension that arises from a song presentation that represents simultaneously a performance by a singing star and the vocalized drama of a diegetic character. The tensions render a "hybrid text" that negotiates "the [filmic] presentation of a musical performance and the harnessing of that performance for a narrative fiction,"[86] as Wolfe puts it.

But what we might call the "Jolson effect" in *The Jazz Singer* is both exemplary and extraordinary. It is exemplary because it demonstrates with utmost clarity how the stage routine through which a star transcended the fictional status of his character (by stepping beyond the stage footlights to interpolate songs in direct address) translated to motion pictures and advertised songs with great success. The status of "Blue Skies," "My Mammy," and other established song hits was renewed by Jolson's performance of them in *The Jazz Singer*. The case of Jolson is also extraordinary because he was the music industry's preeminent performer-plugger. He epitomized the role of the star vocalist who created hits precisely by virtue of stepping past the footlights and out of character. As Charles O'Brien points out, "Rather than being a conventional film melodrama, *The Jazz Singer* had a 'documentary' impact of a radio broadcast, with Jolson offering the sort of high-voltage earnestness that fans of the famed entertainer's stage and radio appearances had come to expect. Instead of incarnating a fictional character, Jolson was said to have played himself."[87]

More revealing of the power of star-song identification, I believe, are the stars who were less quintessential pluggers than Jolson. For instance, Helen Morgan may have been a singing entertainer, but she was not known for stepping beyond the footlights. During her signature performances, she constructed and maintained the persona of a torch singer who lamented her lost loves, while famously draped over a piano. By 1929, moreover, audiences would have associated her name with her more recent achievement as the star in the stage production of *Show Boat* (1927), a musical deemed revolutionary precisely because of its effective integration, not isolation, of songs and narrative. Although there is no doubt that Morgan's performances negotiated the limits of star and character, she maintained a crucial distance from her audience. Even less aligned with the performance mannerisms of Jolson were those of Richard Barthelmess, who was known for acting in silent films and certainly not for singing. The star-song attractions in *Applause* and *Weary River* thus modulate the tension found in *The Jazz Singer*. Despite this modulation, these films remain forceful examples of efforts made at two Hollywood studios to capitalize on the cultural cachet of the star-song attraction in the 1920s.

4

Integrating a Song

THE THREAT TO NARRATIVE PLAUSIBILITY

WHEN WARNER BROS. released *Weary River* in January 1929, reviews published in both the popular and trade press celebrated the commercial value of the film's titular theme song. A report printed in the *New York Evening News* predicted that the song's melody would "catch on, and be popular around town pretty soon"; a reviewer for the *New York Herald-Tribune* commented, "Though [the song is] repeated with dangerous frequency…popularity is hereby predicted for 'Weary River' both as a picture and a theme song"; and a writer for *Variety* anticipated that the number would earn "big royalties [that] will help the picture, as the picture will make the song."[1] The press's concentration on the cross-promotion of *Weary River* and its music no doubt pleased executives at Warner Bros. who, as described in chapter 2, were in the midst of negotiating a massive buyout of the music publishing business.

However, by emphasizing the profits to be netted by the song "Weary River," contemporaneous critics overlooked the ways in which the song serves an important narrative function: It demonstrates to Alice (Betty Compson) that her beau Jerry (Richard Barthelmess) will attain salvation if he relinquishes his criminal lifestyle and takes up singing. The prospect of Jerry's redemption is forecast earlier in the film by the lyrics of the theme song, first crooned by Jerry over the airwaves from a radio broadcast station set in prison. The lyrics demarcate Jerry's past from his present and, in referencing a river that inevitably meets the sea, they imply that Jerry welcomes the comfort to be found in social conformity:

I have been just like a weary river
that keeps winding endlessly;
Fate has been a very cheerful giver
to most every one but me;
Oh, how long it took me to learn
Hope is strong and tides have to turn;
And now I know that every weary river
some day meets the sea.

The recurrent association between Jerry's turn of conscience and his performance of the ballad culminates in the film's closing scene, when Jerry's final performance of "Weary River" over the radio inspires Alice to accept his marriage proposal. With a marriage hanging in balance and a criminal's redemption at stake, "Weary River" ushers in dramatic relief and resolution—and yet, responses to the film in 1929 ignored the song's dramatic functions, focusing instead on its status as a bankable commodity.[2]

The example of *Weary River* speaks to the fundamental contradiction posed by motion picture songs during the transition to sound. On one hand, films foregrounded and repeated songs as discrete moments of performance that could augment studio profits by attracting audiences and boosting sales of sheet music and phonograph records. On the other hand, the established codes of classical cinema entailed the imbuing of songs (and other elements of narrative) with narrative significance. Song presentations therefore simultaneously functioned as isolatable attractions and integrated devices of storytelling. Numerous early sound films resolved this apparent incongruity by fashioning protagonists in the roles of musicians or singers, as in the case of *Applause* and *Weary River*, or by casting already established vocal stars in fictional singing roles, such as Al Jolson in *The Jazz Singer* and *The Singing Fool*. The diegetic setting and narrative circumstances of these films justified multiple and repetitive song presentations. But not all filmmakers could resort to the casting of musical protagonists as the lead characters of their non-musical films.

Some films from this period betray another strategy for song use, one that I believe shares a kinship with the "integrated attraction" identified by scholars of early cinema.[3] As Charlie Keil describes it, the integrated attraction is a device of visual style that balances the demands of novelty and narrativization, and it does so largely because it is motivated by an elaborate set of circumstances that imbue the device with narrative value. For example, Keil suggests that the otherwise arresting nature of an overhead point-of-view shot in the short film *Belle Boyd, A Confederate Spy* (1913) is tempered by the narrative events that lead up to, and hence justify, its appearance as an element of storytelling. This hybrid style, one that "entails both flaunting the exoticism of attractions and aiding in the comprehension of narrative," is found in transitional cinema presented roughly between 1908 and 1917, bridging the previous "cinema of attractions" and the later feature length cinema.[4]

The concept of the integrated attraction underpins several scholarly histories of visual style in American cinema, including Charles Musser's discussion of the narrative impulse inherent to the otherwise attraction-based iris shot in *The Gay Shoe Clerk* (1902); Lea Jacobs's analysis of lighting in Cecil B. DeMille's films produced in 1915–1916, which rendered otherwise spectacular lighting effects as narrative events so that they were "literally a part of the unfolding drama"; and Scott Higgins's careful tracing of how Technicolor, initially "an intrusive device in a black-and-white world of filmmaking," was retooled by Hollywood in the 1930s to serve more conventional functions of classical narrative.[5] In each of these examples, a visually striking device that threatens to strain the self-effacing mechanisms of classical cinema is regarded as integrated, or "harnessed" (per the title of Higgins's book), in the service of classically oriented storytelling.

This chapter considers how motion picture songs of the transitional era functioned as integrated attractions. Although their status as conspicuous units of performance, as described in chapter 3, threatened to disrupt audience absorption in the fictional world, or diegesis, songs were simultaneously harnessed to fulfill a variety of dramatic functions and uphold principles of classical narration. As delineated in the first part of this chapter, the narrative functions of songs depended on their specific contexts. Some songs appeared only once over the course of a film and were likely to be employed in ways that served immediate purposes, such as enhancing a scene's historical or spatial credibility. A setting at a dance hall, for example, might call for background music, at which point a song would play on the soundtrack. These types of songs were called *incidental* songs. By contrast, *theme* songs typically accrued meaning as they repeated over the course of a film.

The mere appearance of incidental and theme songs in transitional-era films is in itself unremarkable. As we discussed in chapter 1, different kinds of songs were performed by theater musicians as accompaniment to films produced during the period of silent cinema, and in films produced in the mid-1930s and beyond, incidental and theme songs work to establish setting, reveal information about characters, and serve other kinds of dramatic purposes. What is distinctive about the use of songs in transitional-era films is the peculiar way in which they are sometimes *overly* motivated by their narrative contexts, so that the narrative conditions for justifying a song seem so carefully orchestrated that the film ceases to function as plausible fiction. Two brief examples: In First National's *Loose Ankles* (1930), Ann (Loretta Young) stands to earn a large inheritance on the condition that she finds a husband approved by her two prudish aunts, both moral reformers. One night, in hopes of a secret rendezvous with a new beau whom her aunts would not endorse as marriage material, she heads out to a nightclub that her reformer uncle, unaware of his niece's plans, is beseeching the police to raid that same evening. When her aunts learn of the unfortunate coincidence, they make a surprise appearance at the club, where their dancing to lively song numbers helps to undo their inhibitions and eventually their prohibitions against Ann's marriage to the suitor of her choice. The chain of narrative events that leads to the appearance of the aunts at the nightclub and the ensuing song performances is tenuous to say the least. In RKO's *Traveling Husbands* (1931), a theme song composed by one of the film title's peripatetic protagonists is announced through awkward dialogue in the opening scene and heard multiple times and in various arrangements over the radio, as though to suggest the song's popular currency and easy assimilation into different musical genres. In one scene, the song's broadcast over the radio serves to distract characters from a crucial narrative event, wherein one of the husbands violates a young call girl and is in turn shot by a woman who comes to the victim's defense. As an integrated attraction, the theme song of *Traveling Husbands* is both highlighted through repetition (to a tiresome degree) and used in the service of classical narrative economy. Later in this chapter, case studies of two other films—RKO's *Check and Double Check* (1930) and MGM's *Possessed* (1931)—will illustrate the argument that when songs were concerned, some of the transitional-era films fell victim to the law of diminishing returns: the more carefully coordinated the motivation for songs, the greater the strain on narrative coherence.

Such an argument, it is worth noting, draws less assuredly from trade papers and studio documents than have the previous chapters, largely because, although studio employees and filmgoers detected and ultimately admonished the awkward incorporation of songs into narrative films, they did not seem to be guided in any self-conscious manner by the principles of the integrated attraction. This being the case, the close analysis of narrative construction may illuminate the strategies for song use that resided on a spectrum defined by the promotion of discrete star-song attractions (chapter 3) at one end and the integration of songs in narratively plausible ways (chapter 5) at the other. As the analyses of *Check and Double Check* (1930) and *Possessed* (1931) will show, sometimes the efforts to justify song performances as commercial attractions resulted in drawing attention to narrative mechanisms and foregrounding precisely what the norms of classical narration seek to efface: the disruptive spectacle of the motion picture song. First, however, it is necessary to consider the extent to which motion picture songs could be endowed with narrative meaning and not just commercial value.

THE NARRATIVE FUNCTIONS OF THEME SONGS

A theme song of the transitional era constituted a "theme" in three ways: by association, by structural function, or by synoptic value. First, as it repeated over the course of a narrative, a theme song accumulated associations with characters and dramatic motifs. In John Ford's first feature-length sound film, an action-adventure piece titled *The Black Watch* (1929), the song "Flowers of Delight" becomes a code for the forbidden love that blossoms between Captain Donald King (Victor McLaglen), an officer in a Scottish regiment during World War I, and Yasmani (Myrna Loy), esteemed princess of a Pashtun tribe in the Khyber Pass. We first hear the song when King, standing in a courtyard, gazes upward through a window to Yasmani's second-story bedroom. A sweet melody played by a clarinet gives way to an off-screen vocal performance by an unidentified male tenor. In subsequent scenes, an instrumental rendering of the theme appears each time King and Yasmani converse with one another, and it eventually underscores the transformation of Yasmani from a revered goddess to a mortal woman in love. "Flowers of Delight" appears on the soundtrack in a pivotal scene, when Yasmani reveals to King her willingness to relinquish her empire in the name of her love for him. (As she explains, "It is sweeter to be a woman to one man than a goddess to thousands.") The song handily signifies the priority of Yasmani's lust for King over her political ambitions.

It is worth noting that although theme songs were repeated over the course of an individual film, they often varied in tempo, key signature, and instrumentation according to the associated mood or narrative trajectory of particular scenes. In *The Girl Said No* (1930), the song "I Don't Want Your Kisses (If I Can't Have You)" is endowed with a different duration and tempo each of the three times it occurs on the soundtrack. The opening titles introduce the song as an instrumental, upbeat two-step dance number, with a brass section blaring the lead four-measure motif in A-flat major. Later, the entire number repeats during a scene set in a nightclub, where protagonist Tom (William Haines) meets his romantic rival's secretary Mary (Leila Hyams). Here the song is played in a more languid manner by the string section of the nightclub orchestra, its change in tempo and style giving Tom occasion to ask Mary to dance and thereby initiate their romance. The motif recurs in the final two minutes of the film, when Tom kidnaps Mary on her wedding day and the couple escapes with the members of the wedding party following in hot pursuit. As they drive away from the camera, the motif plays on the soundtrack with a slight swing, its tempo at half the speed as that heard at the film's outset. The relaxed musical style underlines the romance forecast by the film's final shot. As this brief example demonstrates, a single theme song could, through repetition and variation, cement itself into the memory of audiences and at the same time conform to the dramatic tenor of specific scenes.

Second, as a result of accruing meaning through repetition, theme songs could reveal information to characters and actively shape narrative form. A precondition for this use of theme songs was the audition of those songs by characters situated within the narrative world—in other words, songs had to be presented as diegetic music heard by the pertinent characters. A good example occurs in *Double Cross*

Roads (1930), a romantic drama produced by Fox, wherein the performance of a theme song drives the narrative toward resolution. The relevant scene takes place after former safecracker David (Robert Ames), released from prison and determined to become law-abiding, discovers that his new sweetheart Mary (Lila Lee) had earlier served as a ploy to lure David back to his criminal gang.[6] David resents what he perceives as Mary's betrayal, and he consents to perform a robbery for his gang boss. In the meantime, Mary decides that she is genuinely in love with David, and she resolves to redeem them both by persuading him to abandon his criminal plans. In a stroke of unbelievably great fortune, Mary just happens to attend an outdoor party at the very house that David is about to burglarize. Standing beyond the window of the room where David is picking a safe, Mary attempts to distract him by singing two upbeat popular songs, "Do You Believe in Love at First Sight?" and "Show Me the Way." Neither song gets David's attention, so Mary asks the party band to play "My Lonely Heart," a ballad that she sang twice earlier in the film—first when she met David and subsequently during their courtship. As Mary launches into the song, a cut reveals David crouching in front of the safe. He looks up suddenly, then rises and walks toward the open window, seemingly in recognition of the song's melodic motif. The next set of shots then alternates between Mary, who continues to sing, and David, who stands and listens at the window until the song ends, at which point Mary sobs, clutches her coat, and hurries offscreen. Inside the house, David closes the safe, leaving its contents untouched. The setting of this scene at a party provides a plausible narrative motivation for Mary's performance of "My Lonely Heart," but the primary narrative function of the song is to halt David's criminal activity. When David hears Mary's voice singing what has become "their" theme song, his association between the song and his romantic desire mirrors our own recognition of the song's dramatic significance. Through repetition and association, "My Lonely Heart" becomes a device of narrative economy that quickly resolves the conflict between the two lead characters and brings the film to a close.

The use of a song performance to prompt scenes of dramatic recognition like the one in *Double Cross Roads* seems to have been a regular technique of narration in feature films of the transitional era. In RKO's *Love Comes Along* (1930), Johnny (Lloyd Hughes), a sailor, falls for cabaret singer Peggy (Bebe Daniels, already a Broadway musical star) when his ship docks at a Caribbean port. On the night of their first encounter, Peggy and Johnny rendezvous outside the cabaret, where Peggy sings the ballad "Until Love Comes Long" to him. The tune repeats twice more over the course of the film: once at a fiesta where Peggy is forced to sing for the nefarious Colonel Sangredo and again in the privacy of the Colonel's apartment. During the latter scene, Peggy sings with tears in her eyes, presumably because the Colonel has blackmailed her into renouncing her relationship with Johnny. The film cuts to a shot of Johnny rowing back to his ship, bemoaning what he perceives as Peggy's infidelity. But he stops when he hears Peggy's voice, seemingly emanating dimly from across the water. Johnny cries out to his pal, "Wait a minute listen!" and we return to a tight shot of Peggy weeping as she sings the theme song's refrain. The Colonel creeps toward her, but Johnny, who apparently travels more swiftly than a song verse can turn to a chorus, bursts into the apartment and with a quick punch knocks out his rival. Soon after, when Peggy asks Johnny why he returned to her, he replies, "Because I heard you singing that song... our song. And I knew I couldn't go away alone." As in *Double Cross Roads*, *Love Comes Along* integrates a theme song as an overt device of narration, one that owes to the song's recurrence across the film.

Though it was a frequent technique of early soundtracks, song repetition was not always necessary in order for a song to fulfill a structural function. In Fox Film's crime drama *Man Trouble* (1930), Dorothy Mackaill's single song performance proves to mild-mannered newspaper reporter Graham (Kenneth MacKenna) that her character Joan loves him and not her thuggish boss Mac (Milton Sills). Throughout the film, we hear Joan sing a peppy dance number, "Pick Yourself Up, Brush Yourself Off," to Mac at his club. But toward the end of the film, Graham arrives at the club and witnesses Joan singing a bluesy ballad titled "What's the Use of Living Without Love?" for the first time. Sung as part of the refrain, the song's title has a cadence that places a pause between the words "living" and "without"; that breathing space affords Joan a moment to flinch when she notices Graham watching her. The ensuing triangle of glances, conveyed through a series of edited eyeline matches, reveals that Graham and Mac each recognize Joan's affections for the former. With renewed courage, Graham confronts Mac, and the film moves swiftly to its conclusion. Despite this being the sole performance of "What's the Use of Living Without Love?," the song serves a structural function and promotes narrative economy.

The fact that the narrative efficacy of "What's the Use of Living Without Love?" seems to depend not on repetition but on the content of the lyrics evokes a third attribute of theme songs: their synoptic value. In addition to serving associative and structural functions, theme songs tended to encapsulate a film's primary subject matter by summarizing or mirroring the dramatic theme of the picture with which the song was associated. For instance, the lyrics of "Weary River"—specifically, their allusions to a river that always reaches the sea—convey Jerry's resolve to conform to the norms of a law-abiding society. And it is no surprise that the (admittedly trite) lyrics to "My Lonely Heart," "Until Loves Comes Along," and "What's the Use of Living Without Love?" sum up the gist of each film's romantic plot of a lone individual pining for a sweetheart. Despite their similarities, however, each song was specially written for its associated film, in part because Hollywood executives were attempting to build up song catalogs that could be controlled by their publishing affiliates, and in part because the appropriation of preexisting numbers as theme songs was seen to be problematic, with the songs themselves being relevant in only tenuous ways to the films in which they appeared.[7] For instance, the relationship between the film *Glad Rag Doll* (1929) and the hit song of the same name, published three months earlier, puzzled newspaper film critics. The subject of the song is a gold digger who is "admired [and] desired by lovers who soon grow tired"; in contrast, the subject of the film is a woman presumed by others to be a gold digger but who reveals herself to have good intentions and morals. Writing in the *Chicago Daily Tribune*, Mae Tinee (a pseudonym for various film critics at the paper) complained that the film's title "means nothing at all."[8] Mordaunt Hall of the *New York Times* seemed perplexed by the provenance of the film's title, while a reporter for *Variety* quipped, "Whoever eased that song for title and plug into Warners can tip his cap for promotion work."[9] Although the lyrics of most theme songs took up the banal subject of love, the expectation that a theme song should reflect a film's chief dramatic subject (coupled with the understanding that studios would profit from issuing new songs to the public) encouraged the composition of original material.[10]

Lyrics revealed information to characters (and audiences) in varying capacities, depending on the nature of a film's soundtrack. The soundtracks belonging to the earliest sound films of the transitional era consisted of a synchronized score and effects, but no synchronous dialogue. Characters in these films could not display their "authentic" vocal talents and were instead accompanied by other voices recorded for the film's soundtrack. A good example is *Our Dancing Daughters* (1928), the first in a trilogy of "flapper films" starring Joan Crawford along with Anita Page and Dorothy Sebastian.[11] In the film's opening titles, the eight-bar melodic motif of "I Loved You Then as I Love You Now" plays in a waltz time signature and moderately fast tempo. Following the titles, the melody reappears during the initial meeting between protagonists Diana (Crawford), an extroverted flapper, and Ben (Johnny Mack Brown), a genteel soon-to-be millionaire. Set at a party, the scene features jazz dance music, seemingly performed offscreen by a band. Diana dances the Charleston in front of her friends and, unbeknownst to her, attracts the attention of Ben, who watches from an adjacent room. Later, when Diana's friend introduces her to Ben, the instrumental music segues into a vocal performance by an offscreen male ensemble. They sing the refrain of "I Loved You Then as I Love You Now," now set to a 4/4 time signature, the lyrics characteristically banal:

> I loved you then as I love you now,
> You are mine in my thoughts always.
> Love comes but once to the hearts of men,
> When it does then it always stays.
> You filled a spot in an empty heart,
> And tho' perhaps in the end we part,
> I'll always dream of what might have been,
> For I love you now as I loved you then.

Once established as the love theme for Ben and Diana, the song acquires dramatic significance in the remainder of the film. For one, the lyrics of the refrain ("Tho' perhaps in the end we part") anticipate Ben's decision to marry Diana's rival Ann (Anita Page), whom he believes is more committed to a relationship than the free-spirited Diana. Additionally, the clear reversal that characterizes the first and last lines of the refrain ("I loved you then as I love you now" becomes "I love you now as I loved you then") foretells and summarizes Ben's lasting affections for Diana. The melodic motif also serves a structural role in that its accrued symbolism of unrequited romance creates a bittersweet effect when Ben and Ann send Diana a note of gratitude for a wedding gift. As Diana reads the note, we recognize a transposed reiteration of the theme song motif on the soundtrack, now played as a slow waltz. The motif recapitulates Diana's thoughts: She loves Ben now as she loved him "then," upon their first meeting. Read in conjunction with the film's soundtrack, the note is not a mere gesture of gratitude for a wedding gift but rather evokes the young flapper's memories of love gained and lost. Despite the absence of an onscreen performance of the song, "I Loved You Then as I Love You Now" is nonetheless a vehicle of narration.

The above analysis takes for granted an important point: After hearing the song's lyrics, audiences could remember and recall them when the instrumental version appeared during the film's final scene. But the quality of projected sound in theaters wired during the transitional era was less than hospitable to vocal clarity, and so the likelihood of audiences hearing every word of a song—much less remembering them—was scant.[12] On the other hand, because, as Jeff Smith has noted, a song's title is often sufficient as a source of narrative meaning, the promotion of "I Loved You Then as I Love You Now" outside of the film, primarily by way of sheet music, would have meant that audiences already were (or would become) familiar with the song's basic message. This assumption holds true for other theme songs of the transitional era, whether they appeared in non-synchronous or synchronous films.

Indeed, in contrast with non-synchronous sound films like *Our Dancing Daughters*, soundtracks to part-talkies and all-talkies exploited onscreen vocal performances, resulting in the use of theme songs to express what characters could not articulate in spoken dialogue through sung lyrics. Lyrics therefore added narrative value. Sometimes, such songs came from surrogate sources, such as ancillary characters, phonograph records, and radio broadcasts. In a scene in MGM's *Way Out West* (1930), for example, ranch owner Molly (Hyams) anxiously awaits for the return of a carnival barker, Windy (Haines), whom she has entrusted with funds for deposit at a bank in the nearest town. A solo male voice accompanied by a ukulele croons the opening line of a ballad titled "Singing a Song to the Stars." A cut from a shot of a clock shows Molly, distressed and standing at a window. Another cut takes us to an exterior shot, where a young woman and one of the ranchers sit beneath a tree. The rancher, played by real-life crooner Cliff ("Ukulele Ike") Edwards, strums his ukulele and continues the song, with lyrics that compare his lover's eyes to stars and end by professing his "dreaming, just dreaming of you." Edwards's crooning accompanies two additional shots that show Molly presumably "dreaming, just dreaming" of Windy. Perhaps she is also "singing a song to the stars," making a private wish for Windy's return. Though Molly cannot admit to the other ranchers that she is in love with Windy, the lyrics communicate her feelings very baldly.

A SONG FOR EVERY OCCASION: INCIDENTAL SONGS

In contrast with theme songs, which typically accumulated meaning through their reiteration over the course of a film, incidental songs were motivated by their immediate narrative circumstances: an ancillary singer performing in a nightclub (*Thunderbolt* [1929]), for example, or background music playing on a train (*Possessed* [1931]). Also unlike theme songs, incidental songs belonged to a variety of musical genres, and they exploited musical conventions of instrumentation and melody in order to suggest historical periods and geographic settings. Thus the effectiveness of incidental songs depended upon an audience's familiarity with the cultural connotations of different kinds of music—what Claudia Gorbman has called "connotative cueing" and classical Hollywood composer Dmitri Tiomkin has described as a "telegraphic code."[13] *White Shadows in the South Seas* (1928) reveals its Polynesian setting by featuring an indigenous popular dance tune played on a Hawaiian guitar in its opening sequence. The opening of *In Old Arizona* (1929) signals its central locale, a Mexican town, through the appearance of six street musicians playing various instruments, including a vihuela, the high-pitched five-string guitar often associated with mariachi music. In Westerns and Western hybrids, such as *Sundown Trail* (1931) and *Montana Moon* (1930), cowboys sing archetypal tunes, including "Oh, Susanna," "She'll Be Coming 'Round the Mountain," and "Old Chisholm Trail." Hot jazz numbers performed by diegetic dance bands enliven the party settings in *Their Own Desire* (1929), *Loose Ankles* (1930), and *Check and Double Check* (1930), while sweet jazz accompanies a couple dancing in a restaurant in *Doorway to Hell* (1930). The longest musical cue in Josef von Sternberg's *Thunderbolt* is an enthralling bluesy performance of "Daddy, Won't You Please Come Home" by Theresa Harris, singing in Harlem's Black Cat nightclub. In romantic dramas and comedies centering on the romance of youths, such as *Son of the Gods* (1930) and *Our Modern Maidens* (1929), incidental songs provide occasion for youths to sing in ensemble. And college songs in *Salute* (1929) enhance the setting of a football game in a college stadium. In all of these examples, the power of songs depends upon transparent musical clichés, with codes that had instant audience recognition.

In some cases, incidental songs functioned to advance film narratives in a manner similar to theme songs. In the Oscar-nominated Warner Bros. crime picture *Doorway to Hell* (1930), Chicago gang leader Louie Ricarno (Lew Ayres) is a key suspect in the murder of two rival gangsters. When a policeman arrives at Louie's home to make an arrest, Louie tunes the radio to a station broadcasting a sentimental ballad sung by an unidentified male tenor. The song serves two narrative purposes: first, as a means by which the cop implicates Louie as a suspect in the murder case ("We've got three boys over at the jail who can sing better than that," he tells Louie, continuing, "We're just waiting to pick up a baritone"), and second, by distracting Louie from the sight of his wife cozying up to his best friend.

Whereas theme songs were usually presented by soloists, incidental songs often entailed collective singing. The creation of community through sing-alongs seems to have been especially apparent in the genre of the war film, where one of the genre's defining features, the glorification of male bonding, is realized through song. John Ford's *The Black Watch*, for instance, opens in a Scottish regiment's mess, where some of the officers hold hands and sing "Auld Lang Syne"; the familiar tune returns during the film's final scene, in which the officers' bittersweet reunion commemorates a young soldier's death. In Howard Hawks's drama *The Dawn Patrol* (1930), the song "Stand to Your Glasses" conveys a sense of community among military pilots who have become inured to the threat of death. The refrain rallies the soldiers around a pessimistic tone, singing as they do: "So stand by your glasses steady, / This world is a world of lies. / Here's a toast to the dead already, / Hurrah for the next man who dies." So important was this song deemed to be for the plot that it found its way into a novelization of the film, published first in *Screen Book* magazine and reprinted in the August 24, 1930, issue of the *Buffalo Times*.[14]

The activity of fraternal bonding through incidental song was not limited to the genre of war films, however. In MGM's *In Gay Madrid* (1930), a romantic drama set at a Spanish university, Ramón Novarro's character sings solo before throwing his arms around the shoulders of his friends, who call out the final lyrics in unison. The documentary *With Byrd at the South Pole* (1930) celebrates the return of real-life explorer Admiral Richard Byrd from the South Pole with instrumental motifs of "Hail, Hail, the Gang's All Here" and "It'll Be a Hot Time in the Old Town Tonight," each of which suggests a theme of camaraderie. Incidental songs provided male characters in a range of genres the opportunity to express platonic affection. This function was rarely carried out by theme songs, which tended to highlight the role of the individual soloist.

A CONFLUENCE OF COINCIDENCES: SONG MOTIVATION IN *CHECK AND DOUBLE CHECK* (1930)

In the example of *Double Cross Roads*, discussed above, David hears Mary sing "My Lonely Heart" by way of a fortuitous coincidence: Mary just happens to be standing outside the room containing the safe that David is cracking. The dramatic device of coincidence is thus used in order to plug the film's theme song and supply a narrative pretext for the song's presentation. Yet the baldness of the coincidence makes us all too aware of the narrative mechanisms that have made the serendipitous encounter between the young lovers possible. In this way, the climax of *Double Cross Roads* can be said to be overly determined, and narrative credibility suffers as a result.

A similar but more complicated use of narrative coincidence distinguishes the incorporation of songs in RKO's *Check and Double Check* (figure 4.1), a feature-length film comedy that served above all as a backdrop for the onscreen antics of Freeman Gosden (Amos) and Charles Correll (Andy), white actors whose "black-voice" performances were featured on the country's most popular radio program, *Amos 'n' Andy*.[15]

Most cultural historians' discussion of *Amos 'n' Andy*, and thus of *Check and Double Check*, focus on the texts' racial politics. Amos and Andy were, after all, incarnations of the antebellum minstrel caricatures Jim Crow and Zip Coon, and, as Michele Hilmes has illustrated, the humor of the show resided primarily in the duo's cultural incompetence, making them "permanent immigrants" in an all-black environment—an environment that also rendered the real social implications of racial identity irrelevant.[16] Hence the show appealed to a wide and unusual range of listeners, from those who identified with the challenges experienced by "outsider" ethnic groups to those who found comedic fortification of their racist sensibilities in the show.[17]

Check and Double Check expands on the premise of the radio show by introducing white upper-class characters into Amos and Andy's previously all-black world. Ryan Jay Friedman's deft analysis, in a book chapter aptly titled "Blackness without African Americans," details the ways in which the film's racial ambiguity serves to undercut RKO's publicity campaign, which sought to maintain clear distinctions between the film's white and black(face) characters. In marketing materials and in the film itself, Amos and Andy are identified as "Negroes," and hence they experience a limited degree of social mobility that mirrors that of other black characters (namely, Duke Ellington and the members of his orchestra, two of whom were forced to don skin-darkening makeup); yet the film upends any semblance of a neat racial dichotomy because, after all, Correll and Gosden are white. As we will see, such racial politics, in which elements of "blackness" permeate white culture, are made manifest at the level of the soundtrack.[18]

In addition to easing the anxieties felt by Southern exhibitors over the potential depiction of miscegenation, RKO's advertising campaign for *Check and Double Check* relied heavily on cross-promotion. Steve J. Wurtzler notes that in addition to coordinating an extensive national campaign involving 150 newspapers from across

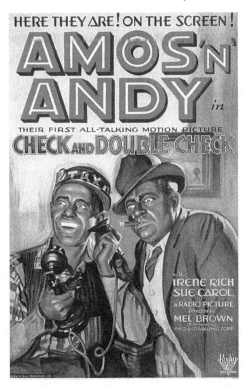

FIGURE 4.1 The theatrical poster from *Check and Double Check* (RKO, 1930) (author's collection).

the country, RKO arranged tie-ups with product sponsors of the *Amos 'n' Andy* radio show (manufacturers of toothpaste, candy bars, and toys); with T. B. Harms, Inc., publisher of the sheet music for songs in the film; and with Victor, for recordings cut by Ellington, Correll, and Gosden. The campaign, in short, was championed by RKO as a "roaring empire of commerce geared to fighting pitch for show world's greatest demonstration of co-operative promotion."[19]

But as far as filmic storytelling is concerned, *Check and Double Check* has not been regarded as a worthy example of narrative economy. When it was initially released, its romantic plot was dismissed by the *New York Times*' Mordaunt Hall as "amateurish," and its primary purchase on audiences today seemingly owes to two ingredients: derogatory depictions, via white blackface, of African American stereotypes, and enthralling jazz performances by Ellington and his band. I would argue that part of the film's clunkiness derives not only from the vapid comedy that characterizes the script, but also from the narrative's over-reliance on the device of coincidence as a means of justifying the presentations of "Three Little Words" and "Old Man Blues."[20] Considered in terms of narrative form, *Check and Double Check* is a revealing example not only of how theme and incidental songs could operate across a single film from the transitional era, but also of a failed attempt to integrate song attractions in a narratively plausible way.

The musical performances in the film owe to the onscreen presentations by Duke Ellington and His Cotton Club Orchestra, as well as the Rhythm Boys, a trio comprised of Bing Crosby, Harry Barris, and Al Rinker. RKO's casting of these musicians was anything but arbitrary, and it represents the studio's attempt to capitalize on the cachet of a brand of black music that had been deemed sanctioned listening for white audiences. Ellington had become the "rage" of the East Coast by the late 1920s, owing to what Harvey G. Cohen describes as the creative and groundbreaking marketing strategies implemented by Ellington and his white manager Irving Mills.[21] Between 1927 and 1930, Ellington had broadcast more than 210 shows from the Cotton Club, reportedly giving most white Americans their first encounter with black music, all the while demonstrating his capacities as a serious artistic figure.[22] Through these productions, Ellington and His Cotton Club Orchestra proved virtuosic performers of hot jazz, the more experimental and frenetic form of jazz strongly associated with black artists, but they were also equally appealing executors of the sweet jazz that dominated radio airwaves and Tin Pan Alley—that is, the jazz that created white listeners.[23] In this way, Ellington has been viewed as the preeminent black musician who broke into the culture of white, mainstream popular music. The Rhythm Boys, meanwhile, epitomized white jazz vocalists of the 1920s and were indelibly linked to the sweet jazz of Paul Whiteman, having been selected by that bandleader in 1926 for the fronting of numerous recordings of his orchestra.[24] Thus the appearance of Ellington, his orchestra, and the Rhythm Boys in *Check and Double Check* capitalized on the musicians' established success, and, perhaps more important, represented RKO's appeal to a white consumer base that had become invested in listening to black music. But the film is also careful to ascribe distinct forms of song to each group: The Rhythm Boys sing the sweet jazz number "Three Little Words," written by Bert Kalmar and Harry Ruby, and Ellington and His Cotton Club Orchestra play "Old Man Blues," a hot jazz tune composed by the bandleader. The performances and their narrative functions are rigorously contrasted.

The diegetic presentation of both songs, however, sits at the point of convergence of three distinct lines of narrative action: (1) the reunion of prospective lovers Jean Blair (Sue Carol) and Richard Williams (Charles Morton), (2) the escapades of Amos and Andy, operators of the Freshair Taxicab Co., and (3) a party hosted by Jean's family, where Ellington's orchestra performs. In order to draw together the three storylines and thus motivate the performance by Ellington's orchestra—a central commercial attraction for audiences—the film exploits a series of coincidences prompted by the film's initial scene, in which the taxicab driven by Amos and Andy breaks down and causes a traffic jam. Their debacle has two payoffs. First, it prevents Amos and Andy's present customers, the Blair parents, from retrieving Richard from the train station. As a result, Richard hires a taxicab and on his way to the Blair house happens upon Jean, who is out for a ride on her horse. We learn later that their initial meeting has important consequences, but for now it suffices to note that in the absence of Amos and Andy's malfunctioning taxicab, Richard and Jean would not have enjoyed a chance encounter with one another in advance of that evening's party. The second outcome of the taxicab failure emerges in the subsequent scene, when, having returned to their office, Amos and Andy receive a call and are offered the job of driving an orchestra to a party. They accept only because they need funds for repairing their defunct vehicle. The orchestra turns out to be Ellington's, and the party turns out to be hosted at the Blair household. Thus the coincidences that lead to the intersection of the plotlines concerning Richard, Jean, Amos, Andy, and Ellington's orchestra can be said to have overly motivated the ensuing song performances.

Several incidental songs underscore the party events. A sweet jazz tune plays after Richard and Jean, having spotted each other from across the dance hall, agree to convene at a nearby lake after the next dance. Richard steps outside and encounters Amos and Andy, who by this point have deposited Ellington and his band at the party but are now confounded by a flat tire on their battered car. Their conversation with Richard unearths another narrative coincidence: Richard's father was the employer of Amos and Andy when they lived in Georgia. When Richard informs the duo of his father's recent passing, the music playing on the soundtrack grows louder, and a plaintive melody presented by the clarinet accentuates the solemn news. The melody continues as Amos reminisces about the benevolence of his former employer. After Richard departs, Amos and Andy manage to start their car, and the scene cuts back to the dance floor.

The incidental song that underscores this scene provides suitably somber accompaniment for Richard's disclosure of his father's death. It also serves a critical narrative function: Because Richard and Jean have agreed to meet "after the next dance," the ensuing music provides an excuse for Richard to wander outside and stumble across the comedians. Their meeting may seem a mere coincidence, but it proves significant when, toward the end of the film, Amos and Andy learn that a property deed they haphazardly discovered could enable Richard to remain in the state of New York and thus pursue his romance with Jean. In the film's penultimate scene, the duo rush to the train station, property deed in hand, and locate Richard just before his departure to Georgia. The incidental but affecting song played during the party scene thus provides a pretext for a chance encounter that forges a critical relationship in the film's larger narrative scheme.

Back in the large hall of the Blair home, Ellington's band plays an interlude, during which the partygoers stop dancing and gather in the center of the room to face the musicians. The subsequent two songs, "Three Little Words" and "Old Man Blues," feature the famous pianist and the Cotton Club Orchestra in different ways. The depiction of "Three Little Words" begins with a frontal long shot of Ellington's orchestra, as shown in figure 4.2.

A trio of male voices, the Rhythm Boys, sings the refrain, but no singers appear on the stage. (According to the entry in the *American Film Institute Catalog*, the Rhythm Boys recorded the song prior to production and were not on set during filming.[25]) The song continues to play offscreen as the editing cuts to shots of the crowd, and then to a shot of Jean exiting the room, presumably to rendezvous with Richard at the lake. In lieu of focusing on the singers or the band, the scene cuts around the space of the dance floor, inhabited by the white partygoers, promoting the sense that the song functions as background music to the white romance rather than as a discrete song-star performance.

In contrast with "Three Little Words," the presentation of the song "Old Man Blues" showcases the musicians of Ellington's orchestra. Here the film cuts between a long shot of the crowd and a series of medium shots featuring the feats of five soloists, in addition to Ellington himself. Confined to the space of the (black) stage, the depiction of the performance of "Old Man Blues" remains independent from the (white) narrative fiction that is taking place on and around the dance floor.

FIGURE 4.2 *Check and Double Check* (RKO, 1930).

At the end of "Old Man Blues," we cut to an exterior scene near a lake. Richard and Jean step out of a rowboat and proceed to sit on a bench, mostly with their backs to the camera. An instrumental and comparatively quiet version of "Three Little Words" can be heard on the soundtrack. The song plays slowly, and its performance comes to articulate what a character cannot: When Richard confesses to Jean, "There's so much I want to say. I just can't seem to express it," vocals appear on the soundtrack, prompting Richard to continue, "Listen. Do you hear what they're singing? That seems to say it so much better than I can." His ostensible ineptitude motivates the couple to remain silent as the entire refrain plays offscreen, though with audible vocals supplied by the Rhythm Boys. The song continues as Richard draws Jean closer and puts his arm around her. He kisses her as the song concludes with its proverbial three little words, and the scene fades to black. Although the reason for Richard's inability to confess his feelings for Jean is unclear, that inability itself motivates the soundtrack's repetition of Ellington's song, which is then conveniently associated with the couple's romance.

Through repetition and association, "Three Little Words" accrues sufficient meaning to serve as a theme song. Its melody appears once more on the soundtrack when Richard, unable to find the document that will permit him to obtain state residency, determines to bid farewell to Jean. Seated at a piano in the foreground of a long shot, Jean taps out the theme song's melody, suggesting that Richard is on her mind. As if on cue, Richard descends from the staircase in the background and says goodbye.

But if "Three Little Words" serves as a theme song, it is one that is overly motivated by way of narrative coincidences and character contrivances. Shoehorned into the narrative arc, the song contrasts well with "Old Man Blues," which, although unnecessary to the narrative trajectory of *Check and Double Check*, likewise provides commercial and aesthetic appeal. "Old Man Blues" exists primarily in order to showcase Ellington and his band, an act that had recently earned national acclaim through a series of radio broadcasts from the Roseland Ballroom and the Cotton Club. Its weak narrative integration may be attributed to the fact that its primary function is to construct and promote the star-song composite of Ellington and his signature tune.

THE PRIORITY OF THE THEME SONG IN *POSSESSED* (1931)

Whereas all of the music cues on the soundtrack of *Check and Double Check* are diegetic, the MGM production of *Possessed* combines diegetic vocal cues with nondiegetic instrumental motifs. Its method of incorporating both kinds of music speaks at once to the endurance of the thematic approach to film scoring—a vestige from the late silent cinema—and to the significance of vocalized songs. During the

coming of sound, the perceived value of motion picture songs influenced the adoption of the thematic approach in two ways: Soundtracks emphasized entire songs
rather than motifs, and they incorporated a vocalized theme song at least once. The
impetus to integrate a vocalized song as a means of investing meaning in subsequent
instrumental renditions sometimes led to awkwardly framed narrative situations, as
exemplified by *Possessed*.

Based on *The Mirage*, a play written by Edgar Selwyn that debuted in 1920, *Possessed*
is a rags-to-riches melodrama cited less frequently for its music than for the problems
it raised at the office of the Motion Picture Producers and Distributors Association
(MPPDA), because the narrative hinges on the fact that Joan Crawford's character,
Marian, and Mark Whitney (Clark Gable) live together out of wedlock.[26] (As Mark
tells Marian, "The surest way to lose a woman is to marry her, and I don't want to
lose you.") To conceal their relationship and maintain respectability, Marian poses
as a wealthy divorcée, Mrs. Moreland. When rumors generated by their relationship
threaten Mark's chances of entering a gubernatorial race, Marian chooses to pretend
that she no longer loves him.

Throughout the film, non-diegetic musical cues (credited to MGM staff members William Axt, Charles Maxwell, and Joseph Meyer) are used to smooth over
transitions between scenes and underscore scenes in which there is no dialogue. For
instance, orchestral music accompanies a shot showing a woman's bejeweled arm
tearing off the pages of a calendar, indicating a temporal ellipsis. A light classical
number plays on the non-diegetic soundtrack when Marian reapplies makeup and
adjusts her jewelry in preparation for meeting Mark's friend. Orchestral music also
plays during a montage depicting Mark's campaign for governor.

But the film's most striking use of music is the theme song "How Long Will It
Last?" composed by Joseph Meyer to words penned by Max Lief. Strains of "How
Long Will It Last?" first appear over the film's opening titles, where it plays in a legato
style with lush orchestration featuring strings and woodwinds that trade off parts of
the A-minor melody between regular interruptions of timpani rolls. As introduced
with the film's opening titles, "How Long Will It Last?" fulfills two narrative functions: First, it serves to recapitulate Marian's entry into the sophisticated world of
Mark Whitney, and second, just as the song title denotes, it suggests the end of their
relationship. The first function is established during the film's opening scenes, which
associate sophisticated culture with diegetic instrumental music. On her walk home
from her job at the paper box factory, Marian watches a train pass through town.
She looks into the windows of the moving cars, and a jazzy instrumental dance
number fades up on the soundtrack, its source revealed as a lavishly dressed couple
dances to the rhythm of the tune in one of the cars. The music fades out as their car
passes, and when the train comes to a halt, Marian is facing a well-dressed man who

compliments her appearance but uses the train as a metaphor to point out their class distinctions. "Only two kinds of people," he tells her, "The ones in and the ones out." In this opening sequence, diegetic instrumental music connotes a sophisticated culture that excludes Marian.

Seeking to escape her rural upbringing, Marian ventures to New York City and finds the man she met at the train. He introduces her to Mark, a millionaire attorney, who is immediately intrigued by her and takes her out to dinner at an extravagant French restaurant. As in the film's opening sequence, the dining scene associates instrumental diegetic music with high-class culture. A tracking shot follows Marian and Mark into the restaurant as lively orchestral music, best described as light classical, appears on the soundtrack, the violins playing staccato in their upper range. The woodwinds take up the melody in a relatively legato style as Mark and Marian are seated. The piece continues as Marian pretends to read from the French menu but orders definitively American food: roast beef, mashed potatoes with gravy, string beans, and apple pie with chocolate ice cream "on top." The conspicuous absence of the phrase "à la mode" from Marian's vocabulary implies her awkward fit into the sophisticated milieu characterized by French cuisine and classical music.

Following the film's affiliation of orchestral music with the social environment that initially excludes Marian, the theme song of *Possessed* signifies Marian's entry into that very environment. However, although the song fulfills a clear dramatic function in its signifying capacity, its presentation disrupts the otherwise steady progression of the film's narrative. Marian first sings "How Long Will It Last?" at a dinner party that takes place three years after her blunder in the restaurant. The scene opens with the camera tracking to an establishing shot of Marian seated at the piano, flanked by her guests. She finishes playing an unidentified piece, and her guests applaud. The man closest to her asks her to sing a song in French. She plunks out a few notes, then laughs and says, "Remember, you asked for it," before launching into a portion of the refrain, sung in French, of "How Long Will It Last?" Throughout her performance, the camera remains at a distance, framing Marian and her surrounding admirers from a slightly high angle. When she finishes singing, another man asks Marian to perform the refrain in German. She does, this time with the camera framing her in a medium shot. A second round of applause ensues. Finally, Mark approaches her and asks, "Isn't there a verse in English?" Marian responds, quietly and suggestively, "I'll tell you the words later," but a guest insists, "There should be no verse in English. After all, English is not the language of love." Perceiving the statement as a dare, Marian sings an entire verse and refrain in English.

The film distinguishes this musical performance from the ones in French and German in two ways. First, Crawford's vocal techniques, which include melodic flourishes and offbeat singing, combine to produce a laxer performance, one that implies an emotional engagement that is noticeably absent from the earlier renditions. Second, a sparse arrangement of strings that emerges on the non-diegetic soundtrack serves to accentuate and intensify the emotional force of the English performance. In anticipation of a scoring strategy that would become an established norm of subsequent Hollywood soundtracks, this scene deploys non-diegetic orchestral music as a means of suggesting Marian's subjective affective state. In these ways, Marian's English performance provides a heightened impression of her character's emotional authenticity, one that is affirmed when an Italian guest concedes, "When a woman sings with her heart, the language is unimportant" after her performance.

Nevertheless, the convergence of several stylistic devices militates against the song's potential to exist as a fully integrated element of narration. Throughout the English performance, the camera remains on Marian, whose face is suddenly illuminated by soft lighting. The scene's visual style, as depicted in figure 4.3, is strongly reminiscent of the framing and editing of Richard Barthelmess during the presentation of songs in *Weary River*, and it isolates Crawford from her diegetic surroundings and in so doing highlights this moment of star-song performance.

The performance is also rendered disruptive by virtue of it having been conspicuously prefaced by the French and German versions. But perhaps most significant, the film has deployed an implausible measure in order to motivate the song performance—namely that, in the span of three years, Marian has learned to speak two foreign languages and play the piano with admirable fluency. Despite the scene's careful attempts to integrate the song into the diegesis, the vocal presentation of "How Long Will It Last?" interrupts the otherwise coherent narrative flow of the film and calls attention to the very contrived mechanisms of form and style that render the performance possible in the first place.

Notable as well is the status of the song within a film whose suggestions of adultery, imported as they were from Selwyn's play, had troubled Jason Joy, director of the self-regulatory committee for the MPPDA—so much so that Joy asked producer Irving Thalberg to abandon the project altogether.[27] Thalberg refused and the film production went ahead as planned, but the point remains that in the context of a contentious phase of preproduction, Meyer and Lief's song was considered a benign addition to the film. Its innocuous nature was evidenced by a letter signed on behalf of Joy and sent to Thalberg, expressing Joy's approval of the song's lyrics and indicating that they, as well as the lyrics for two other songs for MGM films, are "satisfactory with respect to the [Production] Code and contain nothing reasonably censorable."[28] The emphasis placed on the theme song by the film's narrative seems

FIGURE 4.3 *Possessed* (MGM, 1931) film frame.

to capitalize on the safety afforded by the song; it functions as a virtuous channel through which Marian can convey her morally problematic affection for Mark. The fact that Marian's performance is glamorized through aspects of visual style, including a lingering long take, only underlines the song's status as a substitute for the sexual innuendos that were present in the original play and drafts of the script—the same innuendos that proved troublesome to Jason Joy—in turn explaining why so much of the narrative coordinates around the justification of the song's performance.

Once established as a signifier of Marian's transformation into a wealthy socialite, "How Long Will It Last?" is contrasted with other forms of music as a means of distinguishing between high and low culture. In one scene, Marian's hometown sweetheart Wally visits New York and takes Marian to Coney Island. The scene opens with shots of fairground attractions accompanied by a medley of carnival tunes. A cut reveals Wally and Marian riding a carousel, and instrumental music, presumably diegetic, plays the tune of "Little Annie Rooney," a song written and performed in English music halls in the 1890s and popularized at New York's London Theatre. Wally bursts into singing after he tells Marian that he plans on marrying her. Accompanied by the diegetic instrumental music of the carousel, he cries, "Soon we'll marry, never to part / Little Annie Rooney is my sweetheart!" The circus-like musical qualities of "Little Annie Rooney"—the emphasis on brass instrumentation, the chromatic runs of melody, and the marching beat to a

2/2 time signature—contrast vividly with the musical style of "How Long Will It Last?" Through its connection to Wally, moreover, the song is connotative of Marian's rural roots.

The remainder of the film deploys instrumental motifs of "How Long Will It Last?" When Mark's friend arrives one evening with a mistress and dares to compare Marian to his companion, Marian withdraws from the party and wanders toward a window in the apartment's large, empty sitting room. As she stands gazing out, the sound of a cello playing the lead melody of "How Long Will It Last?" can be heard. Mark enters, and the music pauses for a conversation in which Marian tells him, "I am frightened; I feel as though I am walking on the edge of a precipice." When Mark responds, "I'm holding you," and they embrace, the melody of the theme song resumes with high strings and continues until its final cadence.

The association between the theme song and the lovers' relationship is furthered when Marian overhears a conversation between Mark and his politician friends, who encourage him to run for governor and insist that he relinquish his relationship with Marian. Mark discloses to them his plans to marry Marian, but his friends advise that marriage will only verify the prior existence of an illicit affair. In the scene that follows, Marian chooses to sacrifice her love for Mark so that he can run for governor. She rebukes his marriage proposal and pretends to have fallen out of love. Mark orders her to leave, and as she exits and bursts into tears, the main theme from "How Long Will It Last?" appears on the non-diegetic soundtrack, its melody performed by a cello.

Though until now the theme song has anticipated the end of the lovers' relationship, its final manifestation as instrumental underscoring accompanies a plot reversal. In his campaign for governor, Mark delivers a speech at a local hall where hecklers planted by a rival candidate distribute flyers with Marian's picture and demand that Mark reveal the identity of "Mrs. Moreland." Seated in the crowd, Marian stands up, announces, "Mrs. Moreland is nothing to [Mark]," and proclaims Mark's honesty, chivalry, and honor. She exits hurriedly, sobbing, into a rainstorm. Mark suddenly appears and, taking hold of Marian, declares, "I don't care what they do to me back there. If I win, it will be with you. And if I lose, it will still be with you." On the soundtrack, a full orchestra plays the last two lines of "How Long Will it Last?" The shot fades to black and the end title appears as the music resolves.

Through repetition, the instrumental sections of "How Long Will It Last?" become devices of narration. They foretell the fate of the affair between Mark and Marian, and they unite the characters for the sake of narrative closure. But it is important to note that the film can draw on the meaning associated with the instrumental segments only by virtue of their having been prefaced by Crawford's discrete vocalized performance of the song. As a result of the priority placed on the presentation of a vocalized song, Crawford's rendition of "How Long Will It Last?" is integrated by overly determined means.

The variety of narrative functions fulfilled by songs during the transition to sound does not make the period unique in the history of Hollywood film music. As numerous scholars have shown, similar uses of theme and incidental songs are found in films produced during subsequent decades of mainstream cinema. For instance, Heather Laing, in her study of melodramas of the 1940s, examines how diegetic performances achieved emotional expressivity and how non-diegetic music expressed female subjectivity.[29] Both of these practices characteristic of 1940s cinema recall the earlier uses of vocal and instrumental music in *Possessed*, wherein Marian's vocal diegetic rendition of "How Long Will It Last?" serves to externalize her affections for Mark, and later, the non-diegetic instrumental underscoring conveys her subjective desire for Mark's reciprocation. Jeff Smith, who examines popular music in Hollywood cinema since the 1950s, discusses both the capacity for song lyrics to "speak for" characters and the tendency for musical soundtracks of the 1950s through the 1980s to build around melodic motifs derived from theme songs.[30] Claudia Gorbman, in her groundbreaking work *Unheard Melodies: Narrative Film Music*, enumerates a range of functions owed to theme songs and especially highlights their associative powers, while Kathryn Kalinak, in two distinguished books, elaborates upon these functions across a range of film genres and historical periods of Hollywood cinema.[31] These are but a few examples drawn from a rich body of scholarship that conceives of songs as dramatic elements of narration in sound cinema.

Yet the transitional era remains unique insofar as it delimited a brief period in which filmmakers tested and refined their approach to a tension made manifest by the motion picture song. This tension was constituted by, on one hand, the appeal of spectacle, which encouraged the eruption of songs from otherwise plausible fictional worlds, and, on the other hand, the demands of classical narration, which articulated the subordination of spectacle for the sake of narrative cohesion. Given the commercial profile and cultural power of the popular song in the 1920s, one of many questions facing Hollywood producers and filmmakers was how to organize film narratives around the inherent attraction of songs. The result was a fertile period of experimentation with classical plot construction vis-à-vis song integration.

The period did not last long, as the fate of *Possessed*'s theme song exemplifies. Published by MGM's subsidiary, Robbins Music Corp., the sheet music for "How Long Will It Last?" (figure 4.4) displayed two images of Joan Crawford on its cover.

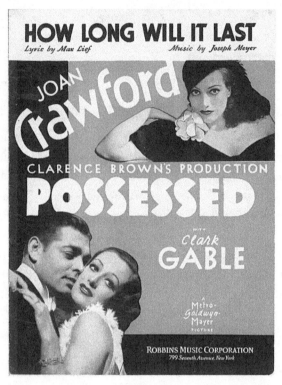

FIGURE 4.4 "How Long Will It Last?" sheet music cover (author's collection).

Crawford also recorded the song, backed by the Gus Arnheim Orchestra, three months prior to the film's release, and although the phonograph recording was never issued, subsequent recordings by Bing Crosby (for Brunswick) and Leo Reisman's orchestra (for Victor Orthophonic) attained moderate sales. Despite the variety of song formats issued by Robbins and the phonograph record companies, and despite the frequent use of the song's lead motif on the film's soundtrack, contemporaneous reviews paid little attention. Neither *Variety* nor the *New York Times* mentioned the number, and although a review in the *Los Angeles Times* noted, "(Crawford) more than adequately portrays the anguish and nobility of an unwedded wife with a song in French and German," the author of the review supplied no reference to the far more significant performance in English.[32] Given the song's conspicuous performance in the film, as well as its modest circulation as a commercial product, the lack of press attention may be puzzling. As the following chapter suggests, the oversight may be considered less a reaction to the song's strained integration than an indication of the negative connotation that the industry came to associate with the concept and practice of the theme song by the end of the transitional era.

Songs and music are now a necessary evil, but they must have story value and must dovetail with the whole scheme of the picture. The writer must be prolific and can't survive by just writing the elementary love song with trite sentimentalities. Hence, the out and out theme song is too obvious and will not be tolerated by producer or public.

L. WOLFE GILBERT (1930)[1]

Ultimately, when the hubbub has died down, a corps of music specialists, with a knowledge of dramaturgy and the exact requirements of the sound film, will be developed; and the motion picture, which has in music a sister art, will reach its full florescence.

PHILIP K. SCHEUER (1929)[2]

5

Curtailing a Song

TOWARD THE CLASSICAL BACKGROUND SCORE

FROM 1928 THROUGH mid-1930, Hollywood's major studios emphasized the commercial and dramatic merits of the motion picture song. While all five companies that represented the studios (Paramount, Fox, Warner Bros., Loew's/MGM, and RCA) affiliated with or acquired majority stock in music publishing firms, studio music departments hired Tin Pan Alley and Broadway composers and lyricists who in turn wrote dozens of theme and incidental songs for motion picture soundtracks. These songs were promoted in print and radio advertisements, and they fulfilled narrative functions in films themselves.

Over the course of the succeeding 18 months, an equally notable transformation occurred, one that saw executives close many of their companies' affiliated branches of music publishing, cut music staff and reduce the salaries of the remaining personnel, and restrict the incorporation of songs in films. Numerous backstage musicals and adaptations of Broadway shows were canceled mid-production, and the use of theme songs in films belonging to non-musical genres greatly diminished. Motion picture songs gradually disappeared from the tops of best-seller lists and were replaced by numbers published independently of films.[3] By the end of 1931, Hollywood's music departments employed less than one-quarter of the staff that they had taken on two years earlier. According to a report in *Variety*, 143 composers and lyricists held studio contracts in 1929; fewer than 30 were on contract by December 1931.[4]

An appealing explanation for the seemingly abrupt shift in industry attitude toward motion picture songs is the effect of the stock market crash in October 1929. "The year 1929 had been one long boom" for the film industry, writes Donald Crafton, who points out that during that year, studios flush with investment monies allocated those funds to experiments with technological novelties like color and widescreen film.[5] In this context of prosperity, the crash in October seemed to forecast especially dire circumstances. Indeed, even while industry representatives attempted to propagate a discourse of optimism in the months following the crash, production budgets decreased, ticket prices diminished, and theaters closed.[6] Thus a studio's choice to trim its extraneous operations, like song publishing, could be seen as a rational economic decision made by a company seeking to maximize profits; as Ross Melnick points out, if media convergence defined the activities of companies in the late 1920s, media *divergence* characterized their operations in the period between 1931 and 1932.[7] The economic impact of the crash could also explain Hollywood's diminishing output of expensive musical productions.

But recourse to the stock market as an explanation for the diminishment of song production and publication perhaps fosters too simplistic a view of movie music in post-crash Hollywood. In particular, it curtails consideration of the fact that grumblings over both the quantity and quality of motion picture songs preceded October 1929. Although pronounced enthusiasm for songs characterized trade press reports on the subject in the late 1920s, the occasional article in *Variety* and *Billboard* foretold the anti-song tenor that would emerge at the outset of the 1930s.[8] So, apparently, did members of the public. In October 1928, a letter to the editor of the *Spokane Spokesman Review*, signed "Harmony Hank," wryly observed, "Striking up a theme song every time the hero and heroine drift into a clutch is like the little boy who drew a picture of a house and wrote about it: 'This is a house.' Give the film fans credit for a little imagination. They don't need theme songs to help them follow the plot."[9] Moreover, although accounts of the "song glut" usually focus on film musicals, which are held responsible for wearing out public appetite for songs, reports in the trade papers indicate concerns about songs in non-musical films.[10] Crafton writes that "the tendency to strip musicals of their music…demonstrates clearly that the genre was rejected not primarily for economic reasons but rather as a response to customers' changing tastes"; the same can be said for non-musical films.[11]

Many of the reports in the trades focused on economic impact, warning that an overproduction of songs would hinder sales of sheet music and records. An article in *Variety* predicted that the sudden flood of theme songs would "mean the survival of the fittest but meantime each is cutting in on the other and hurting the business in general."[12] Other articles cautioned against the watering down of aesthetic value that seemed to have resulted from the song glut. In an article titled "Music Industry on Higher Plane," published in a July 1929 issue of *Billboard*, Irving Thalberg and Jack Robbins, the respective heads of film production and music publishing for the MGM-Robbins partnership, advised readers that theme songs would be written not to appeal to the lowest common denominator of the public but to rather strike a balance of highbrow and lowbrow tastes. They would possess a melodic style more similar to the compositions of Vincent Youmans (of "Tea for Two" fame) and lyrics that strike a balance of "Park avenue and the 10th avenue [*sic*]."[13] Some unease over the erosion of musical quality was evident in forums unrelated specifically to film music. For example, in the September 1929 issue of *International Photographer*, a technical journal for cinematographers, projectionists, and camera and lab personnel, magazine editor Lewis W. Physioc wrote, "The [theme] song is effective when there is a good reason for it, but we fear a monotony of common-place tunes. A beautiful melody is one of the most appealing productions of art, but is the result of inspiration and we hate to think of them being composed promiscuously and to order."[14]

Still worse than the motion picture song's potentially negative impact on sales of ancillary products and musical quality was its apparent incursion into film form: songs "inserted promiscuously" would jeopardize a film's narrative coherence.[15] A *Variety* columnist declared in April 1929, "Melodramas and straight dramatic or dialog pictures are not conducive to plausible song interpolations."[16] What defined a plausible interpolation of songs was not clear, but Thalberg and Robbins suggested that music should be used only during climactic moments or where it proved helpful to heighten dramatic tension.[17] As explained a few years later by Kurt London (author of one of the first books dedicated to the subject of film music), the song glut undermined the differentiation among genres, even non-musical ones. "In consequence of the song-hit craze," London wrote, "there was hardly any difference of style between serious drama and comedy."[18] From this perspective, songs threatened the integrity of genre distinction in addition to narrative coherence.

Then there was the problem of what Edwin Bradley has called the public "exhaustion" and "ennui" for motion picture songs—an outcome of the cyclical nature of Hollywood cinema and its audience's appetite.[19] Instructive in this regard is an analogy to the musical accompaniment that was typical of silent film presentation ten years earlier. Around 1921, Rick Altman observes, audiences began to grow weary of particular musical themes and songs that accompanists integrated into their performances. Once a musical work had attained sufficient familiarity with audience members, it competed with the film for audience attention. Altman describes the process thusly:

[Critics] recognized that accompaniment by title or lyrics shunted the audience's attention from the film to the accompanist.... When first introduced, a
particular piece sidetracks the attention of no more than a handful of spectators already familiar with the music. But once the music becomes a standard
part of the repertory, a substantial portion of the audience is likely to say, "Oh,
that's *Rienzi*" rather than concentrate on the film's action.[20]

Although the threshold of song recognition was less pronounced in sound films
because the vast majority of their motion picture songs were newly written and
unfamiliar to audiences, one can extrapolate from Altman's observation to surmise
that by 1930 theme songs were considered vehicles that shuttled audience attention
away from narrative and toward the act of song presentation. Instead of saying, "Oh,
that's *Rienzi*," perhaps the movie-going public of 1930 was saying, "Oh, that's a *theme
song*." This problem was exacerbated by the convention of the star-song attraction,
which perforce drew attention to the act of song performance—an aesthetic justified by musicals but notably frustrating to the audiences of non-musical films.

As the box-office success of film musicals took a nosedive, and rhetoric that
opposed the use of film songs appeared with increasing frequency in the trade
papers, executives at the major studios took steps toward "de-tuning" sound cinema,
and they did so along both institutional and aesthetic lines. They scaled back publishing operations, minimized references to motion picture songs in advertising, and
reduced the size of music departments by buying off the contracts of Tin Pan Alley
songwriters, retaining instead a lean stock of composers and arrangers who were
regarded as more musically versatile than their Alley counterparts. Indeed, most
of these composers were versed in both classical and popular styles of music, and
their musical education and experience would shape the style and function of film
music in the coming years—most immediately by emphasizing plausibly integrated
songs and intermittent orchestral scoring. Analyses of *In Old Arizona* (1929) and
Safe in Hell (1931), followed by a brief examination of *Arrowsmith* (1931), exemplify
the sound film's capacity to minimize the disruptive potential of songs and increase
the use of orchestral underscoring. As a result of these practices, clearer distinctions
developed between musical and non-musical films.

THE CAMPAIGN AGAINST THE "PROMISCUOUS" THEME SONG

By mid-1930, objections to motion picture songs surfaced regularly in the trades.
Some of these continued to take aim at the sheer quantity of songs injected into
sound films. A *Billboard* critic submitted that the film industry's ability to sustain
its song business would depend on the restrained use of motion picture music.[21]

Variety columnist Bill Swigart proclaimed, "[It is] generally believed among exhibitors throughout the country that if the film producers do not recede in telling a picture story by song, the public will become so tired of squawking tonsils and string symphonies that it will take a long time to bring back the popularity intended for the musical picture."[22]

But, as in 1929, more worrisome than the quantity of songs was the nature of their interpolation. Articles in the trades, sometimes penned by music directors or studio producers, emphasized the importance of the "organic" or "integral" relationship between narrative and number.[23] Ultimately, these terms were deployed in a discourse launched against the theme song, which came to be viewed as a threat to narrative coherence. An article in *Billboard* first extolled the theme song for its commercial value and for providing a moment of "relief" in the narrative, only to submit that "producers are beginning to take a different view of the matter" by ensuring that the "dramatic production is being produced minus that inevitable, and many times unnecessary, song number."[24] Ray Perkins, who at the time was in charge of Warner Bros.' music department, assured readers of *Hollywood Filmograph*, "Our songs are now part of our screen stories. When a picture doesn't call for a theme song there isn't any. In other words, we are now working with the production department to add tuneful melodies to the screen stories in a sensible way."[25] And, in an article titled "Theme Songs Within Reason Or Producers Will Cut 'Em," Felix A. Feist, general sales manager of MGM, made it known to *Billboard* readers in mid-1930 that whereas in sound films to date, "characters burst into song without any valid reason," in the new films, "there will be a reason for a song or it will not be used."[26]

Robert Crawford, executive in charge of musical activities at Warner Bros. and subsidiary First National, was eager to celebrate the company's new approach to music, which he told the *Los Angeles Times* would no longer involve theme songs. "Music is an integral part of a story," he was quoted as saying, and motion pictures would be outfitted with complete scores of music "of the highest operetta type. It is my own belief that it will not be long before we are producing something far greater in its sweep of music than grand opera, which has always been limited by the traditions of the stage."[27] In a special summer issue of *Variety* that featured Warner Bros., Crawford declared:

The dawn of the new music day was heralded by the so-called theme song, but the theme song is now a thing of the past, and it will not return.... The very name seems a trifle antiquated today—so rapidly is the alliance of the screen and music advancing. Music has become an integral part of the screen story, to the great benefit of both.[28]

In August, *Billboard* noted that since "the public was sung to death" by theme songs and story action was "retarded by the musical innovation," the soundtracks of the most successful films of the past year, including *All Quiet on the Western Front* and *Journey's End*, had virtually no musical accompaniment. If at one point "the West Coast became the mecca of the man who had ideas for lilting tunes and rhythmic lyrics," opined the writer, "today the matter is reversed, and the goose that laid the golden egg is no more."[29]

By this time, film musicals were suffering at the box office. Even in regional and rural markets, where musicals had enjoyed long runs in the previous year, exhibitors were reportedly planning to resist the booking of musical productions.[30] Faring the worst of the musical genres were revues, including *King of Jazz* (1930) and *Paramount on Parade* (1930), presumably because their anthology-like presentation of song numbers entailed, by definition, scant trace of narrative integration.[31] One solution was proposed by MGM when it was announced that the studio's writers would insert a story in order to connect the discrete performances in the revue *March of Time*; nonetheless, the film ended up being edited into and released as a series of musical shorts over the course of several years.[32]

In response to both box-office failure and unfavorable critical response, studio executives pledged to curtail if not entirely eliminate the production of musicals.[33] The trades reported Paramount's plans to halt musical productions for six months; MGM's commitment to using songs only with "valid reason"; and Warner Bros.' announcement that it would cease incorporating songs in dramatic pictures produced during the second half of 1930 on grounds that a surplus of songs would "weaken a natural picture plot."[34] In practice, numerous musicals were abandoned mid-production, including *The Merry Widow* (MGM), *Maytime* (Warner Bros.), *Babes in Toyland* (RKO), and *New Movietone Follies of 1931* (Fox).[35] Director Edmund Goulding discarded five of the six songs written by Irving Berlin for *Reaching for the Moon* (1930), retaining only the title song as accompaniment to the film's opening credits.[36] Similarly, only two of the 15 songs written by DeSylva, Brown, and Henderson (DBH) were kept for the comedy *Indiscreet*, a 1930 production that United Artists held off releasing until April 1931. For the production of the operetta *Naughty Marietta*, producer Irving Thalberg proclaimed that the "[r]omantic angle will be emphasized instead of music [because] songs awkwardly inserted or not fitting into the narrative are useless for films."[37] Warner Bros.' adaptation of Cole Porter's Broadway musical *Fifty Million Frenchmen* excluded Porter's entire vocal score; the final film, released in February 1931, uses Porter's songs only as background accompaniment.[38]

The anti-song attitude associated with film musicals influenced the publicity of non-musical films. In echo of earlier efforts to distance film music from its roots in populist Tin Pan Alley, some press material downplayed the entertainment value of motion picture songs and instead focused on heightened musical quality. For instance, an article in the pressbook for *The Arizona Kid* (1930) bore the headline "Old World Melodies Oust Theme Songs" and explains that the stars Warner Baxter and Mona Maris "sing during the production but their songs are old-world Spanish melodies, love songs that probably were composed long before Columbus ventured westward and that have a charm all their own."[39] The pressbook for *The Big House* (1931) included a script for a 30-minute radio program that alternates an announcer's dialogue with musical selections, but the accompanying commentary stressed that the musical selections are "only brief overtures" designed to capture the audience's attention and are "NOT for musical entertainment."[40]

Most pressbooks underlined the narrative functions of songs by using language that alluded to the importance of song integration and motivation. Studio advertising corroborated Feist's declaration by emphasizing the "natural" motivation of song performances. For MGM's release of *Laughing Sinners* (1931), which starred Joan Crawford as a nightclub performer, the pressbook advertised the song "What Can I Do—I Love That Man" by calling it "A Song that Can Stand Promotion":

> This song number fits naturally and easily into the picture. Its insertion has been intelligently handled and it belongs as much to the sequence as the dialogue or the players themselves. As music plugs have been rare in the past year, now would seem to be a good time to go after sheet music stores, broadcasting stations and dance orchestras for whatever publicity you can get out of this number.[41]

A telling example of a studio's reluctance to promote theme songs is First National's pressbook for *The Lash* (1930), which contains no mention of the film's theme song despite its significance during preproduction and production. *The Lash* was based on a Western novel titled *Adios*, and the rights to adapt the novel to screen were obtained by Warner Bros. on the condition that the film's soundtrack include "Adios!," a song published by Feist, Inc.[42] The stipulation launched a series of letters among personnel at Warner Bros., First National, and the novel's publisher, William Morrow and Co. Although the publishing company insisted on the use of "Adios!" as a theme song, studio executive Ray Perkins maintained that First National would use the song as part of the story action but that "it need not be a theme song."[43] Once the film was in production, musical assistant Arthur Franklin on the West Coast wrote to executive E. H. Murphy in New York to inform him of the music department's decision to alter the song's chorus in order to better reflect the film's Mexican setting.[44] In the release print, "Adios!" appears on the soundtrack six times—more frequently than any other piece of music in the film—and is associated with the romance that develops between the plot's two protagonists. It is, in other words, a theme song. The fact that "Adios!" was integrated repeatedly "as part of the action of the picture" and yet *not* promoted as a theme song is indicative of the negative connotation that theme songs had acquired by mid-1930.[45]

"WEST COAST NO MORE A GOLD COAST" FOR SONGWRITERS

With fewer musicals in production, and fewer songs in demand for use in all films, motion picture companies scaled back their music publishing operations—although, at least in the case of Warner Bros., not before attempting to make inroads into the American recording business. In the spring of 1930, the company purchased the music division of Brunswick-Balke-Collender Co., an entertainment conglomerate that included the established Brunswick recording label.[46] Further "hot after its own network," Warner Bros. also acquired control of National Radio Advertising, Inc., a manufacturer of electrical transcriptions for broadcast purposes, thereby enabling the motion picture company to profit from the preparation, sales, and broadcast of recorded programs.[47] These were both inauspicious moves that cost the company $8 million, and in late 1931 Warner Bros. sold its Brunswick-Balke-Collendar holdings to the American Record Corp.[48] A columnist in *Billboard* later declared that Warner Bros. had "flopped" in the music business because its executives had spent nearly $28 million to buy "the shell of a nut without the meat inside."[49] But the company did not abandon song publishing entirely. Although it offloaded its holdings in DBH to the publishing company's original three owners, Warner Bros. retained control over the Music Publishers Holding Corporation, comprising Harms Inc. and all its subsidiaries.

The majors' affiliated publishers also consolidated or closed regional branch offices. Famous Music Corp. paid off the original investments of Warner Bros. and Paramount so that it could operate independently of the motion picture companies.[50] Leo Feist, Inc., then owned by RCA, closed all its offices except for those in New York and Chicago, and Berlin Inc. eliminated branches in Los Angeles and San Francisco while cutting staff in Boston and Chicago.[51] Warner Bros. ordered the closure of Witmark, DBH, and Remick offices across the country.[52] As *Billboard* reported, the company "cannot see the wisdom of supporting a dozen out-of-town offices to exploit songs when the same music-buying public may be reached via the radio from New York and Chicago."[53] Two months later, the company folded up additional branches and consolidated its L.A. offices as a means of alleviating the expense of multiple leases.[54] Robbins, Harms, and Famous shuffled personnel around in order to consolidate offices.[55] In June 1931, Fox's publishing firm, Red Star

Music Co., announced that it would cease operations entirely, at which point the publication of the studio's music was assumed by Sam Fox Publishing Co., a venerable publisher of motion picture music during the silent era.[56]

From the outset of the 1930–1931 filmmaking season, regular reports in *Variety* and *Billboard* began to account for the transformation of the studios' swollen music departments into smaller "skeleton groups" of songwriters. The long-term contracts previously enjoyed by songwriters became unconventional and were replaced by freelance agreements that saw the studios negotiating on a per-song basis. Warner Bros. was forced to retain six songwriters on contract but dismissed Erno Rapee, in addition to Richard Rodgers, Lorenz Hart, and Herbert Fields, who had initially signed up to write three musicals in exchange for a fee of $50,000 apiece.[57] The contracts of Sigmund Romberg and Oscar Hammerstein II were allegedly bought off for $100,000 each after they had written only two of the four operettas for which they were initially engaged.[58] Abel Baer, a songwriter who had signed with Fox and then transferred to Warner Bros. as a result of the company's acquisition of Harms, Inc., returned to his original employer, Feist, Inc., in New York.[59] Also bound for New York by early 1931 were Lew Brown and Ray Henderson of DBH; De Sylva remained in Hollywood.[60] At RKO, Max Steiner received a letter from studio executives in September 1930 ordering him to dismiss all music department personnel not under contract.[61] Some of the discharged songwriters, like Abner Silver, Sammy Fain, and Nacio Herb Brown, formed their own publishing firms.[62] Others who remained often shuttled from studio to studio on short-term contracts, working under department heads: Ben Jackson at Fox; Leo Forbstein and Lou Silvers at Warner Bros. and its subsidiary First National; Nathaniel Finston at Paramount; Hugo Reisenfeld (replaced by Alfred Newman) at United Artists; Max Steiner and/or Victor Baravalle at RKO; and Martin Broones (replaced by Arthur Lange) at MGM.[63] *Billboard* claimed that by dropping songwriters, motion picture producers saved on average more than $100,000 per week.[64] "No more term contracts and fat salaries, which provided gravy for the piano boys up to last year," *Variety* observed.[65]

A few songwriters refused to be bought off. When MGM offered to pay its composers and lyricists 50 percent of their contract value, a "small insurgent group," including Harry Woods and Joseph Meyer, attempted to hold off for 75 percent. *Variety* noted, "When taking the diehard position Metro last week moved the holdouts to remote offices near the railroad tracks and ordered them in cubby holes from nine in the morning until 5:30 in the afternoon, in what appeared to be a smokeout sequence."[66] Woods and Meyer reportedly settled eventually for 64 percent.

The purging of songwriters from music departments took place through mid-1931, but even by the summer of 1930, *Variety* was declaring "West Coast No More a Gold Coast."[67] Perhaps the most vivid account came from Myrtle Gebhart, staff writer for the *Los Angeles Times*, who recounted in an article aptly titled "Tin Pan Alley Says Goodbye":

> When the talkies first came they boomed, "It's Bonanza Time in Hollywood!" But their theme song became truly a "blues." It was repeated, with lugubrious emotion, by countless disappointed song-writers returning east.... The nine principal studios presented 1,086 songs from the singing screen, M-G-M, Warner Bros. and First National leading. The major companies bought outright, or acquired shares in, music-publishing concerns. In swanky new musical libraries, melody was card-indexed. Scores were classified alphabetically: fight, fire and fury music; cakewalk, college, children, chimes and circus airs. They didn't know that you don't placard music and order it in job-lots: animals, birds, seasons, war. They found out, though. All that rhythmic din gave us entertainment indigestion.[68]

The primary constituents of the revamped and comparatively modest music departments were composers, orchestrators, and arrangers who were versed in the styles of light European classics and late 19th-century Romantic idioms, and who at the same time possessed experience writing in the popular song styles of the vaudeville and Broadway stages. As Christopher Palmer has observed, these composers had been educated in the symphonic style of scoring and orchestration, but not in the concert-hall style of modern 20th-century music that was developing alongside the music produced by Hollywood and Broadway entertainment—an important quality given that the studios "assumed the public would refuse to tolerate any music more modern-sounding than the Liszt symphonic poem or the Lehar [*sic*] opera."[69]

An exemplary composer in this context was Max Steiner, who trained in Vienna and conducted music for operettas in London before arriving in New York in 1914. After working as a copyist for Harms, Inc., he began orchestrating and conducting Broadway operettas penned by George Gershwin, Jerome Kern, and Victor Herbert. By the time Steiner arrived at the RKO lot in 1929, he was proficient in a variety of musical styles. Palmer notes that Steiner's roots in Tin Pan Alley, and not Carnegie Hall, explain why "it was only natural that when Steiner started to compose himself, his chosen idiom was initially a kind of flotsam-and-jetsam of late [19]th-century mid-European [R]omantic influences, popular and to a lesser extent classical: a dash of Liszt, a dash of Wagner, dashes of any number of Strausses, Lehár, Friml, Romberg, Victor Herbert, with the occasional seasoning of Gershwin, Berlin or Rodgers reflecting Steiner's later years in the American theatre; but, apart from this, almost nothing of true [20]th-century concert music."[70]

Several of those individuals who had experience blending Romantic and popular music idioms, and who proved to be versatile composers, orchestrators, and arrangers, retained employment during the exodus of songwriters in 1930. At RKO, Steiner worked alongside Roy Webb, who had immersed himself in the study of Bach and Beethoven at Columbia University but had then gone to work on Broadway. Alfred Newman led the music department at United Artists, balancing his training as a classical pianist with his experience on the popular vaudeville and Broadway stage.[71] Hugo Friedhofer at Fox had trained on the cello, immersed himself in the orchestration techniques of Debussy, Ravel, and other late Romantic composers, and worked as a performer, arranger, and composer of silent film music at theaters in San Francisco before being invited to join Fox's music department in 1929.[72] Joseph Meyer at MGM studied violin in Paris and honed his performance skills in a café in San Francisco before writing one of Al Jolson's most successful song hits, "California, Here I Come" (1922), and tunes for several Broadway shows.

By the end of 1931, studio music departments were considerably smaller than they had been two years before. Composers and lyricists who could churn out popular songs served the studios' needs during the "song vogue" of 1928 and 1929, but they were no longer economical investments for producers who sought to maximize efficiency and meet the changing tastes of audiences. The composers who staffed the studio's music departments emphasized intermittent orchestral scoring (to be distinguished from the continuous musical cues that characterized accompaniment to the late silent cinema), and the songs that were deemed necessary were incorporated in generally convincing ways. The soundtracks that resulted anticipated scoring practices that would become associated with the classical Hollywood cinema of the 1930s and 1940s.

AN EARLY PROTOTYPE: SONG INTEGRATION IN
IN OLD ARIZONA (1929)

Credited as both the first talkie Western and the first talkie shot outdoors, Fox's *In Old Arizona* was released on January 20, 1929, at the height of Hollywood's theme song vogue. However, the film succeeds in incorporating songs in narratively plausible ways, and, in so doing, it serves as an early model of song interpolation. With few exceptions, the songs in *In Old Arizona* are delivered not as carefully motivated and discrete presentations but rather as haphazard performances that crop up inconspicuously, and usually as a means for expressing character attributes with narrative efficiency (figure 5.1). The convincing integration of songs in *In Old Arizona* is also suggested by the fact that, despite the number of musical cues in the film, songs

FIGURE 5.1 The formal notification given by Fox Film to ERPI makes clear the multitude of "partial," rather than "entire," songs slated for use by the studio.

during the course of the film are given dramatic significance in consonance with the semantic elements of the Western.

By associating different musical forms with its two lead characters, the Cisco Kid (Warner Baxter) and Sergeant Mickey Dunn (Edmund Lowe), *In Old Arizona* employs songs in the service of enacting dichotomies central to the Western genre: familiar, white culture versus a foreign, non-white ethnic culture; modern urban civilization versus rural tradition; and society versus a lone hero. In light of these pronounced dichotomies, it is no surprise that studio publicity and critical discourse defined the film as a Western, not a musical.[73]

In Old Arizona was a feature-length adaptation of a short story titled "The Caballero's Way," by O. Henry, the pen name of William Sidney Porter. Published in the author's 1907 anthology titled *Heart of the West*, "The Caballero's Way" introduced readers to the character of the Cisco Kid, a ruthless murderer who killed Mexicans "just to see them kick."[74] For a 1917 silent film adaptation titled *Betrayed*, director and actor Raoul Walsh transformed the Kid into a heroic Mexican bandit, a character he sought to revive for his sound remake in 1929, which was co-directed with Irving Cummings and starred

Warner Baxter.[75] As the Kid, Baxter plays a cunning yet sympathetic thief, a Robin Hood of the desert who holds up stagecoaches to acquire trinkets for his beloved yet unfaithful lover Tonia Maria (Dorothy Burgess). The Kid's professional and romantic rival is Dunn, a white officer from the East Coast who receives orders to capture the Kid and kill him if necessary. Dunn sees in Tonia a way to trap the Kid, and so he seduces her. Tonia's ensuing infidelity leads to her death, as well as the Kid's escape.

The principal narrative conflict in *In Old Arizona* derives from a series of binary oppositions established between Dunn and the Kid: Dunn is an urban, white philanderer, while the Kid is a rural Latino and sentimental monogamist. The film's preoccupation with racial, ethnic, and cultural difference is suggested by dialogue in the opening scene, in which a white man preparing to board a stagecoach bids farewell to a white local. "I enjoyed your country very much," he says, "and I'd come back here to stay among people of such good breeding as you are." As he shakes the local's hand, he is bumped by two passersby who are outfitted in foreign garb and who mumble incoherently before continuing on. The man protests: "Listen. Some of these foreigners have to be put in their place, you know that? And I'm the bucko that can do it." The voiced anxiety over foreign culture anticipates Dunn's attitude toward the Mexican Cisco Kid, and, more broadly speaking, hints at the film's emphasis on ethnic and cultural distinctions.

The rest of the film relies on popular songs to suggest the opposition between the Kid and Dunn. Dunn is associated with a collection of preexisting tunes that were written, published, and popularized on New York's Bowery during the 1890s, the embryonic years of Tin Pan Alley. The enormous success of these hits, which included "It'll Be a Hot Time in the Old Town Tonight" and "Daisy Bell," meant that movie audiences of 1929 would have recognized the songs' appearances in *In Old Arizona* as references to the twilight of the previous century. So, while the songs establish the film's historical setting—as *New York Times* reviewer Mordaunt Hall observed, "The songs remind one that the yarn takes place in the days of President McKinley"—their association with Dunn characterizes him as a product of urban, Anglo culture of the late 19th century.[76] The songs that Dunn hums, whistles, and sings can be conceived as contemporaneous with the film's historical setting in the 1890s. In contrast to Dunn's association with the Tin Pan Alley tunes, the Kid is linked to two faux-Mexican popular ballads. Both "Song of the Cisco Kid," supposedly penned by Warner Baxter himself, and the film's hyped theme song "My Tonia" display elements of Latin American music, such as the habañera rhythm, that baldly signify Mexican ethnicity.[77] In this way, the film associates a distinctive style of music with each lead character.

Two scenes early on in the film establish a rigorous opposition between the Kid and Dunn. The Kid first appears when he robs a stagecoach and steals a cashbox and

FIGURE 5.2 Melodic excerpt from "Song of the Cisco Kid" (Warner Baxter).

brooch for Tonia. As he rides off into the desert, we hear him sing the opening line of "The Song of the Cisco Kid": "I'll send my gal to the city / And I'll send my gal to the town" (figure 5.2). Melodically, the short motif betrays prototypical features of a Mexican ballad, particularly in its minor tonality (sung in the key of D-minor), its relatively limited melodic range, and Baxter's portamento style of singing, through which he tends to slide from one note to the next.[78]

In addition, the lyrics frame both "the city" and "the town" as destinations, suggesting that the singer remains at some distance from the referenced urban milieu. Even this brief motif begins to characterize the Kid as an inhabitant of a rural environment. It is worth noting too that the phrase ends on the supertonic (or second) note of the D-minor scale, which precludes a sense of resolution that characterized the performances of theme songs in other motion pictures from early 1929.

The association between the Kid and the faux-Mexican ballad contrasts with the scene that follows. After fading to black from the image of the lone caballero singing in the wilderness, we open on four of Sgt. Dunn's officers, all white, sitting on a fence and singing the carefree refrain of "Daisy Bell," a popular waltz that was better known as "Bicycle Built for Two" and became a national success after it was introduced in music halls on New York's Bowery circa 1892. The lyrics of "Daisy Bell" refer to a modern mode of transportation, "a bicycle built for two," which conjures an image nearly antithetical to that of the Kid's horse cantering on the desert sands. Additionally, the collective performance of "Daisy Bell" stands out against the image of the Kid singing solo. This visual presentation signifies Dunn's social standing as distinct from the Kid's loner tendencies. Above all, however, the song's indelible association with Bowery ethos affiliates Dunn and his officers with the white urban working-class culture of the East Coast in the 1890s.

Subsequent juxtapositions of the Kid and Dunn pit the "Song of the Kid" against the Tin Pan Alley tunes in order to establish another opposition: The Kid yearns for monogamy, while Dunn is a womanizer. In one scene, Dunn enters a barbershop and, having never seen an image of the Kid, fails to recognize the lavishly dressed Mexican man who ushers him to a chair. The Kid then draws a bath in the backroom while the barber gives Dunn a shave. Several times during his conversation with the barber, Dunn interjects the memorable title phrase of "Ta-ra-ra Boom-de-ay!," another tune that was made notorious by performances—especially boisterous ones by Lottie Collins in New York music halls during the early 1890s. Although one of its songwriter, Henry J. Sayers, claimed to have heard the original rendition of the song at Babe Connors's famous St. Louis brothel and sanitized the lyrics for white bourgeois audiences, the lyrics convey a young woman's sexual freedom through phrases like "I'm one eternal big expense, but men say that I'm just immense!" and "Though free as air, I'm never rude; I'm not too bad, and not too good!"[79] In *In Old Arizona*, Dunn sings only the catchy, rhythmic refrain, but the song's enduring success—it inspired many versions—guaranteed that film audiences of 1929 would have appreciated its signification of both Anglo culture and sexual candor. Placed in direct opposition to Dunn's chanting of the "Ta-ra-ra Boom-de-ay!" refrain is the sound (and then sight) of the Kid belting out from the backroom more lyrics to "Song of the Cisco Kid," which now describe his "gal" as young, pretty, and "ready to settle down." The contrast between the Kid's and Dunn's songs, and the singers' respective romantic preferences, is reinforced by the scene's closing dialogue. As they exit the barbershop, Dunn asks the Kid whether he plans to meet some señoritas. The Kid answers, "No. Oh, I like señoritas, but I love only one." Dunn retorts, "Same with me: one at a time."

Later, as Dunn struts into a town saloon, an offscreen male chorus sings "(There'll Be) A Hot Time in the Old Town Tonight." This is followed by the pianist's show-case performance of "She May Have Seen Better Days" (1894), James Thornton's ballad about a fallen woman. A close-up of the pianist cuts to a shot of Dunn advancing toward an apparently inebriated woman in the saloon. The song's lyrics comment on the woman's present state of affairs: "She may have seen better days, when she was in her prime; / She may have seen better days, once upon a time; / Tho' by the wayside she fell, she may yet mend her ways. / Some poor mother is waiting for her who has seen better days." Undisturbed, Dunn proceeds to flirt with the sobbing woman. The film cuts from the clamor of the saloon to a long shot of the Kid and Tonia, who sit together near a window in her home, the setting in the publicity still shown in figure 5.3.

As Tonia gazes upward to the Kid, he strums a ukulele and croons the entirety of "Song of the Cisco Kid." Two long takes, both shot with a static camera, shuttle our attention to the song's lyrics, which consist of the phrases previously sung, as well as two additional lines: "Her flirtin' days are over; / And she's going to settle down." In their expression of the Kid's desire to start a life with a woman whose "flirtin' days are over" and who is "going to settle down," the song's lyrics offer a soulful contrast to Dunn's flirtatious conduct in the saloon. At the same time, the presentation is the film's singular instance of a nonintegrated performance of an entire song. There is no clear motivation for the Kid's performance, which appears rather abruptly, but

FIGURE 5.3 Dorothy Burgess and Warner Baxter as Tonia and the Cicso Kid in *In Old Arizona* (Fox, 1929) (Kobal Collection at Art Resource, NY).

neither does the film attempt to set up the song by way of extenuating narrative circumstances. It is an example of a star-song attraction (see chapter 3) that does not bear the burden of a carefully orchestrated plot.

Whereas "Song of the Cisco Kid" works primarily to establish a binary opposition between the Kid and Dunn, the number advertised as the film's theme song, "My Tonia," fulfills both thematic and structural functions. For one, it serves as a metaphor for infidelity and its associated dangers. Tonia negotiates the attractions of Dunn and the Kid, manipulating both men for her gain, but her violation of cultural (Latina) boundaries and entry into the East Coast milieu as represented by Dunn precipitate her demise. But the song also functions as a device of narration, initially withholding and then revealing information about Tonia's infidelity to the Kid—an especially notable function because, otherwise, the Kid possesses broader story knowledge than any of the film's characters. For instance, in the barbershop, the Kid deceives Dunn by posing as an innocent caballero; on a cattle-wrangling job, he outsmarts three men who try to kill him. The only activity of which the Kid seems unaware is Tonia's betrayal. This discrepancy of knowledge—between Tonia and the Kid, and between the audience and the Kid—propels the narrative toward its resolution, which itself is achieved only through the revelation of Tonia's betrayal.

In Old Arizona portends the importance of "My Tonia" by presenting it repeatedly during the opening orchestral overture and opening titles. (In imitation of the overtures that accompanied silent film presentations in motion picture palaces, many early sound films prefaced opening titles with black leader and a synchronized orchestral overture.) The black screen shuttles our attention to the soundtrack, which comprises a male ensemble twice singing the 16-measure refrain of "My Tonia," the melody of which is in D-major against a habañera rhythm. The overture concludes on a closed cadence only to recommence, modulated up two whole tones, as the film's three opening title cards appear, with one announcing "Words and music of 'My Tonia' by DESYLVA, BROWN & HENDERSON."

The overture and opening titles are the only occasions given for a vocal rendition of the theme song; during the plot, "My Tonia" is rendered as an instrumental piece played on a phonograph record. Its first iteration connotes Tonia's infidelity and occurs early on in the film, in a scene set at Tonia's home. The scene opens on a close-up of a spinning disc on a phonograph, and we hear the characteristic habañera rhythm and melody of "My Tonia." The film cuts to an exterior shot depicting Tonia's maid noticing the arrival of the Kid on his horse. The maid runs inside to retrieve Tonia, and soon we see Tonia pushing a man out the door moments before the Kid appears. Ignorant of Tonia's deceit, the Kid enters her home and, upon hearing the song, begins to make such sentimental statements as "the touch of your hand is like the touch of an angel." Tonia hurries to the kitchen to finish cooking ham and eggs, and a cut reveals the Kid walking over to the record player and placing the needle down, playing again the instrumental sounds of "My Tonia." He calls to Tonia, and a cut reveals her leaning against a doorframe in a seductive pose, smoking a cigarette. The two ensuing shots suggest that Tonia and the Kid are too preoccupied to eat breakfast: A close-up of burnt ham and eggs is followed by a close-up of the record player spinning "My Tonia." By the time the scene fades to black, the theme song has been used twice as musical accompaniment for Tonia's seduction of men.

Tonia's undoing is set in motion when she traverses the conceptual division that the film has established between the Kid and Dunn. Her first encounter with Dunn occurs when, seeking to deliver a message to him from the Kid, she saunters into the town saloon, her sultry movements accompanied by the sounds of a faint piano rag in the background. Dunn's attention is drawn immediately to her, and they initiate teasing banter. In the subsequent scene, the Kid is away on a job, and Dunn visits Tonia at her home. They drink wine, and Dunn reminisces over the East Coast, New York, and the Bowery, claiming that he can hardly wait to get "back to civilization." He also sings to himself, "There'll be a hot time in the old town tonight," a phrase intimating his plans with Tonia, who seems excited by the prospect of encountering an urban setting beyond her rural abode. Dunn agrees to host her at his camp that evening.

As if Dunn's peers were privy to his conversation with Tonia, the next scene opens on a group of them singing the refrain of "The Bowery," another turn-of-the-century tune (introduced in the 1892 Broadway musical *A Trip to Chinatown*) that signifies the rowdy culture of the renowned strip of Manhattan. The song's lyrics tell of a newcomer to New York who stumbles upon the Bowery neighborhood and experiences a series of adventures and revelations ("I had one of the devil's own nights! / I'll never go there anymore" and "The Bow'ry, the Bow'ry / They say such things and they do strange things"). The gist of the song was likely known to audiences of 1929 and can be interpreted as a reflection of Tonia's desire to venture beyond the setting of her rural home, where she is expected to remain faithful to one man. In addition, the song functions to underline the cultural divide between Tonia and Dunn: She tries to join in the singing but cannot pronounce the word "Bowery," pronouncing it instead "brewery" and "bawry" to the amusement of the officers. The playful irony of the song's lyrics also elude Tonia, and she questions why Dunn speaks with passion for the Bowery when the words proclaim, "I'll never go there anymore." Tonia's awkward attempt to assimilate Anglo culture, as represented by Dunn and the popular songs of the 1890s, underlines her immutable association with Mexican culture, as represented by the Kid and his ballads.

The final use of Tonia's namesake theme song reveals her infidelity to the Kid and leads to her death. Toward the end of the film, the Kid arrives at Tonia's home, discovers a horse tied outside, and hears the familiar, scratchy tune of "My Tonia" emanating from her record player. At last, he interprets the song as an indication of Tonia's sexual flings, a notion confirmed when he sees Dunn exiting Tonia's home and buckling his belt. From a concealed spot, the Kid overhears Tonia telling Dunn that she never loved the Kid, and the duo then plot to capture and kill the bandit. Armed with this information, the Kid turns the tables, and the plot moves quickly to a resolution that sees Dunn unintentionally kill Tonia. In this way, "My Tonia" serves as a metaphor for the dangers of transgressing faithfulness to the Kid, as well as one's own ethnic borders—which for Tonia have been summed up in a single musical number and repeated.

The final shot of the film warrants a brief mention. A medium shot shows the Kid staring offscreen in the direction of Tonia's body as he utters the last line of "Song of the Cisco Kid": "Her flirtin' days are over and she's ready to settle down." The passage serves as a bookend to the lyrics sung by the Kid at the film's outset: "I'll send my gal to the city, and I'll send my gal to the town." Now placed at the end of the film, "Song of the Cisco Kid" conveys a sense of irony, for by sending his "gal to the city," the Kid sent Tonia into the arms of Dunn, setting into motion a series of events that ensured that her "flirtin' days are over" and "she's ready to settle down"—six feet under.

In Old Arizona integrates song numbers in coherent and convincing ways across its plot. "Song of the Cisco Kid" and numerous incidental numbers drawn from early publications of Tin Pan Alley are presented as casual performances by the Kid, Dunn, and Dunn's officers. Rather than afford the actors opportunities for star-song attractions, as in *Weary River* (see chapter 3), the songs in *In Old Arizona* almost always function to enhance characterization. Moreover, the film's theme song "My Tonia" is not performed by a singing star, but rather played as an instrumental number on a scratchy phonograph record. Although the theme song comes to serve as a device of narration, insofar as it reveals salient information to the Kid, its presence on the soundtrack is, unlike the songs in *Check and Double Check* (see chapter 4), rendered plausible by its narrative context.

THE INTERMITTENT BLUES OF *SAFE IN HELL* (1931)

With the exception of the overture and opening titles, the music in *In Old Arizona* consists solely of vocal cues. *Safe in Hell*, a First National production directed by William Wellman (*Public Enemy*) and released by Warner Bros. in December 1931, incorporates both vocal and instrumental renditions of popular songs. Based on a play by Houston Branch and originally titled *The Lady from New Orleans*, the film centers on Gilda Karlson (Dorothy Mackaill), a white New Orleans prostitute who mistakenly believes that she has killed a man. With the help of her boyfriend Carl (Donald Cook), she escapes to a Caribbean island. She and Carl marry in an ad hoc ceremony just before Carl, a seafarer, departs for an assigned voyage, promising to return. Gilda is left to repel the unwelcome advances of the numerous criminals who inhabit the island. The most offensive among them is Bruno (Morgan Wallace), the island's executioner, who eventually frames Gilda for possession of a handgun and then tries to blackmail her into having sex with him. Wishing to fulfill her marriage vows, however, Gilda chooses to accept her punishment: death at the hands of Bruno.

The film's musical cues fall into one of three categories:

1. Instrumental and non-diegetic ("Pagan Moon" and unidentified orchestral cues)
2. Instrumental and ambiguously diegetic ("St. Louis Blues" and "The Darktown Strutters' Ball")
3. Vocal and diegetic ("When It's Sleepy Time Down South")

The only vocalized number in the film, "When It's Sleepy Time Down South," is sung by a supporting character and, as we will see, integrated by way of a presentation that minimizes the threat of a disruptive star-song attraction as discussed in chapter 3. In addition, "When It's Sleepy Time Down South" is, like "St. Louis Blues" and "The Darktown Strutters' Ball," a song whose provenance and accrued meanings through the 1910s and 1920s identified it strongly with African American culture. Contrasted with these jazz numbers is the film's theme song "Pagan Moon" (written by Warner Bros. employees Joe Burke, Alfred Bryan, and Al Dubin), which is heard not as a vocal performance but rather as an instrumental number, even in the opening and end titles. Such an unusual (for the time) presentation of a theme song distinguishes *Safe in Hell* not only from early sound films that highlighted theme songs through vocal presentations, as discussed in previous chapters, but also from Hollywood's earliest scored films, such as *Our Dancing Daughters* and *White Shadows in the South Seas* (both 1928), which often incorporated non-synchronous vocal performances in order to accentuate chosen narrative events. Sheet music and recordings of "Pagan Moon" included the song's lyrics penned by Al Bryan and Al Dubin; hence, the vocal-less deployment of the song in *Safe in Hell* may well be indicative of an attempt to diminish attention to the song and yet to capitalize on the possibilities of its thematic and narrative import.

The opening scene of *Safe in Hell* explicates its setting and characterization by drawing on what Peter Stanfield describes as the accumulative symbolic power of W. C. Handy's "St. Louis Blues" (1914).[80] As Stanfield has argued, the numerous uses and recordings of "St. Louis Blues" through the late 1910s and 1920s had by the early 1930s endowed the song with multiple significations, including "blackening" of white identity, urban primitivism, and, in accordance with Handy's own account of the song's provenance, "an excursion into the lower depths" of female sexuality. Following Handy's copyright of the song, "St. Louis Blues" became a staple act of blackface routines and was recorded in a variety of musical styles by Handy himself, Marion Harris, the Original Dixieland Jazz Band, and, in 1930 alone, Louis Armstrong, Rudy Vallee & His Connecticut Yankees, Cab Calloway, the Mills Brothers, and the Boswell Sisters. But arguably the two most distinctive and famous presentations of the song were performed by Bessie Smith, first for a 1925 phonograph recording for Columbia, backed by Louis Armstrong and Fred Longshaw, and second for a 1929 RKO short film. The song was also performed in *Hallelujah*, where it was sung by Nina Mae McKinney (who was featured in *Safe in Hell*). Quickly assimilated to white performance contexts, the song appeared on Broadway in *George White's Scandals of 1926* and *Is Everybody Happy?* (Warner Bros.' 1929 musical biopic of white bandleader Ted Lewis). Through these multiple iterations that capitalized on black culture and the lyrics' references to duplicitous sexual behavior,

Stanfield writes, the song was identified at once with a "black urban underclass" and "transgressive" female sexuality.

By the time of the release of *Safe in Hell* in late 1931, therefore, "St. Louis Blues" could be counted on to serve as a shorthand reference both to the verisimilitude of low-class New Orleans and to Gilda's transgressive female sexuality as enacted through her vocation. In the opening scene, these meanings are conveyed through an instrumental rendition of the song that accompanies an interior shot of Gilda's apartment. Its status neither fully diegetic nor non-diegetic, the tune functions at once to establish the setting of New Orleans and to hint at Gilda's vocation without drawing attention to itself as a song.

A similar effect is generated when "St. Louis Blues" cuts to a lively version of the jazz standard "The Darktown Strutters' Ball." This syncopated, ragtime-like number, written in 1915 by black songwriter Shelton Brooks, was popularized by a 1917 recording by the Original Dixieland Jazz Band. Its foxtrot rhythm made it appealing as a dance number, and its lyrics about an accepted segment of urban night-life—"darktown"—surely resonated with a great many Americans in general and songwriters in particular; at least seven songs written in the 1910s alone referred to "darktown" in their titles.[81] In this scene from *Safe in Hell*, Brook's piece plays in the background as Gilda enters the apartment of a yet-unknown client. She heads to a piano and plunks out a few notes of "The Darktown Strutters' Ball," alerting us to the song's ambiguously diegetic status; what was audible as offscreen music can be construed retroactively as a tune that Gilda has heard either from the street outside the apartment or from inside her head. A man suddenly enters, and Gilda abruptly stops playing when she realizes that he is Piet Van Saal (Ralfe Harolde), the lecher who had led Gilda into prostitution. Piet makes advances toward Gilda, but she resists him, finally knocking him out with a bottle and fleeing from the building as a burning cigarette she inadvertently dropped sets fire to the curtains in the apartment. Flames burst through the open windows of the building as Gilda escapes on the street below. The situation for which Gilda believes she is culpable is underscored by "The Darktown Strutters' Ball," a song that affiliates its jazzy (and hence "black") sounds with the character of the "fallen woman" to which Gilda has consigned herself.

Some time after Gilda flees New Orleans for the ostensible safety of a remote island in the Caribbean, a blues number is used to suggest that she cannot escape her past. While awaiting Carl's return from his mission at sea, Gilda lives in a hotel owned and managed by Leonie (Nina Mae McKinney), a black woman who, like Gilda, hails from New Orleans and becomes to some extent a mentor to her.[82] One night, Gilda's attempts to sleep are thwarted by the noise of a raucous party that is taking place below her room. There, Leonie is singing to the hotel's all-male patrons

a bluesy ballad, "When It's Sleepy Time Down South," the lyrics of which celebrate
a mythical South comprised of "steamboats on the river," "pale moonshine shining
on the fields," "soft winds blowing through pinewood trees," and "mammies falling
upon their knees."[83] Yet, in terms of the scene's visual style, Leonie's performance
is not foregrounded in the way that it might have been had it appeared in *Weary
River* or *Possessed* (discussed in previous chapters). Instead of the frontal framing
and static takes that characterized song presentations in those two films, the camera
here follows McKinney as she circles the table of male diners and pours wine into
their glasses. The impression is that Leonie just happens to be singing; perhaps she is
inspired by the revelry of the moment or by the attention from the men at the table.

This is not to suggest that the selection of "When It's Sleepy Time Down South"
was arbitrary. Its lyrics allude to Leonie's Southern American provenance and imply
that, like Leonie, Gilda belongs to the South. Her attempted incarnation as a virtuous woman on the Caribbean island is irreconcilable with her history as a New
Orleans call girl, particularly in the face of criminals who have already pointed her
out, lasciviously, as "the only white woman on the island." In this way, the performance of "When It's Sleepy Time Down South" capitalizes on the well-rehearsed
nexus between blues music, African American culture, and the "excursion into the
lower depths" of female sexuality.

In addition, the song precipitates Gilda's self-transformation and cements her status, at least among the island's inhabitants, as a fallen woman. Upon hearing Leonie's
performance downstairs, and presumably unnerved by Carl's prolonged absence,
Gilda casts aside her chaste persona and chooses to join the party (figure 5.4), spending the rest of the night drinking with and entertaining the men with jokes. After
the party has ended, Bruno, the deceitful island executioner, tries to force Gilda into
joining him at his house. She spurns him and discloses that she too is a criminal,
having killed a man in New Orleans. In so doing, Gilda reveals the secret that she
has concealed from the very men who have sought to dishonor her. After this disclosure, the men have little reason to pay heed to Gilda's proclamations of moral virtue.
Further, when Piet shows up on the island, apparently having survived the fire at
his apartment building and thus exonerating Gilda from a potential murder conviction, she is executed nevertheless. Her downfall was preordained by the fact that she
remains permanently bound to her past in New Orleans—as implied by her reaction
to "When It's Sleepy Time Down South."

While blues and "bluesy" numbers highlight Gilda's connection to the allure and
danger of New Orleans, "Pagan Moon," a decidedly non-bluesy waltz number—
that is, a decidedly "white" number—is associated with Gilda's hope for a future
with Carl. The melody of the song first appears during the film's opening titles,
after which it continues on the soundtrack as musical underscoring for shots of the

FIGURE 5.4 Gilda (Dorothy Mackaill) entertains in *Safe in Hell* (Warner Bros., 1931).

New Orleans harbor, effectively smoothing over the transition between the extra-diegetic credits and the narrative world. In that world, "Pagan Moon" functions primarily as an expression of Gilda's yearning for Carl's return.[84] In one scene, Gilda grows weary of playing the card game solitaire and, after throwing the cards across the room, she exits to the balcony to watch the sunset over the ocean. The theme music plays as Gilda gazes out at the sea, and it continues as she descends to the main floor of the hotel to collect her mail, hoping to find a letter from Carl. (We discover that Bruno has already inspected the day's mail and has hidden a letter from Carl to Gilda.) Later, "Pagan Moon" appears on the soundtrack when Leonie suggests to Gilda that Carl was disingenuous in his promise to return. "I've been fooled by sailor boys myself," she warns Gilda. After Leonie retreats, the theme song swells on the soundtrack. Gilda rises out of bed and, again, looks out at the ocean. These appearances of "Pagan Moon" invite us to share in Gilda's doubt of Carl's return.

The last iteration of "Pagan Moon" occurs toward the end of the film. Carl returns to the island during the penultimate scene, and he instructs Gilda to take the first boat off the island and meet him in New Orleans. Wanting Carl to remain unaware of her conviction for possessing a handgun, Gilda insists through her tears, "I'll never be bad again. Never again, Carl." They kiss and as Carl hurries offscreen, the strains of "Pagan Moon" emerge again. By this point, the instrumental version of the theme song has accrued sufficient meaning to amplify the poignancy of Gilda's decision to sacrifice her life so that Carl can continue to believe in her reformation.

In three ways, *Safe in Hell* serves as a model for the credible integration of songs: first, by avoiding the use of a vocalized theme song; second, by relegating the sole instance of a vocalized song to the status of an incidental number performed by a supporting character; and third, by employing songs as a means of narration rather than discrete spectacle. The consignment of an instrumental version of "Pagan Moon" to the non-diegetic soundtrack helps to fulfill conventional functions of the theme song (e.g., to evoke in Gilda thoughts and memories of Carl), but also prevents the narrative from calling attention to the song as a performance or dramatic device in its own right. "When It's Sleepytime Down South" is used in order to motivate Gilda's transformation, but it is sung casually by an ancillary character. In these ways, *Safe in Hell* uses popular songs in narratively integrated ways.

It is telling, finally, that scant mention is made of songs in the Warner Bros.' pressbook for the film, not even on the book's standard page of recommended techniques for exploitation.[85] Elsewhere in the book, a short piece discloses that Nina Mae McKinney sings "When It's Sleepy Time Down South," but overall the pressbook is a stark contrast to those examined in chapter 3, its focus remaining on star Dorothy Mackaill and supporting cast member Clarence Muse, the latter earning mention by virtue of the fact that he played Porgy in a 1927 stage production of DuBose Heyward's novel.[86] While Mackaill's alleged interest in music is noted in an article titled "Dorothy Mackaill is 'Blues Enthusiast,'" the ensuing text emphasizes that even though she is an "admirer" of the blues and "an expert at singin' 'em," she does not sing them in *Safe in Hell*. The piece continues, "There are, however, in the grim sequences of 'Safe in Hell,' moments made melodious by the crooning of negro blues singers." Ryan Jay Friedman credits such allusions to a white-controlled film industry that sought to capitalize on the status of African American music as a "fashionable [object] of consumer desire."[87] Although this may be true, it should be noted as well that the pressbook for *Safe in Hell* actually contains comparatively few references to music—the result of the film industry's discourse against motion picture songs.

THE INTERMITTENT CUES OF *ARROWSMITH* (1931)

Arrowsmith, a drama adapted from the Sinclair Lewis novel of 1925 and directed by John Ford, extends the practices of scoring made manifest by the soundtrack of *Safe in Hell*, but also curtails the overall use of music. Produced by Samuel Goldwyn Productions and released by United Artists in December 1931 (the same month of the *Safe in Hell* release), the film contains only a handful of musical cues, suggesting an affinity with the classical Hollywood scores that would emerge a couple of years later. The film traces the story of an ambitious medical doctor (Ronald Colman) who prioritizes his research on the bubonic plague over the welfare of his wife (Helen Hayes). The film's orchestral cues, scored by Alfred Newman, function in two capacities: to bridge the transition between extra-diegetic titles and the narrative, and to punctuate two climactic scenes. In the film's opening shots, a main musical theme functions primarily to smooth over the transition from the titles to the narrative. The music played during the opening titles accentuates the appearance of the first intertitle with a series of staccato notes. The main theme, the melody of which is reminiscent of "Rhapsody in Blue," then plays in a legato style and resolves as the intertitle fades out. A brief fanfare of horns appears during the subsequent shot, a striking composition depicting a series of horse-drawn wagons crawling across the horizon of a prairie vista. The fanfare segues into legato phrasing and quickly fades off the soundtrack. The musical theme returns only during the last two shots of the film, where it again bridges the structural gap between the fictional world of the film and the extra-diegetic title.

While the theme smoothes over the transitions between titles and narrative, it remains absent from all other temporal and spatial transitions across the narrative. Only two additional orchestral cues appear, both serving to amplify the emotional intensity of scenes depicting the spread of the bubonic plague. The first of the two scenes shows a rat crawling along the edge of a Swedish ship and through a porthole. A tremolo in the strings plays on the non-diegetic soundtrack. A cut to the ship's interior bring us to the ship's doctor, who concludes that several crewmen have died because of the bubonic plague. The proclamation is punctuated suddenly by a sforzando chord (or stinger). A similar orchestral cue plays during the second scene, in which Dr. Arrowsmith and his colleagues evacuate a village on a Caribbean island whose inhabitants have suffered an outbreak of the bubonic plague. As the doctors and the village inhabitants sequester the house and property of a plantation owner so that they might convert it into a makeshift hospital, a tremolo in the strings, followed by several sforzando attacks, are heard to accompany shots of the villagers burning their disease-ridden homes. In this way, the orchestral cues accentuate two of the film's climactic scenes.

The soundtrack of *Arrowsmith* is not entirely devoid of songs. When Dr. Arrowsmith and a renowned scientist drink beer in a local tavern and reminisce about a mutual colleague, a leisurely waltz begins to play on the soundtrack. Its source is not revealed, but the music is presumed to be diegetic because the melody of the tune eventually sung by the two men is consonant with the background music. The two belt out, "She had a dark and a-rovin' eye, / And her hair hung down in ring-a-lets, / She was a nice girl," before another man stumbles over to their table and interrupts their haphazard performance.[88] Like other incidental songs of the transitional era, the song sung by the two men functions to establish a bond between them—but the song is rendered as a spontaneous, casual, and brief performance, neither a discrete nor contrived presentation. Insofar as it limits its song use to diegetic, plausibly motivated performances, and employs orchestral music for the sake of accentuating emotionally charged narrative events, the musical soundtrack for *Arrowsmith* anticipated the model that defined classical Hollywood scoring for at least the next two decades.

CONCLUSION

By 1931, the song vogue was over. Leaders of the music and motion picture industries recognized that films were no longer the primary medium for the exploitation of popular songs. Audiences had grown weary of musicals and by extension popular songs in all genres, and the studio executives responded by reducing their output of songs and musicals, reconfiguring their music departments, and divesting some of their holdings in music publishing. They had figured out that the most economic medium for song advertising was radio, because it furnished royalties and enabled companies to test songs on 60 million listeners before investing thousands of dollars on national exploitation campaigns.[89] Meanwhile, practices of scoring entailed the diminished use of entire popular songs and the increasing reliance on intermittent, orchestral cues.

But perhaps the most lasting effect of the industry's response to the song glut was the clarification of the distinction between the musical and non-musical production. By early 1933, when the Warner Bros. release of *42nd Street* initiated a second wave of musical production by Hollywood studios, audiences and critics seemed willing to accept the intrusion of songs in narrative flow given a relatively stable definition of the musical, one that Marty Rubin has since described as a genre that presents musical numbers "that are impossible—i.e., persistently contradictory in relation to the realistic discourse of the narrative."[90] Rubin further points out, "This definition is useful for distinguishing bona fide generic musicals from movies that are merely films with musical performances in them."[91] By 1933, it seems, the diegetic rupture caused by a song became a defining convention of the musical genre. Such a rupture could manifest in both narrative flow (e.g., through a character who possesses no prescribed musical talents suddenly bursting into song) and visual style (e.g., by way of the camera framing a frontal presentation characteristic of Broadway performances). In contrast, in non-musical genres, songs such as those described in this chapter were integrated convincingly, arising as they did from the "realistic discourse of the narrative." If, as Donald Crafton has written of the 1929–1930 season, "it was the rare movie that was *not* a musical in some sense of the term," then by the end of the transition to sound, the definition of non-musical genres was much clearer.[92] And so it was with no small dose of optimism that Lew Michelson, columnist for *Hollywood Filmograph*, proclaimed the return of the theme song outside of the context of the musical:

> The theme song will again find a place of prominence in pictures but in a different form. No more will it be possible to have five or six theme songs in one production.... No more will it be possible for someone to sing a song in a picture for no reason at all, but our theory is the theme song is coming back in a more intelligent form. Yes, the theme song is coming back.[93]

The writer was more prescient than perhaps even he could have known.

Conclusion

THE FATE OF THE MOTION PICTURE SONG

SAYING IT WITH SONGS has examined the institutional and aesthetic roles of the popular song in American cinema during the film industry's transition to sound. In early sound films, songs were promoted as modular attractions and as marketable commodities that enjoyed commercial lives outside of theaters. In order to secure copyright control over these valuable assets, Hollywood's major production companies invested in the businesses of song creation and distribution. In so doing, they inherited the institutional culture of popular music that had been cultivated by the American music industry since the rise of Tin Pan Alley and extended into practices of musical accompaniment for silent cinema. This culture included an emphasis on live performances by stars; the deployment of cross-promotion across printed, recorded, and broadcast media; and the "thematic approach" to musical accompaniment, which both introduced and cemented the popularity of motion picture theme songs on the cusp of Hollywood's transition to sound. The prosperity of the music industry through the 1920s, as well as established practices of film music accompaniment, meant that when the major studios converted to sound and entered into the business of song publishing, they acquired not only financial control over copyrights but also commercial and aesthetic practices that had already proven successful in other media. Extending these practices to the promotion and formal design of early sound films, studio publicity campaigns marketed motion picture songs by means of radio broadcasts, phonograph recordings, and sheet music covers, and filmmakers adopted from the Broadway stage the accepted strategies for nesting songs within narrative structures.

However, the interpolation of song performances as discrete moments of spectacle came to be seen as a threat to the norms of classical narration in non-musical films. The theme song in particular was considered a disruptive device because, by virtue of its repetition during a given film and its existence as an isolatable entity in other media, it solicited attention as a non-narrative element. Motion picture theme songs jeopardized the efficacy of a classical system of narration that sought to maintain norms of stylistic subordination in the service of economic storytelling.

Throughout the transition to sound, therefore, producers and filmmakers experimented with strategies for integrating songs in non-musical films. Some films motivated the appearance of discrete and repetitive song performances by casting characters as musicians and vocalists. The plots of 1929 films *Weary River* and *Applause*, for example, are propelled by virtue of the musical talents ascribed to each film's protagonist even while devices of editing and mise-en-scène highlight the characters' performances as moments of star-song spectacle. Other attempts at song integration employed elements of visual style in order to anchor song performances more firmly within a film's diegetic space and time, but some of these attempts nevertheless strained the threshold of narrative plausibility. In this way, the narrative structures of *Check and Double Check* (1930) and *Possessed* (1931) can be said to suffer from the law of diminishing returns—that is, the more elaborate the narrative circumstances leading to a song presentation, the more cumbersome and even ostentatious the narrative. The most successful attempts at song integration occurred in films that presented excerpts of songs, rather than entire renditions, and that did so by way of haphazard performances, rather than by overtly deliberate presentations. The army sergeant in *In Old Arizona* sings fragments of turn-of-the-century Tin Pan Alley tunes as he conducts his daily business, while his foil, the Cisco Kid, croons portions of a faux-Mexican ballad as he rides in the desert or bathes in town. *Safe in Hell* also attenuates emphasis on popular songs by foregoing a vocalized version of a theme song in favor of a non-diegetic instrumental piece. The film's sole vocal performance, moreover, is an incidental number that is presented by an ancillary character and sung in a relatively casual manner. Both *Safe in Hell* and *In Old Arizona* privilege the demands of classical narration over the presentation of isolated moments of spectacle.

These latter examples are also significant because, as a result of the organization of their musical soundtracks around one or two theme songs, they serve as progenitors to the "theme score," or "monothematic score," that endured through subsequent decades of the classical Hollywood cinema.[1] Characteristic of such films as *Laura* (1944), *High Noon* (1952), *Love Is a Many-Splendored Thing* (1955), and *Around the World in Eighty Days* (1956), the monothematic score, Jeff Smith writes, "organized its melodic and motivic material around a single popular tune rather than a group of leitmotivs,"[2] so that a single theme song was transformed into instrumental motifs that could be integrated as non-intrusive devices of narration. Although the proportion of Hollywood productions with theme songs diminished following the coming of sound, the ways in which songs were narratively motivated in films and extra-textually marketed outside of films echoed some of the strategies that the studios developed during the transitional years.

The subject of song use in classical Hollywood cinema after the transition to sound has occupied much scholarly literature in the field, thus obviating the need for a detailed account here. A brief example, however, may help to illustrate the nature of the monothematic score in the post-transitional era. As Kathryn Kalinak has shown, Max Steiner's musical score for *The Searchers* (1956) is structured around a single theme drawn from Stan Jones's ballad "The Searchers," which is sung by the Sons of the Pioneers during the film's opening titles and closing shots. The ballad's second and seventh verses highlight one of the central themes of the narrative, that is, the concomitant acts of wandering and searching ("What makes a man to wander / What makes a man to roam / What makes a man leave bed and board / And turn his back on home. / Ride away—Ride away—Ride away" and "A man will search his heart and soul / Go searching way out there / His peace o' mind, he knows he'll find / But where Oh Lord, Lord where).[3] Throughout *The Searchers*, Romantic-style melodic motifs that derive from the theme song are associated with John Wayne's character, literally underscoring his odyssey. Although Steiner's score manifests a degree of musical development that was more complex than those of transitional-era scores, its organization around a motif extracted from a theme song recalls the conventions of song use that were common toward the end of the transitional period.

The monothematic score also inspired practices of song plugging that echoed those of the transitional era, though at least on one occasion these practices involved the publication of a song *after* a film's release. That occasion was the response to *Laura*, a film that makes frequent use of different arrangements of a single orchestral theme. Following the film's release by 20th Century-Fox in October 1944, the studio executives were reportedly "deluged with requests for copies of its musical theme," to which they responded by commissioning lyricist Johnny Mercer to collaborate with the film's composer, David Raksin, on the production of a theme song based on the popular melody written for the film.[4] Published by Robbins Music Corp. and recorded by numerous artists (first by Woody Herman and His Orchestra), "Laura" became a hit song in 1945 and has since been regarded as a jazz standard. While Kalinak writes that the success of "Laura" gave rise to the theme score, one might add that the song's success reinvigorated a model for motion picture song use that circulated during the transition to sound.

This is not to say that the strategies that sustained the cross-marketing campaigns of classical Hollywood cinema following the transition were identical to those that arose between 1927 and 1931. Just as music publishers of the early 20th century adapted to and capitalized on concurrent changes in music recording technology, the plugging of motion picture songs continued to rely upon contemporaneous developments in recording and distribution. Jeff Smith and Alexander Doty have observed that the advent of the LP record, the 45-rpm single, and the transistor radio in the late 1940s and 1950s led to the displacement of sheet music counters and a greater emphasis on recorded music and licensing fees.[5] Writing about *High Noon* (1952) and its legendary theme song "High Noon" (better known as "Do Not Forsake Me, Oh My Darlin'"), Smith notes that United Artists launched one of its heaviest campaigns for song promotion by exploiting sheet music, radio, and recordings as a means of increasing the likelihood of the song being played repeatedly and across multiple media formats, thereby increasing the probability of reaching a target audience.[6] As with other examples in the history of music technology, the rise of the LP and other media for recording and broadcasting did not so much replace existent platforms for song distribution so much as they did broaden them, effectively augmenting the marketing strategies that movie producers had implemented in the late 1920s.

THE ENDURANCE OF THE STAR-SONG ATTRACTION: PUTTING THE BLAME ON *GILDA* (1946)

In the abovementioned examples of non-musical films, the few vocalized theme songs that *do* appear are consigned to credit sequences or to non-diegetic soundtracks. What happened to the star-song performance in films belonging to non-musical genres? A brief example, *Gilda* (1946), illustrates how such films accommodated moments of star-song spectacle in narratively plausible ways. Produced in late 1945 and released by Columbia in April 1946, *Gilda* is set in Argentina and stars Rita Hayworth as the wife of shady casino owner Ballin Mundson (George Macready). At first unbeknown to Ballin, Gilda and his newly hired bodyguard Johnny Farrell (Glenn Ford) were involved in a torrid relationship in the past. The soundtrack for *Gilda* features a score by Hugo Friedhofer and two theme songs, "Amado Mio" and "Put the Blame on Mame," both penned by Doris Fisher and Allan Roberts. While motifs from "Amado Mio" are adapted and incorporated as intermittent, non-diegetic underscoring, diegetic performances of "Put the Blame on Mame" occur three times over the course of the narrative, culminating in Hayworth's legendary striptease but functioning primarily to expose and elaborate on the lasting hostility between Gilda and Johnny.

The earliest iteration of "Put the Blame on Mame" is heard by way of a phonograph record in Gilda's boudoir, where the songs serves to bracket a pivotal plot point: Johnny's recognition of Gilda as Ballin's new wife. The passage begins with a shot of Johnny and Ballin entering a darkened room in the latter's home, while the sound of a woman's voice can be heard scat singing the central melody of "Put the Blame on Mame." Initially framing a static two-shot of Ballin and Johnny, the camera tracks rapidly toward Johnny, capturing a reaction that suggests his instant recognition of the sound's source. The two men approach Gilda's bedroom, and a cut takes us to the film's first shot of Gilda, a medium close-up displaying her bare shoulders as she flips her head and smiles, presumably at her husband who has now entered the room. When she sees Johnny, however, Gilda's smile withers, and she pulls up a piece of her gown to cover one shoulder. Meanwhile, an instrumental version of "Put the Blame on Mame" continues to play in the background. Ballin introduces Gilda to Johnny, after which a cut to a long shot shows Gilda rising to turn off a record player now in view. Ballin is excluded from the subsequent series of shots, his voice relegated to offscreen space as a series of shot/reverse shots depict an exchange of glares between Johnny and Gilda. Their conversation, moreover, is laden with innuendoes of a failed relationship. (Gilda, for example, offers the improbable remark that the name Johnny is "such a hard name to remember, and so easy to forget.") After Johnny and Ballin leave Gilda's bedroom, "Put the Blame on Mame" resumes from the offscreen scratchy phonograph record. Not only is the song identified with Gilda, but it is also associated with the acrimonious relationship between her and Johnny—an impression underlined by the terse dialogue that transpires during the pause in the song's appearance on the soundtrack.

Like Joan Crawford's character Marian in *Possessed*, discussed in chapter 4, the character of Gilda is cast as a woman with singing talent.[7] But, unlike Marian, Gilda's musical aptitudes are motivated by plausible narrative circumstances; she is a showgirl. At the same time, devices of visual and sonic style serve to de-emphasize the presence of "Put the Blame on Mame" and instead present the song in a casual way through the presence of Gilda's record player. The remaining two renditions of the theme song afford far greater attention to it—but they too are motivated by Gilda's apparently natural talents for performance.

"Put the Blame on Mame" appears for a second time when Johnny, sleeping in a room at Ballin's casino, is awoken in the early hours of the morning by the sounds of an acoustic guitar and Gilda's improvised singing of the theme song. Johnny rises and walks to a window overlooking the casino room, and we hear (and subsequently see from Johnny's point-of-view) Gilda's soft singing of the song's opening lyrics: "When Mrs. O'Leary's cow kicked the lantern in Chicago town / They say that started the fire that burned Chicago down / That's the story that went around / But here's the real lowdown." The ensuing six shots exclude Johnny from the frame, instead portraying Gilda as the object of the gaze of the casino's unassuming washroom attendant, Uncle Pio (Steven Geray), as Gilda continues to sing the refrain and a second verse. In the seventh shot of the sequence, Gilda hears footsteps and halts her singing. She and Pio look offscreen, and the film cuts to a medium shot of Johnny entering the room, interrupting Gilda's performance for the second time in the film—and a more intimate one at that.[8] Nonetheless, this second presentation affords greater attention to the theme song both by lengthening its duration and including lyrics.

The third and final performance of "Put the Blame on Mame," which takes place during Gilda's striptease at Ballin's casino, turns the message of the song on its head. By this time, Ballin is presumed to be the dead victim of an airplane crash (which, it turns out, he has staged), and Gilda and Johnny have rekindled their romance and married. However, when Gilda discovers that Johnny has married her out of spite—specifically, to punish her for allegedly being unfaithful to Ballin—she seeks a marriage annulment, which Johnny refuses to grant. In this sense, therefore, the lyrics of "Put the Blame on Mame" resonate with the singer's predicament in the latter half of the film. Like "Mame" in the song, Gilda is a woman trapped and blamed for problems that she did not cause. Although she was never unfaithful to Ballin, Johnny somehow deems her culpable for his boss's death.

Moreover, in addition to suggesting Gilda's narrative predicament, "Put the Blame on Mame" in its final performance serves a crucial role in advancing the film's plot. After invading the casino floor—a space that has become Johnny's domain—Gilda uses the song to humiliate her new husband in front of his peers. While singing two uninterrupted verses, she swings her hips, removes a long black glove, flips her hair, and circles around the entire stage. At one point, a cut to a medium-long shot shows Johnny pushing his way through the crowd and staring at Gilda, with a combined expression of disbelief and revulsion on his face. Although several scholars have cited Hayworth's femme-fatale striptease as a disruption of the flow of narrative for the sake of promoting spectacle, the meaning accrued by the song up to this point makes it more a potent and integrated narrative device than a disruptive one.[9] For one, the scene is an expression of Gilda's authority. (I concur with Adrienne L. McLean's observation that "[p]erhaps it is not what Gilda lacks that makes her fascinating but what she has—the ability to sing and dance, to perform professionally, and therefore to lead another life than the one Johnny wants her to lead."[10]) Moreover, the performance instigates a climactic narrative event: Gilda's decision to return to the United States, a choice she makes when, immediately following the striptease, Johnny slaps her face. In the final rendition of "Put the Blame on Mame," therefore, the song serves as ironic commentary on Gilda's situation: She sings of entrapment, but it is Johnny who suffers in front of his peers, and doubly so when it is revealed that Gilda never betrayed her marriage to Ballin.

The ways in which *Gilda* motivates three performances of "Put the Blame on Mame" reverberate with the practices by which theme songs came to be integrated into non-musical films during the transition to sound. Like the rendering of "My Tonia" in *In Old Arizona*, the first rendition of "Put the Blame on Mame" occurs by way of a record player and is presented in an instrumental arrangement and haphazard manner. The second performance, which takes place in the subdued setting of the emptied casino, seems at first to disrupt the narrative flow for the sake of showcasing Hayworth's star image, but its interruption by Johnny undermines the potential of the song to function as an isolatable entity and instead highlights its potential to function as a narrative device; Johnny's interruption signals his ability to overpower Gilda's capacity for self-expression. Lastly, having been associated with Gilda's hostile relationship with Johnny, the song's final, brazen presentation instigates a narrative turning point that draws the film to a close.

It is worth noting that "Put the Blame on Mame" also enjoyed moderate success as a marketable commodity. In 1946, the year of *Gilda*'s release, Decca issued two recordings, the first by the Milt Herth Trio and the Jesters (recorded just six days before the film's release on February 14) and the second by Cass Daly, backed by Vic Schoen and His Orchestra. Another version of the song was recorded in July by Monica "America's Singing Sweetheart" Lewis for the Signature label. Sheet music for both "Put the Blame on Mame" and "Amado Mio" was published by the New York-based Sun Music Co. and featured Hayworth's image on the cover. The song was also performed subsequently in two films, the comedic college drama *Betty Co-ed* (1946) and the musical *Senior Prom* (1958), both distributed by Columbia Pictures. Like so many of the theme songs written and produced during the transitional era, "Put the Blame on Mame" inspired a commercial existence outside the context of the motion picture from which it derived.

CODA

To the question posed at the outset of this book—what were early American sound films "saying with songs"?—I offer three answers. First, they said that motion picture songs could augment and sometimes replace practices of media cross-promotion that emerged around the turn of the century and developed up to the rise of radio in the mid-1920s, just before the studios' conversion to synchronized sound production. I have tried to show that the study of song promotion and narrative integration can be enriched by attending to *non-musical* films, and that in so doing we may set the historical record straight when it comes to championing present-day examples of media convergence.

Second, the earliest Hollywood sound films remain a testament to the richly variegated period of song use that resulted from the studios' conversion to sound and concomitant investment in the music industry. In relation to the classical Hollywood film scores of the 1930s and 1940s, soundtracks of the transitional era are not so much precursors (in the teleological sense) as they are fruitful experiments with two nascent models for film scoring: the popular song score and the orchestral background score.

Third, the transition to sound bears witness to the argument that the defining principles of the classical Hollywood cinema were rooted in causal, coherent storytelling, and not in the formal rupture of this coherence. This observation in turn relates to a principal framework of film analysis—that is, the dichotomy of narrative and spectacle. Whether, as some have argued, filmic spectacle is defined by a song, a star, an action sequence, or even an image itself, the critical framework that pits narrative against spectacle has occupied a prominent position in the history of film analysis.[11] But the functions of motion picture songs in Hollywood's earliest soundtracks ultimately militate against this either/or approach, and their eventual assimilation as integrated narrative devices may be regarded as one way in which the classical cinema recovered its stylistic norms following the conversion to sound.

CONFIRMATORY LICENSE ISSUED BY MUSIC
PUBLISHERS PROTECTIVE ASSOCIATION (1929)[1]

New York, N.Y.......................192..

To
E. C. Mills, as Agent and Trustee,
1501 Broadway, New York, N.Y.
No.........................

Application is hereby made for issuance of confirmatory license under agreement dated as of September 5, 1927, in respect of the musical composition described below.

ELECTRICAL RESEARCH PRODUCTS INC.,

By.................................

Title of Composition..
Composer...Author...............................
Publisher...
Portion Used...No. Times Used.................................
Played or Sung by...
*Proposed Use...
Remarks:
Title of
Photoplay:

(*) Under "Proposed Use," please state if composition rendered as a solo or selection, as incidental music, overture or part of medley. _____

Note: Three copies of this application to be forwarded.
Please do not fill in below.

- - - -

New York, N.Y.......................192..

To
Electrical Products Research Inc.,
New York, N.Y.

License as above applied for is hereby issued, subject to all the conditions and provisions of agreement dated as of September 5, 1927.

....
E. C. Mills, Agent & Trustee

"TIE-UPS OF FILM AND MUSIC" AS REPORTED BY *VARIETY*[1]

WARNER BROS.-F.N.
M. Witmark & Sons
George & Arthur Piantadosi, Inc.
Harms, Inc.
Chappell-Harms, Inc.
DeSylva, Brown & Henderson, Inc.
Remick Music Corp.
Green & Stept, Inc.
Famous Music Corp.
Davis, Coots & Engel, Inc.
New World Publishing Co.
T. B. Harms Co.
Atlas Music Corp.

METRO-GOLDWYN-MAYER
Robbins Music Corp.

FOX
DeSylva, Brown & Henderson, Inc.
(Now with Warners)
R-K-O Pictures
Harms, Inc.
(Now with Warners)

UNIVERSAL
Shapiro, Bernstein & Co.

PARAMOUNT
Famous Music Corp.
(Now with Warners)

PATHE
Green & Stept, Inc.
(Now with Warners)

UNITED ARTISTS
Irving Berlin, Inc.

TIMELINE OF RELATIONSHIPS BETWEEN FILM
AND MUSIC COMPANIES

Date	Company Activity	Publishing Outlet
1928 Aug.	Paramount acquires 50% of Harms, Inc. (and subsidiaries[1])	Famous Music Corp.
1928 Sept.	MGM acquires 50% of Robbins Music Corp.	Robbins Music Corp.
1928 Nov.	Fox agreement with DeSylva, Brown & Henderson and acquires U.S. rights to Salabert (France)	DeSylva, Brown & Henderson Crawford Music Corp.
1929 Jan.	Warner Bros. acquires M. Witmark & Sons	M. Witmark & Sons
1929 Aug.	Warner Bros. acquires Harms, Inc. (and subsidiaries)	Music Publishers Holding Corp.
1929 Oct.	Fox creates Red Star Music Co.	Red Star Music Co. Created as subsidiary
1929 Nov.	RCA (parent co. of RKO) acquires Leo Feist, Inc. and Carl Fischer, Inc.	Radio Music Corp.
	Paramount acquires 80% of Spier & Coslow, Inc.	Spier & Coslow, Inc.[2]

1 Harms was the parent company to T. B. Harms, Chappell & Co. (U.K., soon to be Chappell-Connelly), Green and Stept, Atlas Music Co., and New World Music Co. It also owned 50 percent of shares in Remick Music and 20 percent in DeSylva, Brown & Henderson.

2 Paramount continued to publish film songs with Harms, Inc. (then part of the Music Publishers Holding Corp.).

Appendix 4

AGREEMENT BETWEEN AL DUBIN, THE VITAPHONE CORP.,

AND MUSIC PUBLISHERS HOLDING CORPORATION[1]

Dated:	February 1st, 1930
WITH:	THE VITAPHONE CORPORATION and MUSIC PUBLISHERS HOLDING CORP.
TERM:	1 year, from date. (12 works submitted yearly)
SALARY:	$200. weekly
CAPACITY:	Lyric writer. Reports to Coast Studio, when salary starts.
TRAVELING:	Writer receives transportation from New York to Coast plus $25. expenses (each way) and return.
OPTIONS:	1st – 1 year at $250. weekly; 2nd – 1 year at $300. weekly; to be exercised 30 days before expiration of previous terms.
NOTICE:	Mailed to Writer at Coast Studio, from Los Angeles or New York.
ROYALTIES:	$300. weekly advance from date hereof, during term; accounts rendered 30 days after June 30 and Dec. 31; 3 ¢ on piano copies 19¢ wholesale; 2¢ if less; 33 1/3% on commercial records; 6¢ on copies used in living stage production; 50% on records thereof; etc. (usual clause)
BREACH:	Employer has injunctive relief to prevent breach, besides other rights. Waiver of one not waiver of other breach.

(Continued)

Dated:	February 1st, 1930
PUBLICATION:	At discretion of Publisher. Writer's works may be assigned for publication under separate royalty agreement. On written request by registered mail, unpublished works returned within 6 months thereafter.
EXECUTED:	In New York.
MEMBERSHIP:	Contract subject to Writer's membership in American Society of Composers, Authors and Publishers.
EXPENSES:	If Writer employed away from studio, transportation and reasonable expenses paid.
LOAN:	Writer's services may be loaned, but contract stands.

1 Folder 12637B, Warner Bros. Archives, University of Southern California.

Appendix 5

SUMMARY OF AGREEMENT BETWEEN VITAPHONE
CORPORATION, M. WITMARK & SONS, AND RAY PERKINS[1]

<u>Dated:</u> January 25, 1929
<u>Parties:</u> The Vitaphone Corporation
M. Witmark & Sons
Ray Perkins

<u>Scope of Agreement:</u> Vitaphone and Witmark hereby jointly employ Writer to render his exclusive to lyrics to songs and/or the music therefor both in connection with motion pictures produced by Vitaphone or any of its related or associated companies or separately therefrom for any purpose, for and during the term of this agreement, and to assist in the preparation of songs, lyrics, music and other such similar material used in connection with motion pictures, either separately or in synchronism or timed relation with sound, and in general to perform all other duties pertaining to the work of lyric and/or music writer.

    <u>Assignment of Rights</u> (Par. 3): Writer assigns to Witmark all manuscripts which he may prepare hereunder, together with all his right, title and interest in the same, including the right in Witmark to copyright the same throughout the world in its own name, and the exclusive right to print, reprint, publish, copy and vend the same, it being the intention of the Writer as to all works written or composed by him during the term hereof, to grant to Witmark all rights of any nature which he may have in and to the same, together with the right to enjoy and exercise all uses which Witmark may make of the same. To have and to hold all of these rights exclusively forever throughout the world to Witmark, its successors and assigns.

    <u>Assignment of Royalties</u> (Par. 4): Writer grants to Vitaphone all royalties or payments which may become due him by virtue of any use which Vitaphone may make of any of the works of Writer, and further grants to Vitaphone all payments or royalties which may become due to

Writer for any use which any other company may make of the works in connection with motion pictures or records of sound used in synchronism or timed relation therewith.

Publication (Par. 5): Witmark agrees with respect to all of the works written, composed, owned or controlled by Writer during the term of this agreement, that it will publish all such works accepted by Vitaphone as theme songs or feature songs in any of its feature pictures simultaneously with the release of the picture; that it will immediately publish all such works of which a public production other than by means of motion pictures shall have been secured, and that for all other such works, it will notify Writer within 12 months after receipt by it of the same, which of such works it accepts for publication. However, such notice and such acceptance shall not be deemed an obligation on the part of Witmark to publish the same immediately thereafter.

Royalties Par. 5(b): Upon those works which Witmark accepts and publishes, Witmark agrees to pay to Writer the following royalties: –

If such works are written solely by the Writer both as to words and music or are solely the property of the Writer both as to words and music, then the royalties shall be 3¢ upon each piano arrangement copy of the work published in printed form and sold and paid for.

If the Writer has written or composed either the words or the music thereof but not both, then the royalties shall be 1½¢ upon each and every piano arrangement copy published in printed form and sold and paid for.

If the work is written solely by the Writer both as to words and music or is the sole property of the Writer both as to words and music, then Witmark agrees to pay to the Writer 33-1/3% of all sums of the royalties received by Witmark arising out of or accruing from the use of such composition or any arrangement thereof on parts of instruments serving to reproduce the same mechanically, it being understood and agreed that this provision shall not apply in any instance where such parts of instruments are used in connection with motion pictures either synchronized therewith or otherwise or in theatres or motion picture houses.

If the Writer has written or composed either the words or music thereof, but not both, or owns either the words or music thereof, but not both, then Witmark agrees to pay 16-2/3% of all sums of the royalties received by Witmark arising out of or accruing from the use of such composition or any arrangement thereof on parts of instruments serving to reproduce the same mechanically, it being understood and agreed that this provision shall not apply in any instance where such parts of instruments are used in connection with motion pictures either synchronized therewith or otherwise or in theatres or motion picture houses.

One-half of the foregoing royalties and percentage of royalties shall be payable on numbers published and sold in foreign markets.

One-half of the foregoing royalties shall be payable upon copies sold at less than the regular rate.

No royalties shall be payable upon any copies sold or disposed of as new issues nor on copies distributed gratuitously to the press, and to professional musicians for advertising purposes nor on reproduction in miniature for advertising purposes or publication in any newspaper, magazine or periodical, nor for publication in any collection or volume containing works of other composers, or as part of any medley containing parts of two or more compositions.

Advance Royalty (Par. 5(c)): Witmark agrees to pay Writer against the royalties to be earned on the works accepted and published by Witmark, a drawing account of $100.00 per week, to begin when Author has reported to Vitaphone, Hollywood Studios not later than February 9, 1929.

The drawing account shall be and remain the property of Writer irrespective of the amount of royalty which may accrue.

Salary (Par. 5(d)): Vitaphone agrees to pay Writer a salary of $200.00 per week.

Transportation (Par. 5(d)): Vitaphone agrees to pay Writer all of his transportation expenses including railroad fare, pullman and sleeper excluding excess baggage from New York City to Hollywood Studio, and the sum of $25.00 in lieu of subsistence and other traveling expenses.

Return of Works (Par. 5 (e)): Witmark agrees upon expiration of this agreement to return to Writer within 6 months after written request from Writer, all the works which have not been accepted for publication by Witmark. Upon such return Witmark agrees to assign back to Writer all rights which it acquired in and to the same reserving, however, for and to Vitaphone, the right and privilege to use the same as, or in connection with, motion pictures and on sound records to be used in theatres either separately royalties or other payments accruing to writer and arising from such use.

Term (Par. 13): Continuing from January 25, 1929 to a period ending one year after February 1, 1929.

Option to Extend (Par. 13): Vitaphone and Witmark, or either of them, shall have the option to extend Writer's employment for an additional period of one year from and after the expiration of the basic period, upon the same terms and conditions as herein contained, except that Vitaphone to pay Writer a drawing account of $150.00 per week and a salary of $300.00 per week instead of the amounts provided for in paragraph 5(c) and 5(d) hereof.

Return Transportation (Par. 15): Upon expiration of this agreement, if Writer desires to return to New York City, Vitaphone agrees to pay transportation expenses of Writer from Hollywood, California, to New York City, including railroad fare, pullman and sleeper, but not excess baggage, together with the sum of $25.00 in lieu of subsistence and other traveling expenses.

CREDITS

PARTS OF CHAPTERS 2 and 3 were published in different form in the article "Pop Go the Warner Bros., et al.: Marketing Film Songs during the Coming of Sound," by Katherine Spring, in *Cinema Journal*, Vol. 48, Issue 1, 68–89. Copyright ©2008 by the University of Texas Press. All rights reserved. Part of chapter 3 was published in different form in the article " 'To Sustain Illusion is All That is Necessary': The Authenticity of Song Performance in Early American Sound Cinema," by Katherine Spring, in *Beyond Vitaphone: The Early Sound Short*, spec. issue of *Film History: An International Journal*, Vol. 23, Issue 3, 285–299. Copyright ©2011 by Indiana University Press. All rights reserved.

For their kind permission to reproduce copyright material that appeared in earlier publications, I thank Rebecca Frazier-Smith of the University of Texas Press and Kathryn Caras of Indiana University Press, respectively. For additional permissions, I thank Bob Birchard (Robert S. Birchard Collection), Maggie Clark, Todd Ifft (Photofest Inc.), Donna Pennestri (*Variety*), Daniel Spring, and Jamie Vuignier (Kobal Collection).

INTRODUCTION

1. Quoted in Cal York, "Gossip of All the Studios," *Photoplay* 35.6 (May 1929), 51.

2. A reviewer in 1930 praised *A Hollywood Theme Song* as "one of Sennett's best" and lauded the songs and lyrics composed by Dave Silverstein and William Dugan. "Pictures–Reviewed and Previewed," *Hollywood Filmograph*, November 1, 1930, 20. A 16mm print of the film is housed at the Moving Image Section of the Library of Congress Motion Picture, Broadcasting and Recorded Sound Division. The film's final script and other production documents can be found in *Hollywood Theme Song* (32.f-330), Production Files, Mack Sennett Papers, Special Collections, Margaret Herrick Library, Academy of Motion Picture Arts and Sciences, Los Angeles.

3. The period that is said to define Hollywood's transition to sound depends upon the research question being asked. Donald Crafton's exhaustive overview takes 1926 as a starting point because that year marked the formation of the seminal Vitaphone company and the exhibition of the first feature-length synchronized sound film (*Don Juan*, in August), while the spring of 1931 is a suitable endpoint because by that time the industry had accepted the permanence of synchronized sound film; no major studio was producing silent movies. Lea Jacobs, however, has shown that practices of re-recording instigated by the advent of synchronized sound film technology did not stabilize until the late 1930s, implying in turn a prolongation of the transitional period. Likewise, William M. Drew's study of silent films exhibited on American screens through the 1930s extends what we usually think of as the transitional era. The period demarcated by *Saying It With Songs* is informed by David Bordwell's chapter in *The Classical Hollywood Cinema*, which examines how the coming of sound disrupted techniques of silent film style, such as camera movement and editing pace, before there arose cinematic norms that not only emulated those of late silent cinema, but also endured through the classical era. *Saying It With Songs* contends that norms for the use of songs in film underwent a similar process of disruption and stabilization from 1927 through

1931. Donald Crafton, *The Talkies: American Cinema's Transition to Sound, 1926-1931.* Vol. 4 *of History of the American Cinema*, ed. Charles Harpole (New York: Charles Scribner's Sons, 1997), 10, 18, 267; Lea Jacobs, "The Innovation of Re-recording in Hollywood Studios," Film History 24.1 (2012): 5–34; William M. Drew, *The Last Silent Picture Show: Silent Films on American Screens in the 1930s* (Lanham, MD: Scarecrow Press, 2010); David Bordwell, "The Introduction of Sound," in *The Classical Hollywood Cinema: Film Style and Mode of Production to 1960*, eds. Bordwell, Janet Staiger, and Kristin Thompson (New York: Columbia University Press, 1985), 306. For a series of astute discussions on the notion of historical transition, see *American Cinema's Transitional Era: Audiences, Institutions, Practices*, eds. Charlie Keil and Shelley Stamp (Berkeley, CA: University of California Press, 2004), 1–100.

4. Quoted in Jack L. Warner with Dean Jennings, *My First Hundred Years in Hollywood* (New York: Random House, 1964), 168.

5. Miklós Rózsa, "The Growing Art," *Music and Dance in California and the West*, ed. Richard Drake Saunders (Hollywood: Bureau of Musical Research, 1948), 79.

6. James Buhler, David Neumeyer, and Rob Deemer, *Hearing the Movies: Music and Sound in Film History* (New York: Oxford University Press), 299.

7. Laurence E. MacDonald, *The Invisible Art of Film Music: A Comprehensive History* (New York: Ardsley House, 1998), 11–22; Russell Lack, *Twenty Four Frames Under* (London: Quartet Books, 1997), 80–89, 240–263; Roger Hickman, *Reel Music: Exploring 100 Years of Film Music* (New York: W. W. Norton, 2006). Oft-cited books on the film musical's "birth" during the transition to sound are Richard Barrios, *A Song in the Dark: The Birth of the Musical Film*, 2nd ed. (New York: Oxford University Press, 2009) and Edwin M. Bradley, *The First Hollywood Musicals: A Critical Filmography of 171 Features, 1927-1932* (Jefferson, NC: McFarland, 1996). Bradley acknowledges the "scores of non-musicals from the early sound era that were graced with a song or two" (xi). Miles Kreuger's compilation of material published in *Photoplay* magazine from 1926 through 1933 also emphasizes films that derive primarily from Broadway musical genres. Miles Kreuger, ed., *The Movie Musical, From Vitaphone to 42nd Street* (New York: Dover, 1975). Two books published more recently offer refreshingly well-researched accounts of the period's use of film music: James Buhler, David Neumeyer, and Rob Deemer, *Hearing the Movies*, 295–303, and James Wierzbicki, *Film Music: A History* (New York: Routledge, 2009), 71–130.

8. Although these figures are based on listings in the *Catalog*, and have not all been confirmed through film viewing (as many of the films included in the survey are deemed to be lost), the following numbers illustrate the swift rise and fall of song use in Hollywood's earliest sound films. Each number indicates the percentage of films (in a given production season) that contained at least one song: 1928–1929: 32%; 1929–1930: 52%; 1930–1931: 28%; and 1931–1932: 23%. *American Film Institute Catalog*, available online at http://afi.chadwyck.co.uk/home [June 1, 2011].

9. "Back to Melody," *Time* 24.25 (December 16, 1929): 45–46; B. G. DeSylva, "The Birth of a Popular Song: A Successful Song-Writer Demonstrates, For All to See, Exactly How It Is Accomplished," *Vanity Fair* 28.10 (June 1927): 41, 114.

10. Hilary Lapedis, "Popping the Question: The Function and Effect of Popular Music in Cinema," in *Popular Music* 18.3 (1999): 367–379; Pauline Reay, *Music in Film: Soundtracks and Synergy* (London: Wallflower Press, 2004); Ian Inglis, ed., *Popular Music and Film* (London: Wallflower Press, 2003); Ian Conrich and Estella Tincknell, *Film's Musical Moments* (Edinburgh, UK: Edinburgh University Press, 2006).

11. Crafton, *The Talkies*, 315–316.

12. Kathryn Kalinak, *Settling the Score: Music and the Classical Hollywood Film* (Madison, WI: University of Wisconsin Press, 1992), 66.

13. See, for example, Kalinak, *Settling the Score*; also Philip Furia and Laurie Patterson, *The Songs of Hollywood* (New York: Oxford University Press, 2010).

14. Robert C. Allen, *Vaudeville and Film, 1895-1915: A Study in Media Interaction* (Ph.D. diss., University of Iowa, 1977; New York: Arno Press, 1980), 1. Writing in 1977, Allen noted a few exceptions to the lack of scholarship on media interaction, including Robert McLaughlin's study of Broadway and Hollywood, and J. Douglas Gomery's doctoral thesis, which was subsequently published as Douglas Gomery, *The Coming of Sound* (New York: Routledge, 2005). Like Gomery's book, accounts of the transitional era written by Donald Crafton, Charles O'Brien, Robert Spadoni, and Ryan Jay Friedman are all indispensible resources for scholars of the transition to sound, but their research questions do not concern film music primarily. Crafton, *The Talkies*; Charles O'Brien, *Cinema's Conversion to Sound: Technology and Film Style in France and the United States* (Indiana University Press, 2005); Robert Spadoni, *Uncanny Bodies: The Coming of Sound Film and the Origins of the Horror Genre* (Berkeley, CA: University of California Press, 2007); Ryan Jay Friedman, *Hollywood's African American Films: The Transition to Sound* (New Brunswick, NJ: Rutgers University Press, 2011).

15. During the 1980s and 1990s, America's largest media corporations developed into fully integrated conglomerates. For example, Viacom acquired the MTV network (1985); Warner Communications bought Chappell Music (1987) and merged with Time, Inc. (1999); Walt Disney Co. purchased Miramax Films (1993) and ABC (1995); Viacom acquired Paramount Communications (1994) and united with CBS (1999); and, perhaps most famously, Time-Warner coordinated a $183 billion merger with AOL (2000). See, for examples, Erik Barnouw, *Conglomerates and the Media* (New York: New Press, 1997); Bum Soo Chon, Junho H. Choi, George A. Barnett, et al., "A Structural Analysis of Media Convergence: Cross-Industry Mergers and Acquisitions in the Information Industries," *Journal of Media Economics* 16.3 (2003): 141–157; Eli M. Noam, *Media Ownership and Concentration in America* (New York: Oxford University Press, 2009).

16. Corey Creekmur, "Picturizing American Cinema: Hindi Film Songs and the Last Days of Genre," in *Soundtrack Available: Essays on Film and Popular Music*, eds. Pamela Robertson Wojcik and Arthur Knight (Durham, NC: Duke University Press, 2001), 385. For that matter, one could even point to examples from the period of silent cinema that were inspired by popular songs. Dozens of examples of songs inspired by silent cinema in general (e.g., "Mister Moving Picture Man" in 1912) and silent film stars in particular (e.g., "My Mother's Lullaby," written for Anita Stewart in 1917) are found in Gerald D. McDonald, "A Bibliography of Song Sheets: Sports and Recreations in American Popular Songs: Part IV: Songs of the Silent Film," *Notes*, 2nd ser. 14.3 (June 1957): 325–352. The trade and popular press reported occasionally on film song tie-ups of the silent era. In 1917, for example, *Los Angeles Times* columnist Grace Kingsley reported, "That ever keen and tanny [*sic*] organization, the Universal Film Manufacturing Company, has hit upon a decided novelty in picture production. It is nothing more nor less than putting popular songs into picture form. Thus not only will the lover of 'Poor Butterfly,' for instance, be able to hear his favorite popular song, but he will also see the story, as suggested by the number, unrolled on the film before his eyes." Grace Kingsley, "Frivols.: 'Pop' Song Films Next; Lois Weber Arranging for Studio Site," *Los Angeles Times*, May 18, 1917, II3.

17. David Suisman, *Selling Sounds: The Commercial Revolution in American Music* (Cambridge, MA: Harvard University Press, 2009); Russell Sanjek and David Sanjek, *American Popular Music Business in the 20th Century* (New York: Oxford University Press, 1991); Russell Sanjek, updated by David Sanjek, *Pennies from Heaven: The American Popular Music Business in the Twentieth Century* (New York: Da Capo Press, 1996). The thorough volumes by Russell and David Sanjek supply historians with excellent vantage points from which to view the broad industrial history of American popular music. However, their comprehensive scope—an entire century's worth of the business of popular music—precludes an analysis of the nature and functions of film songs. Other accounts of the relationship between the film and music industries are fascinating reads tinged with nostalgia, such as Gary Mormenstein, *Hollywood Rhapsody: Movie Music and Its Makers, 1900 to 1975* (New York: Schirmer, 1997).

18. Jeff Smith, *The Sounds of Commerce: Marketing Popular Film Music* (New York: Columbia University Press, 1998). A shorter study is provided by Alexander Doty, "Music Sells Movies: (Re)new(ed) Conservatism in Film Marketing," *Wide Angle* 10: 2 (1988): 70–79. Doty traces a "pattern of mainstream movie-and-music commercial interaction" between the 1930s and the 1960s. While Doty acknowledges that songs of early talkies "were merchandised on records, on the radio, and in the form of sheet music to capitalize upon a film's high market visibility," the majority of his essay focuses on soundtracks produced subsequent to Hollywood's conversion to sound.

19. Ross Melnick, *American Showman: Samuel "Roxy" Rothafel and the Birth of the Entertainment Industry, 1908-1935* (New York: Columbia University Press, 2012); Steve J. Wurtzler, *Electric Sounds: Technological Change and the Rise of Corporate Mass Media* (New York: Columbia University Press, 2007).

20. Keating finds an analogy in Donald Crafton's account of slapstick comedy films, in which "the forward progress of the linear narrative is constantly being interrupted by gags that do nothing to help the protagonist achieve his or her goal." Patrick Keating, "Emotional Curves and Linear Narratives," *The Velvet Light Trap* 58.1 (2006): 5.

21. Rick Altman, *The American Film Musical* (Bloomington, IN: Indiana University Press, 1987), 102; Richard Dyer, "Entertainment and Utopia," in Dyer, *Only Entertainment*, 2nd ed. (London: Routledge, 2002), 27; Jane Feuer, *The Hollywood Musical*, 2nd ed. (Bloomington, IN: Indiana University Press, 1993), 68. The alternation model has broad appeal as an explanation for the structure of the musical, as evidenced by recent accounts situated in cognitive film studies, such as Torben Grodal's and Patrick Hogan's underlining of the disruptive nature of songs. Torben Grodal, *Moving Pictures: A New Theory of Film Genres, Feelings, and Cognition* (Oxford, UK: Clarendon; New York: Oxford University Press, 1997), 168; Patrick Hogan, *Understanding Indian Movies* (Austin, TX: University of Texas Press, 2008), 163.

22. Altman, *The American Film Musical*, 110–115.

23. Crafton, *The Talkies*, 315.

24. *Film Daily*, May 5, 1929, 9; *Film Daily*, May 26, 1929, 8.

25. *Film Daily*, August 11, 1929, 8; *Film Daily*, January 5, 1930, 12.

26. *Film Daily*, June 30, 1929; "Summer Talkers Look Big," *Variety*, May 1, 1929, 7. Curiously, the review of *Broadway Babies* in *Variety* makes no mention of a musical genre. "Film Reviews," *Variety*, June 16, 1929, 22, 25.

27. *Motion Picture News* did not provide a genre label but described the film as one that contained "real drama, musical comedy, and comedy." *Motion Picture News*, February 16, 1929, 500.

28. Through 1929, *Film Daily* tended to reserve the descriptors "musical" or "operetta" for Broadway adaptations. *Film Daily*, June 30, 1929, 12; "Summer Talkers Look Good: No Hold Back on Releases," *Variety*, May 1, 1929, 7; *Film Daily*, April 14, 1929, 12; "Film Reviews," *Variety*, May 1, 1929, 26; *Variety*, April 3, 1929, 16.

29. *Motion Picture Almanac 1930* (Chicago: Quigley, 1930), 219; *Film Daily*, January 27, 1929, 4; *Film Daily*, February 10, 1929, 13. For *The Broadway Melody*, see *Motion Picture Almanac 1930*, 213; *Variety*, February 13, 1929, 57; *Film Daily*, February 17, 1929, 10.

30. Max Steiner, "Scoring the Film," in *We Make the Movies*, ed. Nancy Naumberg (New York: W. W. Norton, 1937), 218.

31. Irene Kahn Atkins, *Source Music in Motion Pictures* (Plainsboro, NJ: Associated University Presses, 1983), 31.

32. Bordwell, Staiger, and Thompson, *The Classical Hollywood Cinema*, 13.

33. For examples, see Donald Crafton, "Pie and Chase," in *Classical Hollywood Comedy*, eds. Kristine Brunovska Karnick and Henry Jenkins (New York: Routledge, 1994), 106–119; Elizabeth Cowie, "Storytelling: Classical Hollywood Cinema and Classical Narrative," in *Contemporary Hollywood Cinema*, eds. Steve Neale and Murray Smith (New York: Routledge, 1998), 178–190; Christopher Williams, "After the Classic, the Classical and Ideology: the Differences of Realism," *Screen* 35.3 (1994): 275–292.

34. See, for example, Keating's discussion of song numbers in Busby Berkeley musicals. Keating, "Emotional Curves," 5–8, 10–13.

35. Rick Altman, "Early Film Themes: Roxy, Adorno, and the Problem of Cultural Capital," in *Beyond the Soundtrack: Representing Music in the Cinema*, eds. Daniel Goldmark, Larry Kramer, and Richard Leppert (Berkeley, CA: University of California Press, 2007), 205–224.

CHAPTER 1

1. Paul Whiteman, "Introduction," in Abel Green, *Inside Stuff on How to Write Popular Songs* (New York: Paul Whiteman, 1927), 5.

2. Muriel Babcock, "Tin Pan Alley Invades Town," *Los Angeles Times*, December 9, 1928, C13.

3. Standard histories of Tin Pan Alley may be found in Isaac Goldberg, *Tin Pan Alley: A Chronicle of the American Popular Music Racket* (New York: John Day, 1930; reprinted, New York: Frederick Ungar, 1961); Sigmund Spaeth, *A History of Popular Music in America* (New York: Random House, 1948); Paul Whiteman, with Mary Margaret McBride, *Jazz, Popular Culture in America 1800-1925* (New York: J. H. Sears, 1926; repr., New York: Arno, 1974).

4. The provenance of the moniker "Tin Pan Alley" is unclear. Most histories attribute the source of the name to songwriter and reporter Monroe Rosenfeld, who supposedly wrote an article about the district for the *New York Herald* in 1903. Hazel Meyer, author of *The Gold in Tin Pan Alley*, credits O. Henry (William Sydney Porter) and lyricist Stanley Murphy, but more recent scholarship cites Roy McCardell's piece, "A Visit to Tin Pan Alley, Where the Popular Songs Come From," published in *The World* on May 3, 1903. Keir Keightley, "Taking Popular Music (and Tin Pan Alley and Jazz) Seriously," *Journal of Popular Music Studies* 22. 1 (March 2010): 91–93; Hazel Meyer, *The Gold in Tin Pan Alley* (Philadelphia: Lippincott, 1958), 40.

5. William Arms Fisher, music composer and author of a promotional "history" book issued by a Boston-based music publishing house, Oliver Ditson Co. (a likely competitor to New York houses), dismissed the output of the Alley as "blurbs and ballads and banalities" and declared that

its "frankly commercial pursuit involves a ceaseless and eager following of the taste of the crowd—the discriminate and undiscriminating crowd—an inseparable part of the American scene." William Arms Fisher, *One Hundred and Fifty Years of Music Publishing in the United States: An Historical Sketch With Special Reference to the Pioneer Publisher, Oliver Ditson Company, Inc., 1783-1933* (Boston: Oliver Ditson, 1933), 114. A vibrant account of the factory-like environment of the Alley is David Suisman, *Selling Sounds: The Commercial Revolution in American Music* (Cambridge, MA: Harvard University Press, 2009), 48.

6. Alec Wilder, *American Popular Song: The Great Innovators, 1900-1950*, ed. James T. Maher (New York: Oxford University Press, 1972).

7. David Suisman, *Selling Sounds*; Daniel Goldmark "Creating Desire on Tin Pan Alley," *Musical Quarterly* 90.2 (Summer 2007): 197–229.

8. Suisman, *Selling Sounds*, 22.

9. Suisman, *Selling Sounds*, 45.

10. According to an oft-cited volume by Joel Whitburn, four songs of the ten best-selling phonograph records of songs published by Alley firms were published in the 1920s. These were "The Prisoner's Song," sung by Vernon Dalhart; "My Blue Heaven," by Gene Austin; "Dardanella," by Ben Selvin's Novelty Orchestra; and "Three O'Clock in the Morning," by Paul Whiteman & His Orchestra. The sources on which Whitburn bases his rankings include trade publications, industry sales rankings, and reports of the American Society for Composers, Authors, and Performers. Joel Whitburn, *Pop Memories 1890-1954: The History of American Popular Music* (Menomonee Falls, WI: Record Research Inc., 1986), 631.

11. David Bordwell, *Planet Hong Kong: Popular Cinema and the Art of Entertainment*, 2nd ed. (Madison, WI: Irvington Way Institute Press, 2011), 4.

12. Rick Altman, *Silent Film Sound* (New York: Columbia University Press, 2004), 52.

13. William Leach, *Land of Desire: Merchants, Power, and the Rise of a New American Culture* (New York: Pantheon, 1993), qtd. in Goldmark, "Creating Desire," 229; Russell Sanjek, *Pennies from Heaven: The American Popular Music Business in the Twentieth Century*, revised and updated by David Sanjek (New York: Da Capo, 1996), 32–33.

14. Suisman, *Selling Sounds*, 58.

15. Goldberg, *Tin Pan Alley*, 203–204.

16. Kerry Segrave, *Payola in the Music Industry: A History, 1880-1991* (Jefferson, NC: McFarland, 1994), 1–29. See also Goldberg, *Tin Pan Alley*, 197–233; Edward B. Marks, *They All Sang: From Tony Pastor to Rudy Vallée* (New York: Viking, 1934), 3–21; David Ewen, *All the Years of American Popular Music* (Englewood Cliffs, NJ: Prentice Hall, 1977), 107–108; David Ewen, *The Life and Death of Tin Pan Alley* (New York: Funk & Wagnalls, 1964); Timothy E. Scheurer, "Introduction: The Tin Pan Alley Years (1890-1950)," in *American Popular Music: Readings from the Popular Press, Volume I: The Nineteenth Century and Tin Pan Alley*, ed. Timothy Scheurer (Bowling Green, OH: Bowling Green State University Popular Press, 1989), 88; Nicholas E. Tawa, *The Way to Tin Pan Alley: American Popular Song, 1866-1910* (New York: Schirmer Books, 1990), 48–53; Nicholas E. Tawa, *Sweet Songs for Gentle Americans: The Parlor Song in America, 1790-1860* (Bowling Green, OH: Bowling Green State University Popular Press, 1980), 101–119. The exploitative practices of payola precipitated the 1917 formation of the Music Publishers Protective Association, discussed in chapter 2.

17. Charles K. Harris, *After the Ball: Forty Years of Melody* (New York: Frank-Maurice, 1926), 36, 40.

18. Marks, *They All Sang*, 4.

19. Charles K. Harris, *How to Write a Popular Song* (Chicago: Charles K. Harris, 1906), 56.

20. Philip H. Ennis, *The Seventh Stream: The Emergence of Rocknroll in American Popular Music* (Hanover, NH: Wesleyan University Press, 1992), 42.

21. The retail cost of sheet music fluctuated during the first two decades of the century. In 1900, a piece of sheet music cost between 25 and 60 cents. Woolworth's and its competitors bargained down wholesale prices in order to offer retail prices of 10 cents per piece, which became the standard cost. (In 1918, Woolworth's alone sold 200 million pieces at this price.) Exceptions to the rule were "high class" music and songs by illustrious composers like Irving Berlin, whose works commanded 30 cents per copy. By 1929, according to an article published in *Vanity Fair*, most sheet music for motion picture theme songs sold for 25 cents. Linda L. Tyler, "'Commerce and Poetry Hand in Hand': Music in American Department Stores, 1880-1930)," *Journal of the American Musicological Society* 45.1 (Spring 1992): 75–120; Barney Dougall, "Theme-songs, I Love You," *Vanity Fair* 33:3 (November 1929), 67. See also Sanjek, *Pennies from Heaven*, 23, 34–35.

22. "Last Week's Ten Best Sellers among the Popular Songs," *Billboard*, July 19, 1913, 15. David J. Steffan points out that the publication signaled a critical shift in industry's conception of music popularity, from one based on supplier data to one based on consumer spending. David J. Steffan, *From Edison to Marconi: The First Thirty Years of Recorded Music* (New York: McFarland, 2005), 163. On sales of pianos, see Suisman, *Selling Sounds*, 203.

23. "Introducing Our Phonograph Department," *Billboard*, September 15, 1917, 14.

24. Abel Green and Joe Laurie, Jr. *Show Biz: From Vaude to Video* (New York: Henry Holt, 1951), 316. See also David Ewen, *All the Years*, 280. The song was recorded on July 29, 1928. *Encyclopedic Discography of Victor Recordings*, available online at http://victor.library.ucsb.edu [September 1, 2011].

25. Philip K. Eberly, *Music in the Air: America's Changing Tastes in Popular Music, 1920-1980* (New York: Hastings House, 1982), 24. From figures provided by the Recording Industry Association of America.

26. Christopher H. Sterling and John Michael Kittross, "Table 6-A: Ownership of Radio Receivers, 1922-1959," in *Stay Tuned: A History of American Broadcasting*, 3rd ed. (New York: Routledge, 2001), 862. See also Herman S. Hettinger, *A Decade of Radio Advertising* (Chicago: University of Chicago Press, 1933), 43.

27. Eberly, *Music in the Air*, 61.

28. The value of manufactured upright pianos, the common type of piano found in American homes, dropped from $12.3 million in 1927 to $2.6 million in 1931. "Table No. 748: Musical Instruments—Parts and Materials: Production," in U.S. Dept. of Commerce and Labor, *Statistical Abstract of the United States, 1933* (Washington, DC: U.S. Government Printing Office, 1933), 739.

29. Table XXIII in Hettinger, *A Decade of Radio Advertising*, 218. Hettinger's chart of programming proportions draws from broadcasting records produced by NBC and CBS. Semi-classical music and variety music occupied roughly 15 percent and 5 percent, respectively. (According to a study cited by Sterling and Kittross, a whopping 72 percent of network programming in 1927 consisted of music in some form.) Especially illuminating discussions of the debates over the relative merits of broadcast classical and popular music and, more generally, radio's formation of listener taste may be found in Susan J. Douglas, *Listening In: Radio and the American Imagination* (Minneapolis: University of Minnesota Press, 2004), 83–99; David Goodman, "The Promise of Classical Music," in *Radio's Civic Ambition: American Broadcasting*

and Democracy in the 1930s (New York: Oxford University Press, 2011), 116–180; and Michele Hilmes, *Radio Voices: American Broadcasting 1922-1952* (Minneapolis: University of Minnesota Press, 1997), 49–74.

30. Eberly, *Music in the Air*, 30, 61–63.

31. McCormack's performance was backed by the Victor Salon Orchestra, which had recorded "All Alone" for Victor three weeks prior to the broadcast. The statistics are drawn from Laurence Bergreen, *As Thousands Cheer: The Life of Irving Berlin* (1990; reprinted, New York: Da Capo, 1996), 201. McCormack's recording of "All Alone" quickly reached the top position on the music charts. Russell Sanjek and David Sanjek, *The American Popular Music Business in the 20th Century* (New York: Oxford University Press, 1991), 22; Whitburn, *Pop Memories*, 303, 649. The significance of classical singers in the early days of radio broadcasting is the subject of Victoria Etnier Villamil, *From Johnson's Kids to Lemonade Opera: The American Classical Singer Comes of Age* (Boston: Northeastern University Press, 2004).

32. Benjamin L. Aldridge, *The Victor Talking Machine Company*, ed. Frederic Bayh (Camden, NJ: RCA Sales Corp., 1964), 98. The entire book is available for reading online at http://www.davidsarnoff.org/vtm.html [September 1, 2011].

33. Qtd. in "Famous Stars Sing First Time by Radio to 6,000,000 People," *New York Times*, January 2, 1925, 1, 3. See also "Radio vs. Theater: Operatic Concert By Prominent Artists Raises Discussion as to Whether Radio Is Responsible for Theatrical Slump," *Radio Retailing*, February 1925, 161, 194, cited in Shawn Gary Vancour, "The Sounds of 'Radio': Aesthetic Formations of 1920s American Broadcasting," Ph.D. diss. (University of Wisconsin-Madison, 2008), 335–336.

34. Susan Smulyan, *Selling Radio: The Commercialization of American Broadcasting, 1920-1934* (Washington, DC: Smithsonian Institution Press, 1994), 72–86. Smulyan and several others, ranging from AT&T public relations executive William Peck Banning to American historian Roland Marchand, have argued that advertising agencies were reluctant to regard radio as a national advertising medium and therefore required persuasion on the part of network executives. William Peck Banning, *Commercial Broadcast Pioneer: The WEAF Experiment, 1922-1926* (Cambridge, MA: Harvard University Press, 1946), 90; Roland Marchand, *Advertising the American Dream: Making Way for Modernity, 1920-1940* (Berkeley, CA: University of California Press, 1986), 152.

35. Felix, quoted in Smulyan, *Selling Radio*, 76.

36. Timothy D. Taylor describes several examples of how the psychological effect of popular music was exploited in the service of indirect radio advertising. One notable example is the "effervescent" march that became associated with the *Clicquot Club Eskimos* radio program, sponsored by the makers of similarly effervescent ginger ale. Taylor observes that, like the march, the music selected to advertise products in the days of early radio was chosen not for its "affective qualities but, rather, [for] its ability to reinforce imagery and text, to animate the product." Timothy D. Taylor, *The Sounds of Capitalism: Advertising, Music, and the Conquest of Culture* (Chicago: University of Chicago Press, 2012), 36.

37. Joe Davis, "Sidelights on Music Publishing," *Billboard*, December 8, 1928, 56. The Triangle Music Publishing Co. was a comparatively modest firm that focused on the distribution of "race" music—blues and jazz written and performed by African Americans. In May 1930, Davis, himself white, changed the name of the company to Joe Davis, Inc. A fascinating biography of this underrepresented figure of American popular music history is Bruce Bastin, with Kip Lornell,

The Melody Man: Joe Davis and the New York Music Scene, 1916-1978 (Jackson, MS: University of Mississippi Press, 2012).

38. Joe Davis, "Sidelights on Music Publishing," *Billboard*, December 8, 1928, 56.

39. Ibid.

40. William McKenna, "Popular Songs and the Changing Times," *Billboard*, December 10, 1927, 78.

41. *Radio Continuity: Lucky Strike, 1928-29*, 1929, Bates 945263197-3552, available online at http://legacy.library.ucsf.edu/tid/nsw01a00 [September 15, 2011].

42. Ibid., 237.

43. The same copy, accompanied by an illustration of Earhart and her signature, appeared in a newspaper advertisement. *The Milwaukee Sentinel*, August 2, 1928, 3.

44. Sterling and Kittross, *Stay Tuned*, 124.

45. Stan J. Liebowitz, "The Elusive Symbiosis: The Impact of Radio on the Record Industry," *The Review of Economic Research on Copyright Issues* 1 (2004): 19–28.

46. Dave Laing, "Photography," in *Continuum Encyclopedia of Popular Music of the World*, eds. John Shepherd, David Horn, et al. (London, New York: Continuum, 2003), 296.

47. Ewen, *The Life and Death of Tin Pan Alley*, 165–167.

48. No stranger to self-aggrandizement, Tucker wrote in her autobiography, "I've been singing ['Some of These Days'] for [30] years, made it my theme. I've turned it inside out, singing it every way imaginable, as a dramatic song, as a novelty number, as a sentimental ballad, and always audiences have loved it and asked for it. 'Some of These Days' is one of the great songs that will be remembered and sung for years and years to come, like some of Stephen Foster's." Sophie Tucker, *Some of These Days: The Autobiography of Sophie Tucker* (Garden City, NY: Doubleday, Doran, 1945), 114.

49. Segrave, *Payola in the Music Industry*, 13.

50. Eileen Bowser, *The Transformation of Cinema, 1907-1915*, vol. 2 of *History of the American Cinema*, ed. Charles Harpole (New York: Charles Scribner's Sons, 1990), 103–119.

51. Richard deCordova is careful to distinguish between "picture personalities," who simply made repeated appearances in narrative films from around 1909 and onward, and stars, whose successes relied upon the articulated distinction between public and private lives, even when information about the latter was constructed and mediated heavily by press agents. Just as repeated performances helped to solidify a star's association with a particular song, the repetition of the same star in different films encouraged audiences to return to the movie theater so that they might participate in the alluring process of the identity formation of the star. Richard deCordova, *Picture Personalities: The Emergence of the Star System in America* (1990; Champagne, IL: University of Illinois Press, 2001).

52. Warren Susman, "Personality and the Making of Twentieth-Century Culture," in *Culture of History: The Transformation of American Society in the Twentieth Century* (New York: Pantheon, 1984): 273–277. Michele Hilmes argues that radio amplified the effects of the culture of personality because, unlike the medium of motion pictures, it introduced the voices of national celebrities into the private sphere. Hilmes, *Radio Voices: American Broadcasting 1922-1952* (Minneapolis: University of Minnesota Press, 1997), 58.

53. The theatrical star system can be traced back to at least a century before, when star actors were those who were seen to fuse their personae with those of fictional characters, meaning that audiences would return regardless of the character being played and their expectations would

be activated in favorable ways. In 18th-century Britain, David Garrick was the exemplar star whose identity was yoked to the personalities of his stage characters; in 19th-century France, Frédérick Lemaître was identified with the virtuous, patriotic characters who defended the country's revolutionary heritage. Jean Benedetti, *David Garrick and the Birth of Modern Theatre* (London: Methuen, 2001). By the late 1800s, "matinee idols" and star-based touring companies were established elements of the American theatrical star system.

54. Daniel Goldmark, "Creating Desire on Tin Pan Alley," *Musical Quarterly* 90.2 (Summer 2007): 208. Hundreds of digitized sheet music covers, many of which form the basis for Goldmark's study, can be viewed at the website of the Sheet Music Consortium, http://digital.library.ucla.edu/sheetmusic.

55. Ibid., 207, 226, n. 20.

56. Michael R. Pitts and Frank W. Hoffman, *The Rise of the Crooners: Gene Austin, Russ Columbo, Bing Crosby, Nick Lucas, Johnny Marvin, and Rudy Vallee* (Lanham, MD: Scarecrow, 2001), 58. Musician and executive Nathaniel Shilkret tells a different story, one that has Austin earning the usual $50 per week until his third release, when his weekly salary jumped to $4,000. According to Shilkret, Austin's first recording of "My Blue Heaven" landed the singer $40,000 in royalties. Nathaniel Shilkret, *Sixty Years in the Music Business*, eds. Niel Shell and Barbara Shilkret (Lanham, MD: Scarecrow, 2005), 74–75.

57. Ward Seeley, "Will the Great Artists Continue?" *The Wireless Age* (June 1923), 24–25.

58. Ross Laird, *Brunswick Records: A Discography of Recordings, 1916-1931; Volume 1: New York Sessions, 1916-1926* (Westport, CT: Greenwood, 2001), 27–28.

59. The negative attitude toward broadcasting recorded music over the radio lasted until approximately 1924 and seems to have arisen in response to various factors, including an attempt made on the part of broadcasters to differentiate their products from phonograph records and pressure exerted by Tin Pan Alley music publishers, the union of the American Federation of Musicians, and government regulations. However, recorded music was not prohibited, and by 1929, several network and local stations were airing prerecorded half-hour programs known as electrical transcriptions. To my knowledge, the best account of the role of recordings in early radio is Michael Jay Biel, "The Making and Use of Recordings in Broadcasting Before 1936," Ph.D. diss. (Northwestern University, 1977). See also Hilmes, *Radio Voices*, 51; Mark Coleman, *Playback: From the Victrola to MP3, 100 years of Music, Machines, and Money* (Cambridge, MA: Da Capo, 2005), 38–41; Hettinger, *A Decade of Radio Advertising*, 142–55; David Morton, *Off the Record: The Technology and Culture of Sound Recording in America* (New Brunswick, NJ: Rutgers University Press, 2000), 48–50.

60. William Barlow, *Voice Over: The Making of Black Radio* (Philadelphia: Temple University Press, 1999), 19–28.

61. The nickname reportedly owed to the young musician's obsession with saxophonist Rudy Wiedhoeft.

62. Anthony Rudel, *Hello, Everybody!: The Dawn of American Radio* (Boston: Houghton Mifflin Harcourt, 2008), 222–223.

63. Eberly, 35–36. A superb account of how Vallee cultivated a radio fan base prior to the production and release of *The Vagabond Lover* is provided by Allison McCracken, *Real Men Don't Sing: Crooning and American Culture, 1928-1933*, Ph.D. diss. (University of Iowa, 2000), 112–194.

64. A list of "leading music publishers" is printed in Jack Gordon, *How to Publish Your Own Music Successfully* (Chicago: Jack Gordon, 1925), 137–141. Richard A. Peterson writes that Alley houses typically did not publish country music because artists working in the genre were held in

contempt by both ASCAP and the American Federation of Musicians. A marvelous account of the rise of dominant aesthetic trends in radio of this period is Vancour, "The Sounds of 'Radio.'" Richard A. Peterson, *Creating Country Music: Fabricating Authenticity* (Chicago: University of Chicago Press, 1997), 13–14.

65. As Charles Hamm contends, the term "popular music" should apply to music that is "demonstrably the *most* popular, the ones listened to, bought, and performed by the largest number of Americans." Hamm, *Yesterdays: Popular Song in America* (New York: W. W. Norton, 1979), xix. See also Hamm, "Some Thoughts on the Measurement of Popularity in Music," in *Popular Music Perspectives: Papers from the First International Conference on Popular Music Research, Amsterdam, June 1981*, eds. David Horn and Philip Tagg (Göteborg, DE; Exeter, UK: International Association for the Study of Popular Music), 3–15.

66. Gracyk deems the rankings of recordings from this era to be so misleading as to be "fictitious" and potentially harmful. An ostensibly accurate source is found in an account of sales of particular Victor records up to February 1927, but the list is not inclusive and is intended as a selective sample. B. L. Aldridge, "Appendix IV: Record Sales," *The Victor Talking Machine Company* (New York: RCA Sales Corp., 1964), 114; Tim Gracyk, *Popular American Recording Pioneers, 1895-1925* (New York: Haworth, 2000), 8–11.

67. Whitburn, *Pop Memories*; Julius Mattfield, *Variety Music Cavalcade* (Englewood Cliffs, NJ: Prentice-Hall, 1952); David Ewen, *All the Years of American Popular Music* (Englewood Cliffs, NJ: Prentice-Hall, 1977); Roger Kinkle, *Complete Encyclopedia of Popular Music and Jazz, 1900-1950* (New Rochelle, NY: Arlington House, 1974). Kinkle's encyclopedia applies in Hamm, *Yesterdays*, xix, 326–390.

68. Al Dubin, *The Art of Songwriting* (New York: Majestic Music, 1928); Gordon, *How to Publish*; Abel Green, *Inside Stuff on How to Write Popular Songs* (New York: Paul Whiteman, 1927); Harry J. Lincoln, *How to Write and Publish Music*, rev. ed. (Cincinnati: Union Music, 1926); Walter W. Newcomer, *Song Requirements of Talking Pictures* (New York: Walter W. Newcomer, 1928); E. M. Wickes, J. Berg Esenwein, and Harry Von Tilzer, *Writing the Popular Song* (Springfield, MA: Home Correspondence School, 1916).

69. In a period when ragtime was largely equated with jazz, Lincoln defined the "blues via jazz" subgenre as one in which a ragtime musical form served as a backdrop for lyrics conveying feelings of worry, pain, loneliness, and longing. Lincoln, *How to Write and Publish Music*, 30–39.

70. "Ballads Cutting Out Jazz Music," *Los Angeles Times*, August 31, 1919, III16.

71. Gordon, *How to Publish Your Own Music Successfully*, 31.

72. The source was allegedly a manager of a music counter at a McCrory's location in Brooklyn. *Billboard*, October 15, 1927, 24. Abel Green also distinguished ballads from "popular song sensations [published] just for a quick financial 'clean-up' with little commercial life thereafter." Green, 68.

73. Allen Forte, *The American Popular Ballad of the Golden Era, 1924-1950* (Princeton, NJ: Princeton University Press, 1995). See also Forte, *Listening to Classic American Popular Songs* (New Haven, CT: Yale University Press, 2001).

74. In each of these contexts, Allison McCracken reminds us, male singers exploited the popular ballad's expression of romantic or nostalgic sentiments by singing in a mellow, languid manner. The style culminated in radio crooners of the late 1920s and early 1930s, such as Rudy Vallee and Ozzy Nelson, whose voices were renowned for their velvety, melodious, and allegedly "feminized" qualities. Only a few crooners ended up singing on Hollywood's

soundtracks of the transitional era, but whether sung solo or in ensemble, and whether crooned or sung "straight," the popular ballad permitted the expression of the male voice from within the domain of love-struck and decidedly sentimental masculinity. McCracken, *Real Men Don't Sing*, 33–36, 112–72. See also Hamm, *Yesterdays*, 291–297; Jon W. Finson, *The Voices that are Gone: Themes in Nineteenth-Century American Popular Song* (New York: Oxford University Press, 1994), 65–70.

75. Hamm, *Yesterdays*, 326–390; Forte, *The American Popular Ballad of the Golden Era*, 36–41.

76. Edward A. Berlin, *Ragtime: A Musical and Cultural History* (Berkeley, CA: University of California Press, 1980), 11, 166; Finson, *Voices that are Gone*, 229, 238–239.

77. The number of pieces labeled "ragtime" dwindled toward the end of the 1910s, by which point music reviewers favored the term "jazz." Berlin, *Ragtime*, 73.

78. Peter Muir, *Long Lost Blues: Popular Blues in America, 1850-1920* (Champaign, IL: University of Illinois Press). Further, Jeffrey Melnick attributes the introduction of blues idioms to the assimilation of African American culture by the Jewish songwriters and publishers who populated the Alley. Jeffrey Melnick, *A Right to Sing the Blues: African Americans, Jews, and American Popular Song* (Cambridge, MA: Harvard University Press, 1999).

79. Hamm, *Yesterdays*, 357–372. Hamm quotes from Paul Whiteman's book *Jazz* (New York: H. Sears, 1926), 181–182.

80. Philip Furia, *The Poets of Tin Pan Alley: A History of America's Great Lyricists* (New York: Oxford University Press, 1990); Timothy Scheurer, "'Thou Witty': The Evolution and Triumph of Style in Lyric Writing, 1890-1950," in Timothy Scheurer (ed.), *American Popular Music: Readings from the Popular Press* (2 vols.), Vol. 1: *The Nineteenth Century and Tin Pan Alley* (Bowling Green, OH: Bowling Green State University Popular Press, 1989), 104–119. Charles Hamm observes that by the 1920s, Tin Pan Alley was dominated by songwriters who had been born and raised in New York City: "The style of the music and of the lyrics had become a New York style, and general attitudes as to what a song should be and where it should fit into American culture were also shaped by the climate and taste of New York." A good example of the influence of urban culture on song lyrics is Ulf Lindberg's analysis of the amalgam of pastoral and urban themes in the lyrics set by Lorenz Hart to Richard Rodgers's music for "Manhattan" (1925). Lindberg shows how the lyrics cast a New York sensibility onto an environment that is otherwise as reassuring as home. Ulf Lindberg, "Popular Modernism? The 'Urban' Style of Interwar Tin Pan Alley," in *Popular Music* 22.3 (2003): 283–296. See also Hamm, *Yesterdays*, 374–377; Forte, *The American Popular Ballad of the Golden Era*, 28.

81. Dubin, *The Art of Songwriting*, 8, 17.

82. Abel Green, *Inside Stuff on How to Write Popular Songs*, 9.

83. Newcomer's manual tries to lure aspiring songwriters into having their work prepared for publishers—for a fee, of course. Newcomer, *Song Requirements of Talking Pictures*, 9–10.

84. One amusing objection to "love songs" comes by way of lyrics penned by Eugene West for publication in *Variety*. An excerpt reads, "Yes, I love you, no I love you, when I love you, then I love you– / That I love you applesauce is quite a pest. / Do I love you, sure I love you / And that big bank roll back of you." West, "Those 'Love You' Songs," *Variety*, July 13, 1927, 47.

85. Unconfirmed sales of sheet music are in Goldberg, *The Life and Death of Tin Pan Alley*, 218. See also Whitburn, *Pop Memories*, 650.

86. W. C. Handy, qtd. in David Evans, *Big Road Blues: Tradition and Creativity in the Folk Blues* (Berkeley, CA: University of California Press, 1982), 47.

87. Rick Altman, *Silent Film Sound*, 106–115, 126–131, 182–183, 220–226. See also Rick Altman, "Cinema and Popular Song," in *Soundtrack Available: Essays on Film and Popular Music*, eds. Pamela Robertson Wojcik and Arthur Knight (Durham, NC: Duke University Press, 2001), 19–30; Martin Miller Marks, *Music and the Silent Film: Contexts and Case Studies, 1895-1924* (New York: Oxford University Press, 1997), 31–50.

88. Altman, "Cinema and Popular Song"; Altman, *Silent Film Sound*, 182–183.

89. Altman, *Silent Film Sound*, 224.

90. Ibid., 249–269, 345–365.

91. Marks, *Music and the Silent Film*, 143, 202–206.

92. Royal S. Brown, *Overtones and Undertones: Reading Film Music* (Berkeley, CA: University of California Press, 1994), 52.

93. Joseph Carl Breil and Clarence Lucas, *Selection of Joseph Carl Breil's Themes from the Incidental Music to 'The Birth of a Nation'* (New York: Chappell, 1916); Marks, *Music and the Silent Film*, 128–129.

94. Marks, *Music and the Silent Film*, 128.

95. Gerald D. McDonald, "A Bibliography of Song Sheets: Sports and Recreations in American Popular Songs: Part IV: Songs of the Silent Film," *Notes*, 2nd ser. 14.3 (June 1957): 325–352; Gerald D. McDonald, "A Bibliography of Song Sheets: Sports and Recreations in American Popular Songs: Part IV: Songs of the Silent Film (Conclusion)," *Notes*, 2nd ser. 14.4 (September 1957): 507–533.

96. Rick Altman, "Early Film Themes: Roxy, Adorno, and the Problem of Cultural Capital," in *Beyond the Soundtrack: Representing Music in the Cinema*, eds. Daniel Goldmark, Larry Kramer, and Richard Leppert (Berkeley, CA: University of California Press, 2007), 205–224.

97. Ernst Luz, "Theme Playing as Used and Abused," in "Music and the Picture," *Motion Picture News*, August 14, 1915, 130; Tim Crawford, "The Use and Misuse of Themes," in "Presenting the Picture," *Metronome*, May 1, 1927, 24, qtd. in Altman, *Silent Film Sound*, 376.

98. Altman, *Silent Film Sound*, 378. An example from the film industry in the late 1920s involved Billy Rose, the musical supervisor of Universal's *Show Boat* (1929) who reportedly persuaded film producer Carl Laemmle Jr. to use a new song, titled "Lonesome Road" (co-written by Nathaniel Shilkret), by claiming that audiences were tired of hearing the old hits "Ol' Man River" and "Make-Believe." Shilkret, *Sixty Years in the Music Business*, 75.

99. Jeff Smith conceives of the hook as "a kind of counterpart to Romantic music's [leitmotif]." Like the leitmotif, he writes, "hooks are brief snatches of melody or sonorial novelty, usually only a few notes, which provide a starting point for the development of phrase structures." Smith, *The Sounds of Commerce: Marketing Popular Film Music* (New York: Columbia University Press, 1998), 7–8, 15.

100. Cue sheet for *Speedy* (compiled by James C. Bradford), Stills, Posters and Paper Collections, Motion Picture Department, George Eastman House (Rochester, NY).

101. In its printed form on the cue sheet, the refrain lasts 31 measures; the sheet music, published by Robbins Music Corp., contains the standard refrain lasting 32 measures.

102. Similar examples are found in the cue sheets for *The Awakening* (compiled by Ernst Luz), *Ramona* (compiled by Ernst Luz), and *Manhattan Cocktail* (compiled by James C. Bradford). Stills, Posters and Paper Collections, Motion Picture Department, George Eastman House (Rochester, NY).

103. *Billboard*, April 16, 1927, 24; *Billboard*, July 23, 1927, 20.

104. *Billboard*, December 10, 1927, 78. See also *Billboard*, March 24, 1928, 26.

105. "Inside Stuff—Music," *Variety*, May 9, 1928, 77. Early in the 1927–1928 season, the subject of film song tie-ups attracted minimal press attention. *Variety*'s column "Inside Stuff on Music" and *Billboard*'s "Land O' Melody" occasionally mentioned a film song's publisher, but until May 1928, neither devoted much space to film song tie-ups. For examples, see *Variety*, August 24, 1927, 54; *Variety*, October 5, 1927, 55; *Billboard,* January 28, 1928, 22; *Billboard*, February 4, 1928, 24.

106. "Inside Stuff—Music," *Variety*, May 2, 1928, 63.

107. "Inside Stuff—Music," *Variety*, August 1, 1928, 47.

108. Altman, *Silent Film Sound*, 379. Laurence E. MacDonald similarly writes that the popularity of "Charmaine," "Diane," and "Ramona" in 1927 and 1928 "gave Hollywood producers much food for thought about how to publicize movies." MacDonald, *The Invisible Art of Film Music* (New York: Ardsley House, 1998), 17.

CHAPTER 2

1. Jerry Hoffman, "Westward the Course of Tin Pan Alley," *Photoplay*, September 1929, 38–39, 94, 98; reprinted in Miles Kreuger, ed., *Movie Musicals from Vitaphone to 42nd Street, As Reported in a Great Fan Magazine* (New York: Dover, 1975), 56–59.

2. Jesse L. Lasky, "Answering Pertinent Questions," *Billboard*, March 16, 1929, 24.

3. *Variety* quoted Rapee's three-year compensation at $345,000, but the contract between the musician and Warner Bros. adds up to $260,000 plus a minimum of $400 per week against royalties earned for copies of sheet music sold in North America in addition to monies derived from mechanical rights licenses. Summary of contract between Warner Bros. and Erno Rapee (December 31, 1929), Folder 12633B, Warner Bros. Archives, University of Southern California. See also "$345,000 in 3 Yrs for Rapee," *Variety*, January 15, 1930, 73.

4. Rapee arrived in Los Angeles on February 8, 1930, and Warner Bros. terminated his contract on October 10, 1930. Since late 1928, Rapee had been writing songs for New York-based publishing firm DeSylva, Brown & Henderson. "Theme Song Writer Arrives; He Will Direct All Music for Studio," *Los Angeles Times*, February 9, 1930, A8; Erno Rapee: Cancellation Agreement (October 13, 1930), Folder 12633B, Warner Bros. Archives, University of Southern California; "Rapee Settles $220,000 WB Contract on Coast," *Variety*, October 22, 1930, 3.

5. Richard Florida and Scott Jackson, "Sonic City: The Evolving Economic Geography of the Music Industry," *Journal of Planning Education and Research* 29.3 (March 2010): 310–321.

6. In order to stave off the possibility of any single record company securing a monopoly over the reproduction of specific songs, the provision also stated that once a work had been mechanically reproduced and publicly distributed, anyone could record or reproduce the work provided that the statutory rate was paid to the copyright owner. This provision is known today as the compulsory license.

7. Russell Sanjek, *American Popular Music and Its Business: The First Four Hundred Years*, Vol. 3 (1900-1984) (New York: Oxford University Press, 1988), 108.

8. David A. Jasen, *Tin Pan Alley: An Encyclopedia of the Golden Age of American Song* (New York: Taylor & Francis, 2003), xi-xiii. See also David Ewen, *Great Men of American Popular Song* (Englewood Cliffs, NJ: Prentice-Hall, 1972), 59.

9. See footnote 4, chapter 1.

10. In their history of show business published in 1951, *Variety*'s Abel Green and Joe Laurie Jr. reported that in 1912, cabaret presentations cost approximately $1,000 to stage but grossed

as much as $25,000 per week. Abel Green and Joe Laurie Jr., *Show Biz, from Vaude to Video* (New York: Henry Holt, 1951), 78.

11. Sanjek, *American Popular Music*, 20.

12. Histories of ASCAP that promote what Bennie L. DeWhitt calls the organization's "foundation myths" include "5,000,000 Songs," *Fortune* 7.1 (January 1933), 28; Leonard Allen, "The Battle of Tin Pan Alley," *Harper's Magazine*, 181.5 (October 1940), 516; Richard Ergo, "ASCAP and the Antitrust Laws: The Story of a Reasonable Compromise," *Duke Law Journal* 8.2 (Spring 1959): 258–277; Lee C. White, "Musical Copyrights v. The Anti-trust Laws," *Nebraska Law Review* 30.1 (November 1950): 50–67. Bennie L. DeWhitt, "The American Society of Composers, Authors and Publishers, 1914-1938," Ph.D. dissertation (Emory University, 1977), 5–15.

13. DeWhitt, "The American Society of Composers, Authors and Publishers," 16–23. ASCAP dealt in "small" (or "minor") performing rights, which were the rights to non-dramatic works. "Grand" (or "major") performing rights pertained to entire dramatic productions, such as a musical comedy, rather than to the individual songs contained therein. Edwin Claude Mills, *What is ASCAP?* (New York: ASCAP, 1940), 7.

14. *Herbert v. Shanley Co.*, 242 U.S. 591 (1917), 594.

15. *M. Witmark & Sons v. L. Bamberger & Co.*, 291 Fed. 776 (D.C., 1923); *Remick & Co. v. American Automobile Accessories Co.*, 5 Fed. 2d 411 (C.C.A. 6th, 1925); and *Remick & Co. v. General Electric*, 16 F.2d 829 (S.D.N.Y. 1926). Accounts of the Society's often turbulent negotiations with broadcasters appear in Louis G. Caldwell, "The Copyright Problems of Broadcasters," *Journal of Radio Law* 2:2 (April 1932), 287–314.

16. Rick Altman, *Silent Film Sound* (New York: Columbia University Press, 2004).

17. "Minutes of a Conference Held at Fifty-Six West Forty-Fifth Street in Offices of the American Society of Composers, Authors and Publishers," September 20, 1922, New York City, 32; qtd. in Philip Ennis, *The Seventh Stream: The Emergence of Rocknroll in American Popular Music* (Hanover, NH: Wesleyan University Press, 1992), 47.

18. *Film Daily*, August 6, 1922, 70.

19. "Leading Film Circuits Bow to Composers' Royalty Rule," *Variety*, April 1, 1921, 47. The cited theater chains were First National, Southern Enterprises, Sanger Co., William P. Gray, and the Stanley Co.

20. "Publishers Win Movie Music Suit; Court Decides Theatres Must Pay License Fee on Copyrighted Compositions," *New York Times,* July 18, 1924, 7.

21. DeWhitt, "The American Society of Composers, Authors and Publishers," 423.

22. *M. Witmark & Sons v. Calloway*, 22 F.2d 412 (D.C.E.D. Tenn., 1927).

23. "The Forum," *Billboard*, July 23, 1927, 41. The letter writer's name was withheld by request.

24. Rick Altman recounts some of the ways in which exhibitors and publishers resisted ASCAP in *Silent Film Sound*, 352.

25. American Society for Composers, Authors and Publishers, *The Story of ASCAP: An American Institution* (New York: ASCAP, 1946), 10. Two oft-cited cases that exemplify ASCAP's legal triumphs are *Harms v. Cohen*, 279 Fed. 276 (D.C.E.D. Pa., 1922) and *M. Witmark & Sons v. Pastime Amusement Co.*, 298 Fed. 470 (E.D.S.C., 1924), aff'd 2 F.2d 1020 (C.C.A. 4th, 1924).

26. Sanjek, *American Popular Music*, 54. See also Walter L. M. Lorimer, "2¢ Plain, Why Pay More?" *UCLA Law Review* 10:3 (March 1963): 561–574. According to Isidore Witmark of M. Witmark & Sons, when Warner Bros. premiered its first synchronized sound feature film, *Don Juan*, in August 1926, its score, composed by William Axt and David Mendoza, contained

music copyrighted by Robbins Music Co., and Robbins brought suit against Vitaphone. Isidore Witmark and Isaac Goldberg, *Story of the House of Witmark: From Ragtime to Swingtime* (New York: L. Furman, 1939), 423.

27. "Vita Offers $104,000 Yearly for Music," *Variety*, October 6, 1926, 40.

28. The agreement was one of several features that comprised Otterson's appeal to the majors. A detailed account of Otterson's pitch is provided by Douglas Gomery in *The Coming of Sound: A History* (New York: Routledge, 2005), 64–75. Donald Crafton conceives of the studios' support of ERPI's music-licensing department as an example of the cooperative strategies fostered by the studios in order to share the risk involved in the transition to sound. Donald Crafton, *The Talkies: American Cinema's Transition to Sound, 1926-1931*, Vol. 4 of History of the American Cinema, ed. Charles Harpole (New York: Charles Scribner's Sons, 1997), 131, 184. See also "Big Royalties Seen in Vitaphone Deal," *New York Times*, December 21, 1927, 29. The deal with Mills was referred to as the Mills Agreement retroactively, and the first use of the phrase that I have found appears in the summary of *General Talking Pictures Corporation et al. v. American Telephone and Telegraph Co. et al.*, 18 F. Supp. 650 (1937). A copy of the Agreement is included in records of the case *John G. Paine v. Electrical Research Products, Inc.* (Exhibit B), United Artists Corporation Records, Series 2A: O'Brien Legal File, Wisconsin Center for Film and Theater Research.

29. *John G. Paine v. Electrical Research Products, Inc.* (Exhibit B, Section 3). On October 16, 1928, Mills waived the restriction that stated that copyrighted music had to be reproduced exclusively on ERPI products.

30. On May 11, Paramount, United Artists, and MGM signed. Fox did not sign until November 1930, but the studio's contract was effective May 11, 1928. The other major, RKO, was not formed until October 1928. See Gomery, *The Coming of Sound*, 75.

31. "Music Business Sold Film Talking Rights Too Cheaply, Now Believes," *Variety*, August 8, 1928, 49; "Music Men Disgruntled on Sound Film's $100,000 Bargaining for Terms," *Variety*, July 11, 1928, 47.

32. "Big Royalties Seen in Vitaphone Deal," *New York Times*, December 21, 1927, 29; "Protest Society's Classifications," *Variety*, January 11, 1928, 54.

33. An agreement between Mills and RCA was reached in late August 1928. "Bombshell Cast in Am. Society Meeting on 'Classifications,' " *Variety*, April 4, 1928, 55, 57; "Resolutions and Amendments Proposed for American Society," *Variety*, April 11, 1928, 55; "Music Business Sold Film Talking Rights Too Cheaply, Now Believes," *Variety*, August 8, 1928, 49.

34. "Music Men Disgruntled on Sound Film's $100,000 Bargaining for Terms," *Variety*, July 11, 1928, 47; "Producers Invade Music Field: Move Seen as Means to Secure World's Rights and Increased Revenue; Society Denies Any Conflict," *Motion Picture News*, November 24, 1928, 1579.

35. "Sam Fox Scoring Par's Features for 2 Years," *Variety*, December 14, 1927, 55.

36. "Inside Stuff—Music," *Variety*, August 22, 1928, 59; "Inside Stuff—Music," *Variety*, August 29, 1928, 56.

37. Throughout the 1920s, Kern and Gershwin continued to publish under company subsidiaries T. B. Harms and New World Music, respectively. Jerome H. Remick Music Co. became the Remick Music Corp. in May 1928 when Jerome Remick handed over the company to its longtime general manager and secretary Joe Keit. See "J. H. Remick Quits Music," *Billboard*, May 19, 1928, 29; "New York Melody Notes," *Billboard*, May 26, 1928, 27.

38. The fact that Harms received 50 shares designated as class A stock, and Paramount received 50 shares designated as class B stock, might suggest that Harms secured more substantial voting

rights (as is typical but not necessarily true of shareholders of class A stock). In any event, it was agreed that Harms, Inc., would operate for five years as the sales agent for Famous Music Corp., in exchange for 20 percent of the corporation's gross income up to $250 and 15 percent of gross income beyond that cap. A copy of the agreement may be found in Agreement, July 25, 1929, Between Warner Bros. Pictures, Inc. and Max Dreyfus, Louis Dreyfus, et al., Folder 16084B, Warner Bros. Archives, University of Southern California. See also "To Publish, Market Para. Theme Songs," *Billboard*, October 27, 1928, 26; "Coslow and Spier Sign 5-Year Par Agreement," *Variety*, November 6, 1929, 65.

39. "Coslow and Spier Sign 5-Year Par Agreement," *Variety*, November 6, 1929, 65.

40. "M-G-M Buys in on Robbins Music Firm 51%—Robbins Remains; Sees Big Future in Theme Music," *Variety*, September 26, 1928, 55; "M-G-M Robbins Completed," *Variety*, January 9, 1929, 65.

41. Louis B. Mayer, head of MGM, had selected "Wedding of the Painted Doll" for the soundtrack of *The Broadway Melody* while executives of Robbins and MGM on the East Coast were completing contractual agreements. "Inside Stuff—Music," *Variety*, February 13, 1929, 57.

42. "DeSylva, Brown & Henderson's First Year Finds Remarkable Record," *Variety*, February 15, 1928, 55.

43. "Rapee Takes Charge of Firm's Sound Music," *Variety*, November 14, 1928, 57; Letter from Rapee to DeSylva, Brown & Henderson, Inc. (November 19, 1928), Folder 12633B, Warner Bros. Archives, University of Southern California.

44. "WB-Jolson as Music Firm through Berlin," *Variety*, December 26, 1928, 51. Berlin's songs also appeared in Paramount's *The Cocoanuts* (1929), an adaptation of the Broadway musical.

45. Before the agreement between Warner Bros. and Berlin took place, executives of Universal Pictures had offered Berlin a contract that would have seen the composer write 18 songs for the studio's sound films. For reasons that remain unclear, the deal failed to materialize, although a number of songs published by Berlin appeared in Universal films of 1929. "Irving Berlin in Hookup with Universal on Songs," *Billboard*, August 18, 1928, 16; "Berlin Furnishes Theme Songs to U for No Pay," *Variety*, September 26, 1928, 55.

46. On the basis of what *Variety* termed a "friendly association" with United Artists executive Joseph M. Schenck, Berlin composed and published numerous theme songs for the studio's pictures, including "Coquette" for the Mary Pickford melodrama of the same name (1929), "Where Is the Song of Songs for Me?," sung by Lupe Velez in D. W. Griffith's *Lady of the Pavements* (1929), and "With You," "Alice in Wonderland," and "Puttin' On the Ritz," for *Puttin' On the Ritz* (1930).

47. Gomery, *The Coming of Sound*, 60.

48. According to a report in *Billboard*, Warner Bros. considered shelving *The Singing Fool* because the studio did not own the rights to "Sonny Boy." " 'Sonny Boy' Out as Title for Picture," *Billboard*, December 15, 1928, 18.

49. "Film Firms May Publish Music," *Variety*, September 12, 1928, 57. See also Crafton, *The Talkies*, 195.

50. Marcus Witmark served as the firm's titular owner because none of his three sons was of legal age when they started the company in 1886. A vivid if idiosyncratic history of the firm was published as Isidore Witmark and Isaac Goldberg, *Story of the House of Witmark: From Ragtime to Swingtime* (New York: L. Furman, 1939).

51. "Witmark Getting Out Movie Catalog on Talkies of Output for 43 Years," *Billboard*, October 13, 1928, 14.

52. Witmark and Goldberg, *Story of the House of Witmark*, 428–429.

53. The purchase of the Witmark song catalogs furnished Warner Bros. with the copyrights to individual songs but not to entire productions. For example, when MGM acquired the rights to produce Victor Herbert's *Naughty Marietta* in 1930, the studio did not require permission from Warner Bros. to produce a screen adaptation, although Witmark owned rights to the songs from the original stage production. (Incidentally, MGM did not produce the film until 1935.) Also, though M. Witmark & Sons shared a music library with publisher Tams, Inc., the agreement with Warner Bros. did not include the Tams collection. "Tams Deal With W.B. is Denied," *Billboard*, July 27, 1929, 21; "Warners Buy Interest in Music Publishers," *Film Daily*, January 15, 1929, 1–2; "Witmarks Line Up With Warners for Music Publishing Combo," *Variety*, January 16, 1929, 57.

54. "Pop Music Revolution," *Variety*, May 1, 1929, 63; "Music Publishers Find Talkies Boon," *Billboard*, May 18, 1929, 20; *Hollywood Filmograph,* May 11, 1929, 6.

55. August 15, 1929, was the closing date for an agreement signed on July 25. See Agreement, July 25, 1929, Between Warner Bros. Pictures, Inc. and Max Dreyfus, Louis Dreyfus, et al., Folder 16084B, Warner Bros. Archives, University of Southern California. See also "Warner Brothers Get Music Concern," *New York Times*, August 15, 1929, 41; "Warners-Harms Big Deal," *Variety*, August 21, 1929, 5, 57; "Warners Get Harms," *Billboard*, August 24, 1929, 26. For reports on the Warner Bros./Harms deliberations, see the following articles in *Variety*: "Warner-Harms Deal All Cold?" May 29, 1929, 57; "Inside Stuff—Music," June 5, 1929, 56; "Harms Deal On," June 26, 1929, 56; "Warner's 100% Denial," July 31, 1929, 57.

56. "Warners-Harms Big Deal," *Variety*, August 21, 1929, 5.

57. See Sanjek, *American Popular Music*, 55. Of the 140,364 Warner Bros. shares delivered to the stakeholders (worth $7,720,020), 60,364 were cashed at a value of $55 apiece and distributed. $252,255.65 was allocated in total to MPHC, Harms, and DBH in order to cover income taxes and outstanding advances. The remaining $3,067,764.35 was dealt across individual stakeholders in the publishing companies, with Buddy DeSylva taking in the most ($515,132.14) and the remainder allocated to Lew Brown, Ray Henderson, Max Dreyfus, Robert Crawford, Jerome Keit (owner of Remick), and four individuals who had owned partial stock in Harms's subsidiaries. Crawford was also appointed to serve as director of the MPHC, the advisory board of which comprised the presidents of the subsidiaries. In 1930, Dreyfus became president of the MPHC, and Crawford served as co-vice president alongside publisher E. H. Morris. Folder 16084B, Warner Bros. *Archives, University of Southern California; Motion Picture Almanac, 1931* (New York: Quigley, 1931), 451.

58. "Warners-Harms Big Deal," *Variety*, August 21, 1929, 5.

59. Ibid.; also "Pop Music Revolution," *Variety*, May 1, 1929, 63.

60. "Pop Music Revolution," *Variety*, May 1, 1929, 63.

61. " 'U' Buys Gershwin's Rhapsody," *Billboard*, October 26, 1929, 21. The provenance of this case is worth noting because it highlights the power of a musical piece's popularity during the 1929–1930 filmmaking season. When Paul Whiteman agreed to appear in Universal's musical revue *King of Jazz*, he believed that composers at Feist, Inc. would write the film's music and that Feist would supply the songs to Universal free of charge in exchange for royalties from sheet music and record sales. Yet Whiteman's indelible association with George Gershwin's "Rhapsody in Blue" provoked Universal's insistence on including the piece in the film, despite the fact that the work's publisher was New World Music Corp., a subsidiary of Harms (and therefore of Warner Bros.). See "$100,000 for 'Rhapsody' If It's Played in Picture," *Variety*, April 3, 1929, 63.

62. "Musical Firms' Tie-ups and Possibilities in Picture Field are Vastly Important Just Now," *Variety*, April 17, 1929, 71.

63. "Warners-Harms Big Deal," *Variety*, August 21, 1929, 5.

64. Ibid.

65. Ibid.

66. "Fox's Red Star Music Co. Start of Film Concern's Own Organization," *Variety*, October 16, 1929, 65; "Writers Going with Fox's Red Star Co.," *Variety*, October 23, 1929, 73; "Fox Red Star Publishers Will Handle Songs Abroad," *Variety*, October 30, 1929, 79; "Fox Red Star to Farm Out," *Variety*, November 6, 1929, 65; "Fox Red Star Co. With Complete Dept. Lineup," *Variety*, December 18, 1929, 57.

67. RCA controlled both the Radio Music Corp. and NBC, and NBC broadcasters could play, without taking out supplementary licenses, songs from the Fischer and Feist catalogs. "Fischer-Feist-N.B.C. Form New Music Company," *Billboard*, December 14, 1929, 26, 73; "RCA and Feist in Film-Music Tie-up," *Billboard*, February 15, 1930, 3; "Feist and Fischer Guaranteed Average Profit by Radio Music," *Variety*, December 11, 1929, 71; "Back to Melody," *Time Magazine*, December 16, 1929, 45–46; "Warners Act Against Radio," *Billboard*, April 12, 1930, 20.

68. "Coslow and Spier Sign 5-Year Par Agreement," *Variety*, November 6, 1929, 65.

69. Table 1: ASCAP Income From All Sources, 1914-1932, DeWhitt, "The American Society of Composers, Authors and Publishers," 416.

70. "Musicians Storm Hollywood As a Result of Sound Wave," *Billboard*, December 1, 1928, 21; "Tin Pan Alley's Tune and Word Makers Mostly West, Wondering, Like Others," *Variety*, December 12, 1928, 55; "Songsmiths in Coast El'ado," *Variety*, March 27, 1929, 57; "Song Writers Flock to Hollywood," *Motion Picture News*, September 29, 1928, 999; "Tin Pan Alley Denizens Live in Hollywood Now," *Los Angeles Times*, May 28, 1929, A1.

71. Fanya Graham, "Song Writers Desert Gotham for Filmland," *Hollywood Filmograph* 10 (August 1929), 30.

72. "Music and Talent," James Little, *Motion Picture Almanac, 1930* (New York: Quigley, 1930), 131.

73. Dorothy Hawley Cartwright, "Tuning Up the Talkies: Watching the Music Departments Function," *Talking Screen* 1:6 (August 1930): 54.

74. Al Kingston, "Movie Tunes," *Hollywood Filmograph*, May 11, 1929, 22. The "Henry's" referred to might well be Henry's Café, which was located at 6315 Hollywood Blvd. near Vine St. See Marc Wanamaker and Robert W. Nudelman, *Early Hollywood: Images of America* (Mount Pleasant, SC: Arcadia, 2007), 115.

75. "McIntyre Misinformed of Song-Writing Game," *Billboard*, January 10, 1931, 22. The unidentified author of this article contends that another columnist had wrongly cited Kern, DeSylva, and Berlin as the top "money makers of 1930, not knowing that a small army of lyric writers and composers enjoyed the best year of their careers in 1930, including Joe Burke, Al Dubin, (and) Wolfe Gilbert."

76. Thomas S. Hischak, *Through the Screen Door: What Happened to the Broadway Musical When It Went to Hollywood* (Lanham, MD: Scarecrow, 2004).

77. "Film Theme Song Near Monopoly of Publishing Trade," *Variety*, October 17, 1928, 73.

78. Songwriters included Johnny Burke, Harry Pease, Byron Gay, Joseph McCarthy, and Jimmy Monaco. Pat Flaherty, a former executive of DBH, was signed as Red Star's musical director. "Film Theme Song Near Monopoly of Publishing Trade," *Variety*, October 17, 1928, 73; "Warners' Music Writers Leave Fox's Lot—Fox's Own Organization?" *Variety*, September 11, 1929, 65; "Fox Sings Song Writers for New Music Company," *Billboard*, November 2, 1929, 3; "24 Composers on Fox Lot," *Billboard*, February 8, 1930, 21.

79. The contracts and agreements referred to in this paragraph are in Folder 12637B, Warner Bros. Archives, University of Southern California.

80. Crafton, *The Talkies*, 196.

81. The formation of music departments can be seen as one phase in the studio system's history of departmentalization and hierarchization. David Bordwell, Janet Staiger, and Kristin Thompson, *The Classical Hollywood Cinema: Film Style and Mode of Production to 1960* (New York: Columbia University Press, 1985), 123–127, 135–137.

82. "Par-Publix Biggest Musical Organization on Record; Composers, Directors, Etc.," *Variety*, July 11, 1928, 4.

83. Donaldson had also founded, in 1928, a publishing firm, Donaldson, Douglas & Gumble, which quickly became a subsidiary of Harms. Following the creation of Famous Music Corp. by Harms and Paramount, Donaldson was assigned to the studio's music department.

84. "9 Warner Songwriters," *Billboard*, May 18, 1929, 20; Graham, "Song Writers Desert Gotham for Filmland," 30.

85. Crafton, *The Talkies*, 195–196.

86. "Axt to Write Music for Talking Pictures," *Billboard*, May 25, 1929, 21.

87. Ernst Klapholz, qtd. in "Interview with Arthur Lange and Ernst Klapholz," *The Cue Sheet* 7.4 (December 1990): 147.

88. Bill Swigart, "Studio Music," *Variety*, January 8, 1930, 121; Cartwright, "Tuning Up the Talkies," 54–55, 75.

89. Swigart, "Studio Music," 121.

90. David Ewen, *The Life and Death of Tin Pan Alley: The Golden Age of American Popular Music* (New York: Funk and Wagnalls, 1964), 322–326.

91. "Year In Music," *Variety*, January 2, 1929, 21. See also "The Theme Song," *Variety*, January 2, 1929, 28.

92. "Inside Stuff—Music," *Variety*, March 20, 1929, 72.

93. "Inside Stuff—Music," *Variety*, August 28, 1929, 50. See also "Year in Music," *Variety*, January 8, 1930, 119.

94. Richard Koszarski, *Hollywood on the Hudson: Film and Television in New York from Griffith to Sarnoff* (New Brunswick, NJ: Rutgers University Press, 2008).

95. Gerald Bordman, *American Musical Theatre: A Chronicle*, 2nd ed. (New York, Oxford: Oxford University Press, 1992), 439–460; Brian Rust, *The Victor Master Book, Vol. 2 (1925-1936)*, indexes by Malcolm Shaw and Nevil Skrimshire (Stanhope, NJ: Walter C. Allen, 1970); Brian Rust, *The Columbia Master Book Discography, Volume III: Principal U.S. Matrix Series, 1924-1934* (Westport, CT: Greenwood, 1999); Ross Laird, *Brunswick Records: A Discography of Records, 1916-1931; Volume 2: New York Sessions, 1927-1931* (Westport, CT: Greenwood, 2001).

CHAPTER 3

1. Abel Green, "Words About Music," *Variety*, July 3, 1929, 96.

2. Alexander Walker, *The Shattered Silents: How the Talkies Came to Stay* (London: Elm Tree, 1978), 2.

3. "Special Radio Hour Reviews," *Variety*, April 4, 1928, 54. The review is attributed to *Variety* editor Sid Silverman and music reporter (and soon-to-be editor) Abel Green.

4. Michele Hilmes, *Hollywood and Broadcasting: From Radio to Cable* (Champaign, IL: University of Illinois Press, 1999), 53; Donald Crafton, *The Talkies: American Cinema's Transition to Sound, 1926-1931*, Vol. 4 of History of the American Cinema, ed. Charles Harpole (New York: Charles Scribner's Sons, 1997), 44.

5. Richard Barrios, *A Song in the Dark: The Birth of the Musical Film*, 2nd ed. (New York: Oxford University Press, 2009), 107.

6. The figure for sales of sheet music comes from an admittedly dubious document—a publication produced by ASCAP—but the figure is repeated in other primary and secondary sources. American Society of Composers, Authors and Publishers, *Nothing Can Replace Music: Newspaper Editorials and Comments on Music and Radio* (New York: ASCAP, 1933), 1. The figure for film grosses appears in "Those Theme Songs," in *New York Times Encyclopedia of Film: 1937-1940*, ed. Gene Brown (New York: Times Books, 1984), qtd. in Alexander Walker, *The Shattered Silents*, 82.

7. Paul Whiteman's recording of 1928 also thrived on the charts, clocking in 12 weeks in the top spot, and Ruth Etting's recording remained at the top for four weeks. Joel Whitburn, *Joel Whitburn's Pop Memories 1890-1954: The History of American Popular Music* (Menomonee Falls, WI: Record Research Inc., 1986).

8. "New Music Publishing," *Variety*, August 29, 1928, 57.

9. "Explaining Values of Films' Theme Songs for Plugging and Revenue," *Variety*, November 7, 1928, 6.

10. *Variety*, June 13, 1928, 55; "Picture Song Working for Pub. and Screen," *Variety*, October 31, 1928, 56. See also "Film Theme Song Near Monopoly of Publishing Trade," *Variety*, October 17, 1928, 73.

11. Histories of American musical theater overwhelmingly privilege accounts of entire shows over the close analysis of narrative plotting. Raymond Knapp offers a welcome aberration, not to mention an incisive account of the state of the field and its scholarly gaps, in *The American Film Musical and the Formation of National Identity* (Princeton, NJ: Princeton University Press, 2005).

12. The 1920s were peak years for Broadway that saw, in addition to a succession of song hits, audiences paying up to $3.50 for admission to a show and nearly 50 new productions opening in a single season. 40 percent of the theaters that made up the Broadway district by 1929 had been built in the last five years of the decade. Kathleen Morgan Drowne and Patrick Huber, *The 1920s* (Westport, CT: Greenwood, 2004), 22.

13. Gerald Bordman, *American Musical Theatre: A Chronicle*, 3rd ed. (New York: Oxford University Press, 2001), 454–455; Ethan Mordden, *Make Believe: The Broadway Musical in the 1920s* (New York: Oxford University Press, 1997), 107–109.

14. Charles Hamm, *Irving Berlin: Songs from the Melting Pot: The Formative Years, 1907-1914* (New York, Oxford, UK: Oxford University Press, 1997), 184.

15. Mordden, *Make Believe*, 86.

16. Bordman, *American Musical Theatre*, 428.

17. They also plugged "Lady of the Evening," "What'll I Do?" and "All Alone."

18. Joel Whitburn, *Joel Whitburn's Pop Memories 1890-1954*, 649. "Somebody Loves Me" also ranks 20th on Charles Hamm's list "Top Forty: The Most Often Recorded Songs in America, 1900-1950," which is compiled from data found in Roger Kinkle, *The Complete Encyclopedia of Popular Music and Jazz, 1900-1950* (New Rochelle, NY: Arlington House, 1974). See also Charles Hamm, *Yesterdays: Popular Song in America* (New York: W. W. Norton, 1979), 478–488.

19. Numerous Broadway historians credit the use of narrative in musical comedies to the Princess Theatre shows, penned by composer Jerome Kern, lyricist P. G. Wodehouse, and librettist Guy Bolton, between 1915 and 1920. The relatively small size of the venue—299 seats—encouraged the trio to develop so-called "intimate" musicals in which songs arose plausibly from narrative situations. At the time, Bolton explained that he and his collaborators were attempting to create musical comedies that "depend as much upon plot and the development of their characters for success as upon their music." The trio conceived of song lyrics as a means of revealing narrative information and advancing the plot. Of course, the interdependence of songs and narrative was not new, for Offenbach, Gilbert and Sullivan, and George M. Cohan had all made efforts in the same direction. But, unlike the works produced during the late 1890s and early 1900s, the Princess Theatre shows contrasted starkly with the episodic structure of musical revues. Bordman, *American Musical Theatre*, 376.

20. The examples of *Sally* and *Lady, Be Good!* are cited in Mordden, *Make Believe*, 47.

21. Laurence Schwab and B. G. DeSylva, *Good News: A Musical Comedy in Two Acts* (New York: Samuel French, 1932), 44.

22. Two more songs, "You Can't Keep a Good Girl Down" and "The Church Around the Corner," derived from Kern's draft for a Princess Theatre show, *The Little Thing*, but they were debuted in *Sally*.

23. Mordden, *Make Believe*, 184.

24. Hamm, *Irving Berlin*, 184.

25. Ibid., 187.

26. David Ewen, *The Life and Death of Tin Pan Alley* (New York: Funk & Wagnalls, 1964), 114.

27. "Swanee" is said to have catapulted George Gershwin to fame. Jolson's performance inspired the sales of more than one million copies of sheet music and as many records in 1919 alone.

28. Bordman, *American Musical Theatre*, 447.

29. Gerald Bordman, *American Musical Comedy: From Adonis to Dreamgirls* (New York, Oxford, UK: Oxford University Press, 1982), 133.

30. Richard Fehr and Frederick A. Vogel, *Lullabies of Hollywood: Movie Music and the Movie Musical, 1915-1922* (Jefferson, NC: McFarland, 1993).

31. *Paramount Special Introductory Press Book*, Paramount Pictures Pressbooks Collection, Special Collections, Margaret Herrick Library, Academy of Motion Picture Arts and Sciences (Los Angeles).

32. Qtd. in David Cook, *A History of Narrative Film*, 3rd ed. (New York: W. W. Norton, 1996), 243. The coming of sound was disastrous for the careers of many theater musicians. Donald Crafton, *The Talkies: American Cinema's Transition to Sound, 1926-1931, Vol. 4 of History of the American Cinema*, ed. Charles Harpole (New York: Charles Scribner's Sons, 1997), 218–221; Preston Hubbard, "Synchronized Sound and Movie-House Musicians, 1926-29," *American Music* 3.4 (Winter 1985): 429–441; James P. Kraft, "Musicians in Hollywood: Work and Technological Change in Entertainment Industries, 1926-1940," *Technology and Culture* 35.2 (April 1994): 292–299.

33. *Variety*, February 13, 1929, 23.

34. *Variety*, March 6, 1929, 36–37; *Variety*, March 13, 1929, 35; *Variety*, May 29, 1929, 40; *Variety*, June 19, 1929, 19; *Variety*, July 3, 1929, 44–45; *Variety*, December 4, 1929, 39.

35. *Variety*, June 19, 1929, 15.

36. The three exceptions are the books for *The Wedding March* (1928), *Nothing But the Truth* (1929), and *Betrayal* (1929). The scores of all three films include a theme song.

37. Paramount Pictures Pressbooks Collection, Special Collections, Margaret Herrick Library, Academy of Motion Picture Arts and Sciences (Los Angeles).

38. Ibid.

39. Ibid.

40. Ibid.

41. *Cinema Press Books* (microfilm), Margaret Herrick Library, Academy of Motion Picture Arts and Sciences (Los Angeles).

42. Ibid.

43. Ibid.

44. United Artists Corporation Records, Series 1.4: Warner Brothers Pressbooks, 1928-1941, Wisconsin Center for Film and Theater Research (Madison, WI).

45. "Lobby Music Stands Bring Money to Paramount Coffers," *Billboard*, April 5, 1930, 19.

46. Ibid.

47. "Inside Stuff—Music," *Variety*, July 10, 1929, 49.

48. "Exploitation Tips," *Billboard*, September 15, 1928, 24. Incidentally, although "Jeannine, I Dream of Lilac Time" was published by Leo Feist, Inc., a firm unaffiliated with a major production company, Feist nevertheless cross-promoted the song with the film's production company, First National. An advertisement taken out by the publishing company in *Variety* alluded to the studio, film title, and star Colleen Moore. *Variety*, August 1, 1928, 30; *Variety*, August 26, 1928, 37.

49. "Exploitation," *Billboard*, March 23, 1929, 27; "Exploitation," *Billboard*, November 9, 1929, 22.

50. *Cinema Press Books*.

51. Ibid.

52. Ibid.

53. *Paramount Special Introductory Press Book*, Paramount Pictures Pressbooks Collection.

54. *Los Angeles Times*, April 12, 1928.

55. Paramount Pictures Pressbooks Collection. The pressbook informs readers that the composer "has written several important song hits for motion pictures" and that the theme song "Redskin" is sung in the film by Helen Clark (a pseudonym for Victor soprano recording artist Emma Johnson).

56. *Cinema Press Books*.

57. Ibid.

58. Additional examples appear in the Warner Bros. pressbooks, particularly those for *Glad Rag Doll* (1929), which highlights the work of songwriters Jack Yellen and Milton Ager, and *The Squall* (1929), whose theme song was written by Grant Clarke and Harry Akst, the team behind "Am I Blue?" from Warner Bros. recently released production *On With the Show!* (1929). United Artists Corporation Records, Series 1.4: Warner Brothers Pressbooks, 1928-1941.

59. Paramount Pictures Pressbooks Collection.

60. Hilmes, *Hollywood and Broadcasting*, 45.

61. *Variety*, December 16, 1928, 15.

62. "Exploitation Tips," *Billboard*, April 5, 1930, 21.

63. Sam Janney, *Loose Ankles: A Comedy in Three Acts* (New York: Longmans, Green, 1928). Brock Pemberton produced and directed the play's five-month run at the Biltmore Theatre in New York from August 1926 through January 1927. First National initially released an adaptation of the script as a silent film, *Ladies at Play*, in 1926. In 1930, the studio adapted the story again for

sound cinema, hired director Ted Wilde (who had directed Harold Lloyd's *Speedy* in 1928), and reverted to the play's original title, *Loose Ankles*.

64. The song was also featured in two Vitaphone shorts, *Dance of the Paper Dolls* and *The Jazz Rehearsal*, released in November 1929 and May 1930 respectively.

65. "Loose Ankles" was recorded on the Brunswick record label in April 1930 by Andy Kirk and His Twelve Clouds of Joy, featuring vocalist Bill Massey. I have not come across evidence of piano rolls for the song, and certainly the market for rolls had dwindled by the late 1920s. Incidentally, the song's composer, Pete Wendling, was a renowned performer for QRS, the country's largest producer of piano rolls in the earlier part of the century.

66. *Motion Picture Almanac 1930* (Chicago: Quigley, 1930), 212.

67. No fewer than six additional recordings of the song, including those featuring Ruth Etting and Frankie Trumbauer & His Orchestra, were made by various record labels in September and October 1929.

68. For an enlightening discussion of the film's transgressive representation of burlesque performers, as well as its fetishization of female bodies, see Jeffrey P. Smith, "'It Does Something to a Girl. I Don't Know What': The Problem of Female Sexuality in *Applause*," *Cinema Journal* 30.2 (Winter 1991): 47–60.

69. *Weary River* was initially released as a part-talkie, alternating scored, intertitled sequences with sequences featuring synchronized dialogue. Warner Bros. released a silent version of the film in April 1929. *Motion Picture Almanac 1930*, 219; *Film Daily*, January 27, 1929, 4; *Film Daily*, February 10, 1929, 13.

70. "WB-Jolson as Music Firm through Berlin," *Variety*, December 26, 1928, 51.

71. Peter Stanfield discusses various recordings of the ballad and its renderings in several films, although not in *Weary River*. Stanfield, *Body and Soul: Jazz and Blues in American Film, 1927–63* (Urbana, IL: University of Illinois Press, 2005), 44–77.

72. *Film Daily*, January 8, 1929, 4. According to another advertisement, a review in *Evening World* also compared the voice of Barthelmess to that of Al Jolson. *Film Daily*, January 30, 1929, 10–11.

73. *Film Daily*, January 8, 1929, 4.

74. Crafton, *The Talkies*, 509.

75. *Exhibitors Herald-World* (New York: Quigley, 1929).

76. Barthelmess was one of several actors mentioned in *Photoplay*. Others accused of voice doubling were Corinne Griffith, Louise Brooks, Laura La Plante, and Barry Norton. Mark Larkin, "The Truth about Voice Doubling," *Photoplay*, July 1929, 32–33, 108–110; reprinted in Miles Kreuger, ed., *The Movie Musical from Vitaphone to 42nd Street: As Reported in a Great Fan Magazine* (New York: Dover, 1975), 34–37.

77. Ibid.

78. Author's emphasis. *Variety*, January 30, 1929, 14.

79. A more detailed account of industry and public response to the news of Barthelmess's voice doubling may be found in Katherine Spring, "'To Sustain Illusion is All That is Necessary': The Authenticity of Song Performance in Early American Sound Cinema," *Beyond Vitaphone: The Early Sound Short*, spec. issue of *Film History: An International Journal* 23.3 (2011): 285–299.

80. United Artists Corporation Records, Series 1.4: Warner Brothers Pressbooks.

81. *Variety*, January 30, 1929, 22.

82. *Variety*, June 12, 1929.

83. Charles Wolfe, "Vitaphone Shorts and *The Jazz Singer*," *Wide Angle* 22.3 (July 1990): 67.

84. Qtd. in Charles O'Brien, *Cinema's Conversion to Sound: Technology and Film Style in France and the U.S.* (Bloomington, IN: Indiana University Press, 2005), 72.

85. Wolfe, "Vitaphone Shorts and *The Jazz Singer*," 67.

86. O'Brien, *Cinema's Conversion to Sound*, 72.

CHAPTER 4

1. *New York Herald-Tribune*, January 25, 1929; *New York Evening News*, January 25, 1929; *Variety*, January 30, 1929, 22. Other reports in local newspapers indicated that song pluggers seized on the marketability of the theme song, as evidenced by this excerpt from a piece published in the *Wichita Beacon*: "Nearly every person in Wichita who has a whistler and who can whistle, is busy on 'Weary River,' the new tune introduced this week at the Palace by Richard Barthelmess. Few tunes have caught on so quickly as this one." *Wichita Beacon*, April 4, 1929. These newspaper clippings are found in the Richard Barthelmess Scrapbooks, #31 of 50, Special Collections, Margaret Herrick Library, Academy of Motion Picture Arts and Sciences (Los Angeles).

2. The narrative functions of "Weary River" were not overlooked entirely. One writer for the *Christian Science Monitor* commented that the film is "built around a theme-song," and another writer for the *New York Wall Street News* noted that the song is "interwoven into the story." But the majority of reviews emphasized discussions of the song's commercial impetus. Both articles are found in the Richard Barthelmess Scrapbooks, #31 of 50, Special Collections, Margaret Herrick Library, Academy of Motion Picture Arts and Sciences (Los Angeles). *Christian Science Monitor*, January 29, 1929; *New York Wall Street News*, January 29, 1929.

3. Charlie Keil, "Integrated Attractions: Style and Spectatorship in Transitional Cinema," in *Cinema of Attractions Reloaded*, ed. Wanda Strauven (Amsterdam: Amsterdam University Press, 2006), 193–203. A good summary of the scholarship that challenges the opposition between attractions and narrativization in early cinema is found in Charles Musser, "Rethinking Early Cinema: Cinema of Attractions and Narrativity," *Yale Journal of Criticism* 7:2 (Fall 1994): 203–232.

4. Keil, "Integrated Attractions," 199.

5. Musser, "Rethinking Early Cinema"; Lea Jacobs, "Belasco, DeMille and the Development of Lasky Lighting," *Film History* 5:4 (December 1993): 405–418; Scott Higgins, *Harnessing the Technicolor Rainbow: Color Design in the 1930s* (Austin, TX: University of Texas Press, 2007).

6. The only known surviving print of *Double Cross Roads*, housed at the UCLA Film and Television Archive, is labeled "Foreign version with Silent Intertitles." In this version, the character of Mary is referred to as "Marie." I have chosen to respect the spelling of the character's name in the script cited by the entry in the American Film Institute Catalog.

7. This point is underlined by the author of *Song Requirements of Talking Pictures*, a "song-poem" manual published in 1928 with the intent of luring would-be songwriters into having their work prepared for publishers—for a fee, of course. Specious though he may have been, Newcomer cautions the novice songwriter against writing motion picture theme songs unless he or she has already secured a contract with a motion picture producer, lest the writer fail to tie his or her song to a specific movie plot in convincing ways. Walter W. Newcomer, *Song Requirements of Talking Pictures* (New York: Walter W. Newcomer, 1928), 6–8.

8. Mae Tinee, "Surprise Key to this Movie, 'Glad Rag Doll': Recalling 'Things Are Seldom What They Seem,'" *Chicago Daily Tribune*, May 7, 1929, 41.

9. *Variety*, June 5, 1929, 26; Mordaunt Hall, "The Screen," *New York Times*, June 3, 1929, 32.

10. An article published in *Vanity Fair* toward the end of 1929 delineated three categories of song subjects: parental love, unrequited love, and moral education. Theme songs belonging to the first two categories far outnumbered those of the third, but Dougall's observation underlined a fundamental property of theme songs: They tended to arise in specific and delimited narrative situations. Barney Dougall, "Theme-songs, I Love You," *Vanity Fair* 33:3 (November 1929): 67.

11. The subsequent films were *Our Modern Maidens* (1929) and *Our Blushing Brides* (1930). Only the latter was recorded with synchronous sound.

12. Jeff Smith and Murray Smith caution against overextending the analysis of the meanings of song lyrics and insist on the importance of examining the narrative contexts in which film song lyrics can be heard. Jeff Smith, *The Sounds of Commerce: Marketing Popular Film Music* (New York: Columbia University Press, 1998), 166–168; Murray Smith, "The Sound of Sentiment: Popular Music, Film, and Emotion," *16:9* (November 2006), http://www.16-9.dk/2006-11/side11_inenglish.htm (accessed July 1, 2010).

13. Claudia Gorbman, *Unheard Melodies: Narrative Film Music* (Bloomington, IN: Indiana University Press), 58, 84–89; Dmitri Tiomkin, "Composing for Films," in *Film Music: From Violins to Video*, ed. James Limbacher (Metuchen, NJ: Scarecrow, 1974), 60–61.

14. "Novela Week," *Buffalo Times*, August 24, 1930. This item is found in the Richard Barthelmess Scrapbooks, #34 of 50, Special Collections, Margaret Herrick Library, Academy of Motion Picture Arts and Sciences (Los Angeles).

15. The inaugural program of *Amos 'n' Andy* was broadcast on March 19, 1928, through WMAQ, a Chicago station. By August of the following year, it had become a sponsored program (by Pepsodent) on NBC's Blue Network, covering the Northeastern and Upper Midwestern United States. Transmission through NBC's Orange Network, for the Pacific Coast, began in November 1929 and resulted in coast-to-coast broadcasts of the show. *Amos 'n' Andy* was NBC's first program to be distributed by syndication across the country. For Melvin Patrick Ely, author of *The Adventures of Amos 'n' Andy*, the show's appeal "crossed boundaries of region, social standing, age, ethnic origin, and even race"; Michele Hilmes and William Barlow, however, have each offered a nuanced analysis of the ambivalence and sometimes controversy that characterized listener responses to the blackface comedy that defined the show. Melvin Patrick Ely, *The Adventures of Amos 'n' Andy: A Social History of an American Phenomenon* (New York: Free Press, 1992), 9; Michele Hilmes, *Radio Voices: American Broadcasting, 1922–1952* (Minneapolis: University of Minnesota Press, 1997), 75–96; William Barlow, *Voice Over: The Making of Black Radio* (Philadelphia: Temple University Press, 1999) 35–48.

16. Barlow, *Voice Over*, 40; Hilmes, *Radio Voices*, 88, 91.

17. Hilmes, Radio Voices, 91–92. Hilmes also examines the ways in which the show's characterization of black identity relied less on the program's self-references to race than on dialects, accents, and ungrammatical English that audiences would associate with Jim Crow and Zip Coon. Hilmes, *Radio Voices*, 87–88.

18. Ryan Jay Friedman, *Hollywood's African American Films: The Transition to Sound* (New Brunswick, NJ: Rutgers University Press), 153–179.

19. *Exhibitors Herald-World*, October 11, 1930; qtd. in Steve J. Wurtzler, Electric Sounds: Technological Change and the Rise of Corporate Mass Media (New York: Columbia University Press, 2007), 21.

20. The film's soundtrack includes two other incidental songs, "Nobody Knows But the Lord" and "Am I Blue?," the latter of which had already allegedly sold half a million copies of sheet music after Ethel Waters sang it in the Warner Bros. musical *On With the Show!* (1929). But it was Ellington's performance that captured the attention of reviewers. Ed O'Malley, for instance, gushed in *Hollywood Filmograph*, "The auditor gets a five minutes' twirl of Duke Ellington's famous jazz orchestra (colored and gee! lads, how they can hiccough through those trumpets and saxophones!)." Ed O'Malley, "Preview: Amos 'N' Andy in 'Check and Double Check,'" *Hollywood Filmograph*, September 27, 1930, 21. Unconfirmed sales figures for sheet music of "Am I Blue?" are printed in Isaac Goldberg, *Tin Pan Alley: A Chronicle of American Popular Music* (New York: John Day, 1930; New York: Frederick Ungar, 1961), 218.

21. The relationship between Ellington and Mills would be considered exploitative by today's standards, given that Mills retained 45 percent of compensation received by Ellington's performances and recordings, and that an additional 10 percent went to Mills's lawyer. Harvey G. Cohen, "The Marketing of Duke Ellington: Setting the Strategy for an African American Maestro," *Journal of African-American History* 89.4 (Autumn 2004): 291–315. See also Barlow, *Voice Over*, 23–24.

22. Philip K. Eberly, *Music in the Air: America's Changing Tastes in Popular Music, 1920-1980* (New York: Hastings House, 1982), 49; qtd. in Cohen, "The Marketing of Duke Ellington," 298.

23. Cohen, "The Marketing of Duke Ellington," 299.

24. Along with Paul Whiteman and His Orchestra, the Rhythm Boys also performed in *King of Jazz* (1930), Universal's feature-length musical released two months before the release of *Check and Double Check*.

25. Entry for *Check and Double Check* (1931), *American Film Institute Catalog*, available online at http://afi.chadwyck.co.uk/home [June 1, 2011].

26. Gregory D. Black, *Hollywood Censored: Morality Codes, Catholics, and the Movies* (Cambridge, UK: Cambridge University Press, 1996), 60–61; Colin Schindler, *Hollywood in Crisis: Cinema and American Society, 1929-1939* (New York: Routledge, 1996), 96.

27. Black, *Hollywood Censored*, 60.

28. John V. Wilson to Irving Thalberg, August 8, 1931, Production Code Administration Files, Margaret Herrick Library, Academy of Motion Picture Arts and Sciences (Los Angeles).

29. Heather Laing, *The Gendered Score: Music in 1940s Melodrama and the Woman's Film* (Aldershot, UK; Burlington, VT: Ashgate, 2007).

30. Jeff Smith, *The Sounds of Commerce: Marketing Popular Music* (New York: Columbia University Press, 1998).

31. Gorbman, *Unheard Melodies*; Kalinak, *How the West Was Sung*: Music in the Westerns of John Ford (Berkeley, CA: University of California Press, 2007). Kathryn Kalinak, *Settling the Score* (Madison, WI: University of Wisconsin Press, 1992).

32. Norbert Lusk, "Joan Crawford-Clark Gable Combination Powerful Lure to Eastern Film Audiences," *Los Angeles Times*, December 6, 1931, B13; *Variety*, December 1, 1931, 15; Mordaunt Hall, "The Screen," *New York Times*, November 28, 1931, 31. In a list of films shown during the final week of November, the *New York Times* disclosed that "Miss Crawford sings a new song" in *Possessed*. "Broadway's New Films," *New York Times*, November 29, 1931, X6.

CHAPTER 5

1. L. Wolfe Gilbert, "Song Writing for Pictures," *Variety*, January 8, 1930, 119.

2. Philip K. Scheuer, "Picture-Lyric Trend Queried," *Los Angeles Times*, August 4, 1929, B13.

3. "Inside Stuff—Music," *Variety*, March 5, 1930, 54; "Popular Numbers Steadily Nosing Out Congested Catalogs of Picture Tunes," March 26, 1930, 73; "Music Men Again on Top," *Variety*, August 27, 1930, 75.

4. "Music Now in the Studios," *Variety*, December 29, 1931, 40.

5. Donald Crafton, *The Talkies: American Cinema's Transition to Sound, 1926-1931* (New York: Scribner, 1997), vol. 4, *History of the American Cinema*, ed. Charles Harpole, 183–187.

6. Crafton quotes an investment advisor who claimed, "The motion-picture-going habit is so deeply rooted in the American public that even in times of business depression, theater attendance is little affected." Crafton, *The Talkies*, 181–215.

7. Ross Melnick, *American Showman: Samuel "Roxy" Rothafel and the Birth of the Entertainment Industry, 1908-1935* (New York: Columbia University Press, 2012), 343.

8. One of many examples was an article in *Billboard* wherein the author warns, "If we are in for a course of theme songing—if everything we do is to be motivated by musical patterns, there will be a chorus of disgust unrivaled in all the concerts the world has ever known." "Music Engineering," *Billboard*, December 28, 1929, 4.

9. "Forum," *Spokane Spokesman Review*, October 7, 1928. This item is found in the Colleen Moore Scrapbooks, Special Collections, Margaret Herrick Library, Academy of Motion Picture Arts and Sciences (Los Angeles).

10. Edwin M. Bradley, *The First Hollywood Musicals: A Critical Filmography of 171 Features, 1927 through 1932* (Jefferson, NC: McFarland, 1996), 277.

11. Crafton, *The Talkies*, 360.

12. "Too Many Songs," *Variety*, November 21, 1928, 24. See also "Inside Stuff—Music," *Variety*, December 12, 1928, 58; Abel Green, "Disc Reviews," *Variety*, July 24, 1929, 72.

13. "Music Industry on Higher Plane," *Billboard*, July 13, 1929, 26.

14. Lewis W. Physioc, "Pictures Problems," *International Photographer* 1.8 (September 1929): 7.

15. "Music Industry on Higher Plane," *Billboard*, July 13, 1929, 26.

16. "Inside Stuff—Pictures," *Variety*, April 17, 1929, 18. The article ends by condemning "Woman Disputed, I Love You" as a "horrible example" of song interpolation. One year earlier, the journal had extolled that song's virtues as a marketing tool.

17. "Music Industry on Higher Plane," *Billboard*, July 13, 1929, 26.

18. Kurt London, *Film Music: A Summary of the Characteristic Features of its History, Aesthetics, Technique; and possible Developments*, trans. by Eric S. Bensinger (London: Faber & Faber, 1936; reprinted New York: Arno, 1970), 120–121.

19. Bradley, *First Hollywood Musicals*, 277.

20. Rick Altman, *Silent Film Sound* (New York: Columbia University Press), 318.

21. "Film World Marvels at Screen's Song Hits," *Billboard*, March 8, 1930, 19.

22. "Along the Coast," *Variety*, May 21, 1930, 56. See also "Picture Title Plugs Dropped," *Variety*, February 26, 1930, 69.

23. For example, in a special article he penned for *Variety*, Erno Rapee wrote, "Starting with the 'theme song,' a tuneful bit that could be fitted here and there into a story, music has grown in importance until it has become organically a part of the whole picture." Erno Rapee, "Vitaphone and the American Composer," *Variety*, June 25, 1930, 2.

24. "Film World Marvels at Screen's Song Hits," *Billboard*, March 8, 1930, 19.

25. "Songs Must Fit Action in Pictures—Ray Perkins," *Hollywood Filmograph*, 5.

26. "Theme Songs Within Reason Or Producers Will Cut 'Em," *Billboard*, May 31, 1930, 24.

27. "Talking Films Bring Music to Masses," *Los Angeles Times*, May 4, 1930, B11.

28. Robert Crawford, "90% of America's Music Hollywood Written," *Variety*, June 25, 1930, 1.

29. "Musical Films are Taboo: Song Writers Returning East in Great Numbers," *Billboard*, August 23, 1930, 3, 91. A poll conducted by *Film Daily* of 333 newspapers, trade papers, and fan publications concluded that the ten best pictures released between December 1, 1929, and November 30, 1930, were *All Quiet on the Western Front, Abraham Lincoln, Holiday, Journey's End, Anna Christie, The Big House, With Byrd at the South Pole, The Divorcee, Hell's Angels*, and *Old English*. None of these were musicals, though the soundtracks of *With Byrd at the South Pole, The Divorcee*, and *Anna Christie* each incorporated at least one song in its entirety. (Additionally, *All Quiet on the Western Front* was released with a title theme song written by Lou Handman and Bernie Grossman.) The only musical that won an Academy Merit Award for the 1929–1930 season was *King of Jazz*; the award was given to Herman Rosse for "Art Direction Achievement."

30. "Producers Ponder as Small Towns Shun Musical Films," *Billboard*, August 2, 1930, 19.

31. "Picture Audiences Turning 'Thumbs Down' on Revues," *Billboard*, June 14, 1930, 18.

32. "Matter of Talker Songs Sharply Argued by Studios and Writers," *Variety*, July 9, 1930, 3.

33. Bill Swigart, "Along the Coast," *Variety*, June 18, 1930, 83; "Inside Stuff—Music," *Variety*, July 16, 1930, 51; "'30 in the Land of Nod," *Variety*, December 31, 1930, 20.

34. "Musicals Now Studios' Own Problems," *Variety*, September 17, 1930, 4; "Theme Songs Within Reason Or Producers Will Cut 'Em," *Billboard*, May 31, 1930, 24; "Warners Curtailing Theme Songs in Pcts.," *Variety*, July 9, 1930, 57.

35. Bradley, *First Hollywood Musicals*, 277.

36. Laurence Bergreen, *As Thousands Cheer: The Life of Irving Berlin* (1990; reprinted, New York: Da Capo, 1996), 293.

37. "Matter of Talker Songs Sharply Argued by Studios and Writers," *Variety*, July 9, 1930, 3.

38. "Music Films are Taboo," *Billboard*, August 23, 1930, 3, 91.

39. Cinema Pressbooks on Microfilm, Margaret Herrick Library, Academy of Motion Picture Arts and Sciences (Los Angeles).

40. Ibid.

41. Ibid.

42. United Artists Corporation, Series 1.7: Warner Bros. Contract and Legal Files, *The Lash*, Wisconsin Center for Film and Theater Research (Madison).

43. Letter from Thayer Hobson to Jacob Wilk, April 14, 1930; Letter from R. W. Perkins to Jack Warner, May 16, 1930, Series 1.7: Warner Bros. Contract and Legal Files, *The Lash*.

44. Letter from Arthur Franklin to E. H. Murphy, June 17, 1930, Series 1.7: Warner Bros. Contract and Legal Files, *The Lash*.

45. Although Warner Bros. had not purchased shares in the song's publisher Leo Feist, Inc., and would therefore not profit from sales of phonograph recordings, the contractual agreement between studio and publisher provided Warner Bros. with 2¢ per copy of "Adios!" sheet music sold in the United States and Canada. Contract dated May 13, 1930, between Harry Archer, Irving Caesar, Leo Feist, Inc., and Warner Bros. Pictures Inc. Series 1.7: Warner Bros. Contract and Legal Files.

46. "Warners Hot After Own Network," *Variety*, June 18, 1930, 83.

47. "Warner Bros. Go Heavily Into Radio Field," *Variety*, June 25, 1930, 3.

48. "Warners Sell Brunswick Co.," *Variety*, November 10, 1931, 61.

49. "Warners Flop in Song Game," *Billboard*, June 6, 1931, 18; "Warner Reign Nearing End," *Billboard*, June 27, 1931, 20.

50. "Famous Pays Off," *Variety*, December 17, 1930, 58.

51. "Leo Feist Closing All Minor Branches," *Billboard*, February 21, 1931, 5; "Feist Closes Boston," *Variety*, February 25, 1931, 62; "Coast Offices Move," *Variety*, February 25, 1931, 62; "Berlin Cuts Overhead," *Variety*, March 4, 1931, 64; "Arranging Dept. Out and Salaries Cut at Berlin's," *Variety*, April 29, 1931, 83. A report from Chicago stated, "Music situation locally is in a precarious way, with most of the offices overstaffed. With conditions what they are some of the music boys are talking of doubling up on space and cutting down the overhead." "Music Pubs Offices in Chicago Costly," *Variety*, May 6, 1931, 67.

52. For example, leases on Remick offices located in Detroit, Philadelphia, and Boston were cancelled as of May 2, 1931. Memo from Geo. W. Crowley Jr. to Mr. A. McBeath (n.d.), Folder 16085A, Warner Bros. Archives, University of Southern California. See also *Variety*, August 3, 1930, 65; *Billboard*, May 3, 1930, 27; *Billboard*, May 24, 1930, 26.

53. *Billboard*, March 7, 1931, 22.

54. Warner Bros. continued to pare down its office space through early 1932. "Old Methods Passing Out," *Billboard*, March 7, 1931, 22; "Harms Moving in With Other WB Music Firms," *Variety*, May 6, 1931, 66; "WB Publishers Doubling Up on Office Space for $3,000 Saving and Letouts," *Variety*, January 12, 1932, 61.

55. "Coast Shakeup As Music Offices Start Cutting Down," *Variety*, December 3, 1930, 65.

56. In November 1930, Jay Witmark succeeded Pat J. Flaherty as general manager of Red Star. Flaherty was allegedly released after giving publication rights of songs in a Fox picture to another company. In December 1931, Fox reportedly disbanded its music department, retaining only Ben Jackson and his assistant Marcelle Silver. "Open Door Policy For Songsters Is Witmark Policy," *Motion Picture News*, November 1, 1930, 55; "Sam Fox as Red Star's Music Distributor," *Variety*, June 16, 1931, 57; "Jay Witmark May Publish," *Billboard*, June 13, 1931, 22; "Fox Studio Breaks Up Its Music Department," *Variety*, December 8, 1931, 61.

57. Rapee proceeded to work as NBC's general music director and, eventually, as conductor of the Radio City Music Hall Orchestra. *Variety*, September 24, 1930, 65; "Warner Bros. Still Paying," *Billboard*, May 9, 1931, 23; "Rapee Settles $220,000 WB Contract on Coast," *Variety*, October 22, 1930, 3; Bradley, 279.

58. They signed with the studio for a fee of $100,000 apiece per film against 25 percent of profits. Frederick Nolan, *The Sound of Their Music: The Story of Rodgers & Hammerstein* (New York: Applause Theatre & Cinema Books), 64–65.

59. "Abel Baer Back With Feist," *Billboard*, November 29, 1930, 23.

60. "Melody Trio Splits as DeSylva Remains West," *Variety*, March 11, 1931, 68.

61. Max Steiner, "Scoring the Film," in *We Make the Movies*, ed. Nancy Naumberg (New York: W. W. Norton, 1937), 219.

62. "Silver Turns Publisher," *Billboard*, November 1, 1930, 25; "Nacio Herb Brown to Publish," *Billboard*, November 22, 1930, 24.

63. The different names supplied for each studio reflect discrepancies in two sources: "Personnel of Studios," *Film Daily Yearbook of Motion Pictures of 1930*, ed. J. W. Alicoate (New York: Film

Daily, 1930), 627–631; and "Studio Personnel," *Motion Picture Almanac 1930* (Chicago: Quigley, 1930), 192–195. But it is known that Arthur Lange initially worked at MGM, then at RKO and Paramount, before signing with Fox, and that Martin Broones remained at MGM until December 1931. "Studio is maintaining only a skeleton group to handle the little work necessary to record-ings," reported *Variety* at that time. "Broones Out at M-G," *Variety*, December 22, 1931, 53; "The American Film Institute's Hugo Friedhofer Oral History," interview conducted by Irene Kahn Atkins, in *Hugo Friedhofer: The Best Years of His Life; A Hollywood Master of Music for the Movies*, ed. Linda Danly (Lanham, MD: Scarecrow, 2002), 33.

64. The figure was calculated by multiplying the estimated number of songwriters in Hollywood (300) by an average weekly pay of $350. "Dropping of Song Writers Saves $100,000 Weekly," *Billboard*, December 6, 1930, 5.

65. "No Contracts for Music Writers Planned for Future Studio Setup," *Variety*, March 11, 1931, 68.

66. "M-G Lads Settle for 64% After a Battle," *Variety*, December 19, 1930, 57.

67. "West Coast No More a Gold Coast, Declare All the Film Songwriters," *Variety*, July 30, 1930, 97, 100; "Musical Films Are Taboo: Song Writers Returning East in Great Numbers," *Billboard*, August 23, 1930, 3. See also "Red Star Cut," *Variety*, February 26, 1930, 69; "Warner Group to Cut Down Overhead," *Variety*, August 13, 1930, 65; "Movie Musicals in Balance; Staff Curtailment Rumored," *Billboard*, July 16, 1930, 3. Lew Pollack's contract with Warner Bros. expired in May 1931, but Warner Bros. was required by contract to retain six of its key song-writers: Harry Warren, Buddy Green, Sammy Stept, Archie Gottler, Al Dubin, and Joe Burke. "Melograms," *Billboard*, May 9, 1931, 22; "Warner Bros. Still Paying," *Billboard*, May 9, 1931, 23. Months later, when Al Dubin returned to Hollywood to compose a score for the Warner Bros. musical *Side Show* (1931), *Variety* called his a "pioneer trip," noting that "the songwriter is the first in months to make the east-west jump." *Variety*, April 29, 1931, 83.

68. Myrtle Gebhart, "Tin Pan Alley Says Goodbye," *Los Angeles Times*, May 10, 1931, K9.

69. Christopher Palmer, *The Composer in Hollywood* (New York, London: Marion Boyars, 1990), 25. See also *ASCAP Biographical Dictionary*, 4th ed. (New York, London: R. R. Bowker, 1980); Gary Mormenstein, *Hollywood Rhapsody: Movie Music and Its Makers, 1900 to 1975* (New York: Schirmer, 1997); John Russell Taylor, *Strangers in Paradise: The Hollywood Émigrés, 1933-1950* (New York: Holt, Reinhart and Winston, 1983); Tony Thomas, *Film Score: The Art & Craft of Movie Music* (Burbank, CA: Riverwood, 1991).

70. Palmer, *Composer in Hollywood*, 21–22.

71. Born in New Haven, Connecticut, Newman studied with the eminent Polish pianist and composer Sigismond Stojowski before heading to Broadway, where he conducted the orchestras for numerous hit revues and musical comedies, among them shows written by the Gershwins, Richard Rodgers, Lorenz Hart, Cole Porter, Jerome Kern, Vincent Youmans, and Sigmund Romberg.

72. "A Portrait of Hugo Friedhofer by Linda Danly," in Danly, *Hugo Friedhofer*, 6.

73. *Motion Picture Alamanac 1930* (Chicago: Quigley, 1930), 215.

74. "The Caballero's Way," *Literature Collection*. Available online at http://www.literaturecol-lection.com/a/o_henry/73/ [November 15, 2011].

75. Walsh was slated to portray the Kid in *In Old Arizona* but lost his right eye in a car accident shortly after filming commenced. Irving Cummings assumed the role of director, and Warner Baxter was cast as the Kid.

76. Mordaunt Hall, "The Screen," *New York Times*, January 21, 1929, 26.

77. The film's synchronization license (figure 5.1) credits Warner Baxter with the composition of "Song of the Cisco Kid." "My Tonia" was written by DeSylva, Brown, and Henderson, whose self-named publishing company had become Fox's exclusive song publisher in November 1928. In line with contemporaneous techniques of movie song promotion, Nick Lucas made a hit recording of "My Tonia" on the Brunswick record label in December 1928, just before the film's release one month later.

78. Whereas Warner Baxter sings smoothly and clearly, the Kid in O. Henry's story sings with a voice described as "like a coyote with bronchitis."

79. David Ewen, *The Life and Death of Tin Pan Alley: The Golden Age of American Popular Music* (New York: Funk and Wagnalls, 1964), 81–83. Ewen writes, "It is hardly possible to hear (the song's) strains today without visualizing a line of chorus girls throwing their garters at men in the audience (the height of stage naughtiness in the 1890s!)." Sigmund Spaeth relates, "In the original Connors interpretation, the motion (that accompanied the refrain) was of the type known today as the 'bump.' " Sigmund Spaeth, *A History of Popular Music in America* (New York: Random House, 1948), 258.

80. Peter Stanfield, "An Excursion into the Lower Depths: Hollywood, Urban Primitivism, and 'St. Louis Blues,' 1929–1937," *Cinema Journal* 41:2 (Winter 2002): 84–108. Ryan Jay Friedman provides a consummate analysis of *Safe in Hell*'s representation of race in *Hollywood's African American Films: The Transition to Sound* (New Brunswick, NJ: Rutgers University Press, 2011), 120–126.

81. David J. Steffan, *From Edison To Marconi: The First Thirty Years Of Recorded Music* (Jefferson, NC: McFarland), 132.

82. A studio contract reveals that McKinney was paid $333.33 per week, plus return transportation from New York, for her work on the film. Victor Marconi, slated to play a supporting role as one of the island's inhabitants, earned four times as much. Minimum Contract for Artists (May 14, 1931), Folder 2879, Warner Bros. Archives, University of Southern California (Los Angeles).

83. The song was written in mid-1930 by Clarence Muse (who had starred in Fox Film's 1929 all-black musical *Hearts in Dixie*) and the Creole brothers Leon and Otis René, allegedly for the purpose of having Muse sing it in *Under a Virginia Moon*, a play directed in 1930 by George Fawcett at his Vine St. Theater in Hollywood. The play flopped, but the song was republished and popularized by recordings both by Louis Armstrong (in April 1931) and Paul Whiteman (in October 1931), with vocals by Mildred Bailey and the Jesters. "The Fawcett Family," *Variety*, Wednesday, June 25, 1930, 127; "Inside Stuff—Music," *Variety*, December 8, 1931, 61.

84. They are not sung on the film's soundtrack, but some of the lyrics of "Pagan Moon" might have denoted, for audiences familiar with them, a lost past that resonates with Gilda's memories of Carl. (For example, "I can remember that night in your arms / Underneath the pagan moon.") It is plausible to assume that some spectators of 1931 knew the lyrics, because the song was recorded by a number of artists around and shortly following the time of the film's release on December 12, 1931. The Ted Black Orchestra recorded the song for Victor on December 7, and Abe Lyman and His Orchestra struck a recording for Brunswick on December 24. Backed by the Carl Fenton Orchestra, Bing Crosby crooned "Pagan Moon" on his CBS show "Presenting Bing Crosby" on January 7, 1932. At the end of the month, the song appeared in another Warner Bros. production, a Merrie Melodies animated short titled "Pagan Moon."

85. United Artists Corporation Records, Series 1.4: Warner Brothers Pressbooks, 1928-1941, Wisconsin Center for Film and Theater Research (Madison, Wisconsin).

86. Alan Gevinson, *American Film Institute Catalog: Within Our Gates: Ethnicity in American Feature Films, 1911-1960* (Berkeley, CA: University of California Press, 1997), 785. The play was adapted by Dorothy Heyward, wife of DuBose.

87. Friedman, *Hollywood's African American Films*, 29.

88. These lyrics derive from a 19th-century British folk song, "The Pirate Ship," and appear in the Sinclair Lewis novel from which *Arrowsmith* was adapted. In 1950, the tune was rewritten as "The Roving Kind" and inspired a hit recording by Guy Mitchell.

89. "Future Chief Music Income from Royalties, with Sheets and Recording Unimportant, It Seems to Publishers," *Variety*, April 22, 1931, 67; "Morris Firm Shows Profit," *Billboard*, April 25, 1931, 29.

90. Martin Rubin, "Busby Berkeley and the Backstage Musical," in *Hollywood Musicals: The Film Reader*, ed. Steven Cohan (London and New York: Routledge, 2002), 57.

91. Ibid.

92. Crafton, *The Talkies*, 315–316.

93. Lew Michelson, "Lyrics and Music," *Hollywood Filmograph*, January 17, 1931, 19.

CONCLUSION

1. Kathryn Kalinak, *Settling the Score: Music and the Classical Hollywood Film* (Madison, WI: University of Wisconsin Press, 1992), 170; Jeff Smith, *The Sounds of Commerce: Marketing Popular Film Music* (New York: Columbia University Press, 1998), 45.

2. Smith also examines variants of the monothematic score that persisted through the 1990s. Smith, *Sounds of Commerce*, 45, 214–227.

3. Kathryn Kalinak, *How the West Was Sung: Music in the Westerns of John Ford* (Berkeley, CA: University of California Press, 2007), 158–180.

4. Kalinak, *Settling the Score*, 170–179. A complete analysis of *Laura* is found in *Settling the Score*, 159–183.

5. Smith, *Sounds of Commerce*, 32–33; Alexander Doty, "Music Sells Movies: (Re)New(ed) Conservatism in Film Marketing," *Wide Angle* 10.2 (1988): 71.

6. Smith, *Sounds of Commerce*, 59–60.

7. Unlike Crawford in *Possessed*, however, Hayworth lip-synched her song performances for *Gilda*. The songs were dubbed by Anita Ellis.

8. Of this passage, Adrienne L. McLean writes, "It is a privileged moment.... We are alone with Gilda and her song: we feel her pain at being what she is, a woman, one of a sex always blamed when the world goes wrong." Adrienne L. McLean, " 'It's Only That I Do What I Love and Love What I Do': 'Film Noir' and the Musical Woman," *Cinema Journal* 33.1 (Autumn 1993): 5. See also Adrienne L. McLean, *Being Rita Hayworth: Labor, Identity, and Hollywood Stardom* (Piscataway, NJ: Rutgers University Press, 2004), 144–171.

9. The argument that the song is disruptive of narrative linearity is made by Richard Dyer, "Resistance through Charisma: Rita Hayworth and *Gilda*," in E. Ann Kaplan, ed., *Women and Film Noir* (London: BFI, 1978), 91–99; Laura Mulvey, "Visual Pleasure and Narrative Cinema," *Screen* 16.3 (Autumn 1975): 11-12; Kaja Silverman, *The Subject of Semiotics* (New York, Oxford, UK: Oxford University Press, 1983), 230.

10. McLean, "'It's Only That I Do What I Love and Love What I Do,'" 7.

11. Some examples can be found in Tom Gunning, "The Cinema of Attractions: Early Film, its Spectator and the Avant-garde," in *Early Cinema: Space, Frame, Narrative*, ed. Thomas Elsaesser (London: BFI, 1990), 56–62; Donald Crafton, "Pie and Chase: Gag, Spectacle and Narrative in Slapstick Comedy," in *Classical Hollywood Comedy*, eds. Kristine Brunovska Karnick and Henry Jenkins (New York: Routledge, 1994), 106–119; Geoff King, *New Hollywood Cinema: An Introduction* (New York: Columbia University Press, 2002), 219.

APPENDIX 1

1. Exhibit B, Schedule B of *John G. Paine v. Electrical Research Products, Inc.*, July 1929 (Series 2A, Box 87-1, United Artists Collection, Wisconsin Center for Film and Theater Research). The supervisor of the music department at ERPI was Ottalie Mark, who was regarded as an expert in music copyrights for motion pictures after she had worked under Samuel "Roxy" Rothafel and Erno Rapee in New York. When Warner Bros. began experimenting with Vitaphone at the old Vitagraph Studio in Brooklyn, Mark was hired to handle music copyrights, but she was soon wooed by ERPI manager Donald S. Pratt and placed in charge of issuing ERPI synchronization licenses to the studios. Isidore Witmark and Isaac Goldberg credit Mark with creating the "first and most complete music copyright files for synchronization purposes in the world." She went on to become head of BMI's research department. *Story of the House of Witmark: From Ragtime to Swingtime* (New York: L. Furman, 1939), 427.

APPENDIX 2

1. *Variety*, August 21, 1929, 57.

APPENDIX 5

1. Folder 12637B, Warner Bros. Archives, University of Southern California.

BIBLIOGRAPHY

BOOKS AND PERIODICALS

"5,000,000 Songs," Fortune 7.1 (January 1933): 27–33, 84–86.

Aldridge, Benjamin L. *The Victor Talking Machine Company*, ed. Frederic Bayh. Camden, NJ: RCA Sales Corp., 1964.

Alicoate, J. W., ed. "Personnel of Studios." In *Film Daily Yearbook of Motion Pictures of 1930*, 627–631. New York: Film Daily, 1930.

Allen, Leonard. "The Battle of Tin Pan Alley," *Harper's Magazine*, 181.5 (October 1940): 514–523.

Allen, Robert C. "Vaudeville and Film, 1895-1915: A Study in Media Interaction," Ph.D. diss., University of Iowa, 1977; New York: Arno, 1980.

Altman, Rick, ed. *Genre: The Musical*. London: Routledge and Kegan Paul, 1981.

Altman, Rick. *The American Film Musical*. Bloomington, IN: Indiana University Press, 1987.

———. "Cinema and Popular Song." In *Soundtrack Available: Essays on Film and Popular Music*, eds. Pamela Robertson Wojcik and Arthur Knight, 19–30. Durham, NC: Duke University Press, 2001.

———. "Early Film Themes: Roxy, Adorno, and the Problem of Cultural Capital." In *Beyond the Soundtrack: Representing Music in the Cinema*, eds. Daniel Goldmark, Larry Kramer, and Richard Leppert, 205–224. Berkeley, CA: University of California Press, 2007.

———. *Silent Film Sound*. New York: Columbia University Press, 2004.

American Society of Composers, Authors and Publishers, *ASCAP Biographical Dictionary*, 4th ed. New York; London: R. R. Bowker, 1980.

———. *Nothing Can Replace Music: Newspaper Editorials and Comments on Music and Radio*. New York: ASCAP, 1933.

———. *The Story of ASCAP: An American Institution*. New York: ASCAP, 1946.

Anderson, Gillian. *Music for the Silent Films, 1894-1929*. Washington, DC: Library of Congress, 1988.

Banfield, Stephen. *Jerome Kern*. New Haven, CT: Yale University Press, 2006.

Banning, William Peck. *Commercial Broadcast Pioneer: The WEAF Experiment, 1922-1926*. Cambridge, MA: Harvard University Press, 1946.

Barlow, William. *Voice Over: The Making of Black Radio*. Philadelphia: Temple University Press, 1999.

Barnouw, Erik. *Conglomerates and the Media* New York: New Press, 1997.

———. *A Tower in Babel: A History of Broadcasting in the United States to 1933*. New York: Oxford University Press, 1966.

Barrios, Richard. *A Song in the Dark: The Birth of the Musical Film*, 2nd ed. New York: Oxford University Press, 2009.

Bastin, Bruce, with Kip Lornell. *The Melody Man: Joe Davis and the New York Music Scene, 1916-1978*. Jackson, MS: University of Mississippi Press, 2012.

Bazelon, Irving. *Knowing the Score: Notes on Film Music*. New York: Van Nostrand Reinhold, 1975.

Benedetti, Jean. *David Garrick and the Birth of Modern Theatre*. London: Methuen, 2001.

Bergreen, Laurence. *As Thousands Cheer: The Life of Irving Berlin*. New York: Da Capo, 1996 [1990].

Berlin, Edward A. *Ragtime: A Musical and Cultural History*. Berkeley, CA: University of California Press, 1980.

Biel, Michael Jay. "The Making and Use of Recordings in Broadcasting Before 1936," Ph.D. diss., Northwestern University, 1977.

Black, Gregory D. *Hollywood Censored: Morality Codes, Catholics, and the Movie* Cambridge, UK: Cambridge University Press, 1996.

Bloom, Ken. *Hollywood Song: The Complete Film and Musical Companion*. New York: Facts on File, 1995.

Bordman, Gerald. *American Musical Comedy: From Adonis to Dreamgirls*. New York; Oxford, UK: Oxford University Press, 1982.

———. *American Musical Revue: From the Passing Show to Sugar Babies*. New York; Oxford, UK: Oxford University Press, 1985.

———. *American Musical Theatre: A Chronicle*, 2nd ed. New York; Oxford, UK: Oxford University Press, 1992.

Bordwell, David, Janet Staiger, and Kristin Thompson. *The Classical Hollywood Cinema: Film Style & Mode of Production to 1960*. New York: Columbia University Press, 1985.

Bordwell, David. *Planet Hong Kong: Popular Cinema and the Art of Entertainment*, 2nd ed. Madison, WI: Irvington Way Institute Press, 2011.

Bowser, Eileen. *The Transformation of Cinema, 1907–1915*. Vol. 2, *History of the American Cinema*, ed. Charles Harpole. New York: Charles Scribner's Sons, 1990.

Bradley, Edwin M. *The First Hollywood Musicals: A Critical Filmography of 171 Features, 1927-1932*. Jefferson, NC: McFarland, 1996.

Breil, Joseph Carl, and Clarence Lucas. *Selection of Joseph Carl Breil's Themes from the Incidental Music to 'The Birth of a Nation.'* New York: Chappell, 1916.

Brown, Gene, ed. *New York Times Encyclopedia of Film: 1937-1940*. New York: Times Books, 1984.

Brown, Royal S. *Overtones and Undertones: Reading Film Music*. Berkeley, CA: University of California Press, 1994.

Buhler, James, David Neumeyer, and Rob Deemer. *Hearing the Movies: Music and Sound in Film History.* New York: Oxford University Press, 2009.

Burton, Jack. *The Blue Book of Hollywood Musicals.* New York: Century House, 1953.

Caldwell, Louis G. "The Copyright Problems of Broadcasters," *Journal of Radio Law* 2:2 (April 1932): 287–314.

Catalog of musical compositions published by Harms, Inc. compiled to January 31, 1933; New World Music Corporation, January 31, 1933; M. Witmark & Sons, August 1, 1932; T. B. Harms Company, January 31, 1933; Remick Music Corporation, September 14, 1932; Shubert Music Publishing Company, January 31, 1933. New York: National Broadcasting Co., 1933.

Chon, Bum Soo, Junho H. Choi, George A. Barnett, et al., "A Structural Analysis of Media Convergence: Cross-Industry Mergers and Acquisitions in the Information Industries," *Journal of Media Economics* 16.3 (2003): 141–157.

Cohen, Harvey G. "The Marketing of Duke Ellington: Setting the Strategy for an African American Maestro," *Journal of African-American History* 89.4 (Autumn 2004): 291–315.

Coleman, Mark. *Playback: From the Victrola to MP3, 100 Years of Music, Machines, and Money.* Cambridge, MA: DaCapo, 2005.

Conrich, Ian, and Estella Tincknell. *Film's Musical Moments* Edinburgh, UK: Edinburgh University Press, 2006.

Cook, David. *A History of Narrative Film*, 3rd ed. New York: W. W. Norton, 1996.

Cowie, Elizabeth. "Storytelling: Classical Hollywood Cinema and Classical Narrative." In *Contemporary Hollywood Cinema*, eds. Steve Neale and Murray Smith, 178–190 New York: Routledge, 1998.

Crafton, Donald. "Pie and Chase." In *Classical Hollywood Comedy*, eds. Kristine Brunovska Karnick and Henry Jenkins, 106–119. New York: Routledge, 1994.

———. *The Talkies: American Cinema's Transition to Sound, 1926-1931. Vol. 4, History of the American Cinema*, ed. Charles Harpole. New York: Charles Scribner's Sons, 1997.

Creekmur, Corey. "Picturizing American Cinema: Hindi Film Songs and the Last Days of Genre." In *Soundtrack Available: Essays on Film and Popular Music*, eds. Pamela Robertson Wojcik and Arthur Knight, 375–406. Durham, NC: Duke University Press, 2001.

Danly, Linda, ed. *Hugo Friedhofer: The Best Years of His Life; A Hollywood Master of Music for the Movies.* Lanham, MD: Scarecrow, 2002.

DeCordova, Richard. *Picture Personalities: The Emergence of the Star System in America.* Champagne, IL: University of Illinois Press, 2001.

DeWhitt, Bennie L. "The American Society of Composers, Authors and Publishers, 1914-1938," Ph.D. diss., Emory University, 1977.

Doty, Alexander. "Music Sells Movies: (Re)new(ed) Conservatism in Film Marketing," *Wide Angle* 10:2 (1988): 70–79.

Douglas, Susan J. *Listening In: Radio and the American Imagination* Minneapolis: University of Minnesota Press, 2004.

Drew, William M. *The Last Silent Picture Show: Silent Films on American Screens in the 1930s.* Lanham, MD: Scarecrow, 2010.

Drowne, Kathleen Morgan, and Patrick Huber, *The 1920s.* Westport, CT: Greenwood, 2004.

Dubin, Al. *The Art of Song Writing.* New York: Majestic Music, 1928.

Dyer, Richard. "Entertainment and Utopia." In *Only Entertainment*, 2nd ed., 19–35. London: Routledge, 2002.

Dyer, Richard. "Resistance through Charisma: Rita Hayworth and *Gilda*." In *Women and Film Noir,* ed. E. Ann Kaplan. London: BFI, 1978.

Eberly, Philip K. *Music in the Air: America's Changing Tastes in Popular Music, 1920-1980.* New York: Hastings House, 1982.

Ely, Melvin Patrick. *The Adventures of Amos 'n' Andy: A Social History of an American Phenomenon.* New York: Free Press, 1992.

Ennis, Philip. *The Seventh Stream: The Emergence of Rocknroll in American Popular Music.* Hanover, NH: Wesleyan University Press, 1992.

Ergo, Richard. "ASCAP and the Antitrust Laws: The Story of a Reasonable Compromise," *Duke Law Journal* 8:2 (Spring 1959): 258–277.

Evans, David. *Big Road Blues: Tradition and Creativity in the Folk Blues.* Berkeley, CA: University of California Press, 1982.

Ewen, David. *All the Years of American Popular Music.* Englewood Cliffs, NJ: Prentice-Hall, 1977.

——. *Great Men of American Popular Song.* Englewood Cliffs, NJ: Prentice-Hall, 1972.

——. *History of Popular Music.* New York: Barnes and Noble, 1961.

——. *The Life and Death of Tin Pan Alley.* New York: Funk & Wagnalls, 1964.

Fabrizio, Timothy C., and George F. Paul. *The Talking Machine: An Illustrated Compendium, 1877-1929.* Atglen, PA: Schiffer, 1997.

Fehr, Richard, and Frederick A. Vogel. *Lullabies of Hollywood: Movie Music and the Movie Musical, 1915-1922.* Jefferson, NC: McFarland, 1993.

Feuer, Jane. *The Hollywood Musical,* 2nd ed. Bloomington, IN: Indiana University Press, 1993.

Finson, Jon W. *The Voices That Are Gone: Themes in Nineteenth-Century American Popular Song.* New York: Oxford University Press, 1994.

Fisher, William Arms. *One Hundred and Fifty Years of Music Publishing in the United States: An Historical Sketch with Special Reference to the Pioneer Publisher, Oliver Ditson Company, Inc., 1783-1933.* Boston: Oliver Ditson, 1933.

Florida, Richard, and Scott Jackson. "Sonic City: The Evolving Economic Geography of the Music Industry," *Journal of Planning Education and Research* 29.3 (March 2010): 310–321.

Forte, Allen. *The American Popular Ballad of the Golden Era, 1924-1950.* Princeton, NJ: Princeton University Press, 1995.

——. *Listening to Classic American Popular Songs.* New Haven, CT: Yale University Press, 2001.

Friedman, Ryan Jay. *Hollywood's African American Films: The Transition to Sound.* New Brunswick, NJ: Rutgers University Press, 2011.

Furia, Philip. *The Poets of Tin Pan Alley: A History of America's Great Lyricists* New York: Oxford University Press, 1990.

Furia, Philip, and Laurie Patterson. *The Songs of Hollywood.* New York: Oxford University Press, 2010.

Gelatt, Ronald. *The Fabulous Phonograph: From Edison to Stereo* (revised ed.). New York: Appleton-Century, 1965.

Gevinson, Alan. *American Film Institute Catalog: Within Our Gates: Ethnicity in American Feature Films, 1911-1960.* Berkeley, CA: University of California Press, 1997.

Goldberg, Isaac. *Tin Pan Alley: A Chronicle of American Popular Music.* New York: Frederick Ungar, 1961.

Goldmark, Daniel. "Creating Desire on Tin Pan Alley," *Musical Quarterly* 90.2 (Summer 2007): 197–229.

Gomery, Douglas. *The Coming of Sound: A History*. New York; London: Routledge, 2005.

Goodman, David. *Radio's Civic Ambition: American Broadcasting and Democracy in the 1930s*. New York: Oxford University Press, 2011.

Gorbman, Claudia. *Unheard Melodies: Narrative Film Music*. Bloomington, IN: Indiana University Press, 1987.

Gordon, Jack. *How to Publish Your Own Music Successfully*. Chicago: Jack Gordon, 1925.

Gracyk, Tim. *Popular American Recording Pioneers, 1895-1925*. New York: Haworth, 2000.

Green, Abel, and Joe Laurie, Jr. *Show Biz from Vaude to Video*. New York: Henry Holt, 1951.

Green, Abel. *Inside Stuff on How to Write Popular Songs*. New York: Paul Whiteman, 1927.

Green, Stanley. *Encyclopedia of the Musical Film*. New York: Oxford University Press, 1981.

Grodal, Torben. *Moving Pictures: A New Theory of Film Genres, Feelings, and Cognition*. Oxford, UK: Clarendon; New York: Oxford University Press, 1997.

Gunning, Tom. "The Cinema of Attractions: Early Film, Its Spectator and the Avant-Garde." In *Early Cinema: Space, Frame, Narrative*, ed. Thomas Elsaesser, 56–62. London: BFI, 1990.

Hamand, M. Carol. "The Effects of the Adoption of Sound on Narrative and Narration in the American Cinema," Ph.D. diss., University of Wisconsin-Madison, 1983.

Hamm, Charles. "Some Thoughts on the Measurement of Popularity in Music." In *Popular Music Perspectives: Papers from the First International Conference on Popular Music Research, Amsterdam, June 1981*, eds. David Horn and Philip Tagg, 3–15. Göteborg, DE: International Association for the Study of Popular Music, 1981.

——. *Irving Berlin: Songs from the Melting Pot: The Formative Years, 1907-1914*. New York; Oxford, UK: Oxford University Press, 1997.

——. *Yesterdays: Popular Song in America*. New York: W. W. Norton, 1979.

Harris, Charles K. *After the Ball: Forty Years of Melody*. New York: Frank-Maurice, 1926.

——. *How to Write a Popular Song*. Chicago: Charles K. Harris, 1906.

Hettinger, Herman S. *A Decade of Radio Advertising*. Chicago: University of Chicago Press, 1933.

Hickman, Roger. *Reel Music: Exploring 100 Years of Film Music*. New York: W. W. Norton, 2006.

Higgins, Scott. *Harnessing the Technicolor Rainbow: Color Design in the 1930s*. Austin, TX: University of Texas Press, 2007.

Hilmes, Michele. *Hollywood and Broadcasting: From Radio to Cable*. Urbana, IL: University of Illinois Press, 1990.

——. *Radio Voices: American Broadcasting, 1922-1952*. Minneapolis: University of Minnesota Press, 1997.

Hischak, Thomas S. *Through the Screen Door: What Happened to the Broadway Musical When It Went to Hollywood*. Lanham, MD: Scarecrow, 2004.

Hogan, Patrick. *Understanding Indian Movies*. Austin, TX: University of Texas Press, 2008.

Hubbard, Preston. "Synchronized Sound and Movie-House Musicians, 1926-29," *American Music* 3.4 (Winter 1985): 429–441.

Inglis, Ian, ed. *Popular Music and Film*. London: Wallflower, 2003.

Jablonski, Edward. *Gershwin: With a New Critical Discography*. New York: Da Capo, 1998.

Jacobs, Lea. "Belasco, DeMille and the Development of Lasky Lighting," *Film History* 5:4 (December 1993): 405–418.

——. "The Innovation of Re-recording in Hollywood Studios," *Film History* 24.1 (2012): 5–34.

Janney, Sam. *Loose Ankles: A Comedy in Three Acts*. New York: Longmans, Green, 1928.

Jasen, David A. *Tin Pan Alley: An Encyclopedia of the Golden Age of American Song*. New York: Taylor & Francis, 2003.

Kahn Atkins, Irene. *Source Music in Motion Pictures*. Plainsboro, NJ: Associated University Presses, 1983.

Kalinak, Kathryn. *How the West was Sung: Music in the Westerns of John Ford* Berkeley, CA: University of California Press, 2007.

———. *Settling the Score: Music and the Classical Hollywood Film*. Madison, WI: University of Wisconsin Press, 1992.

Karlin, F. *Listening to Movies: The Film Lover's Guide to Film Music* New York: Schirmer, 1994.

Keating, Patrick. "Emotional Curves and Linear Narratives," *Velvet Light Trap* 58.1 (2006): 4–15.

Keightley, Keir. "Taking Popular Music (and Tin Pan Alley and Jazz) Seriously," *Journal of Popular Music Studies* 22.1 (March 2010): 90–97.

Keil, Charlie, and Shelley Stamp, eds. *American Cinema's Transitional Era: Audiences, Institutions, Practices*. Berkeley, CA: University of California Press, 2004.

King, Geoff. *New Hollywood Cinema: An Introduction*. New York: Columbia University Press, 2002.

Kinkle, Roger. *The Complete Encyclopedia of Popular Music and Jazz, 1900-1950*. New Rochelle, NY: Arlington House, 1974.

Knapp, Raymond. *The American Film Musical and the Formation of National Identity*. Princeton, NJ: Princeton University Press, 2005.

Koszarski, Richard. *An Evening's Entertainment: The Age of the Silent Feature Picture, 1915-1928*. *Vol. 3, History of the American Cinema*, ed. Charles Harpole. New York: Charles Scribner's Sons, 1997.

———. *Hollywood on the Hudson: Film and Television in New York from Griffith to Sarnoff*. New Brunswick, NJ: Rutgers University Press, 2008.

Kraft, James P. "Musicians in Hollywood: Work and Technological Change in Entertainment Industries, 1926-1940," *Technology and Culture* 35.2 (April 1994): 289–314.

Kreuger, Miles, ed. *The Movie Musical from Vitaphone to 42nd Street: As Reported in a Great Fan Magazine*. New York: Dover, 1975.

Lack, Russell. *Twenty Four Frames Under*. London: Quartet, 1997.

Laing, Heather. *The Gendered Score: Music in 1940s Melodrama and the Woman's Film*. Aldershot, UK; Burlington, VT: Ashgate, 2007.

Laird, Ross. *Brunswick Records: A Discography of Records, 1916-1931; Volume 1: New York Sessions, 1916-1926*. Westport, CT: Greenwood, 2001.

Lapedis, Hilary. "Popping the Question: The Function and Effect of Popular Music in Cinema," *Popular Music* 18:3 (October 1999): 367–379.

Lastra, James. *Sound Technology and the American Cinema: Perception, Representation, Modernity*. New York: Columbia University Press, 2000.

Leach, William. *Land of Desire: Merchants, Power, and the Rise of a New American Culture*. New York: Pantheon, 1993.

Levy, Louis. *Music for the Movies*. London: Sampson Low, Marston, 1948.

Liebowitz, Stan J. "The Elusive Symbiosis: The Impact of Radio on the Record Industry," *Review of Economic Research on Copyright Issues* 1 (2004): 93–118.

Limbacher, James, comp. and ed. *Film Music: From Violins to Video*. Metuchen, NJ: Scarecrow, 1974.

Lincoln, Harry J. *How to Write and Publish Music*, rev. ed. Cincinnati, OH: Union Music, 1926.

Lindberg, Ulf. "Popular Modernism? The 'Urban' Style of Interwar Tin Pan Alley," *Popular Music* 22.3 (2003): 283–296.

London, Justin. "Leitmotifs and Musical Reference in the Classical Film Score." In *Music and Cinema*, eds. James Buhler, Caryl Flinn, and David Neumeyer, 85–96. Hanover, NH: University Press of New England, Wesleyan University Press, 2000.

London, Kurt. *Film Music: A Summary of the Characteristic Features of its History, Aesthetics, Technique; and Possible Developments*, trans. Eric S. Bensinger. New York: Arno, 1970 [1936].

Lorimer, Walter L. M. "2¢ Plain, Why Pay More?" *UCLA Law Review* 10:3 (March 1963): 561–574.Luz, Ernst. "Theme Playing as Used and Abused," in "Music and the Picture," *Motion Picture News*, August 14, 1915: 130.

MacDonald, Laurence E. *The Invisible Art of Film Music: A Comprehensive History*. New York: Ardsley House, 1998.

Manvell, Roger, and John Huntley. *The Technique of Film Music*. London: Hastings House, 1957.

Marchand, Roland. *Advertising the American Dream: Making Way for Modernity, 1920-1940*. Berkeley, CA: University of California Press, 1986.

Marks, Edward B. *They All Sang: From Tony Pastor to Rudy Vallee*. New York: Viking, 1934.

Marks, Martin Miller. *Music and the Silent Film: Contexts and Case Studies, 1895-1924*. New York: Oxford University Press, 1997.

Mattfield, Julius. *Variety Music Cavalcade: Musical Historical Review 1620-1961: A Chronology of Vocal and Instrumental Music Popular in the United States*. Englewood Cliffs, NJ: Prentice-Hall, 1952.

McCracken, Allison Maura. "Real Men Don't Sing: Crooning and American Culture, 1928-1933," Ph.D. diss., University of Iowa, 2000.

McDonald, Gerald D. "A Bibliography of Song Sheets: Sports and Recreations in American Popular Songs: Part IV: Songs of the Silent Film," *Notes*, 2nd ser. 14.3 (June 1957): 325–352.

———. "A Bibliography of Song Sheets: Sports and Recreations in American Popular Songs: Part IV: Songs of the Silent Film (Conclusion)," *Notes*, 2nd ser. 14:4 (September 1957), 507–533.

McLean, Adrienne L. "'It's Only That I Do What I Love and Love What I Do': 'Film Noir' and the Musical Woman," *Cinema Journal* 33:1 (Autumn 1993): 3–16.

———. *Being Rita Hayworth: Labor, Identity, and Hollywood Stardom*. Piscataway, NJ: Rutgers University Press, 2004.

Melnick, Jeffrey. *A Right to Sing the Blues: African Americans, Jews, and American Popular Song*. Cambridge, MA: Harvard University Press, 1999.

Melnick, Ross. *American Showman: Samuel "Roxy" Rothafel and the Birth of the Entertainment Industry, 1908-1935*. New York: Columbia University Press, 2012.

Meyer, Hazel. *The Gold in Tin Pan Alley*. Philadelphia: Lippincott, 1958.

Millard, Andre. *America on Record: A History of Recorded Sound*. Cambridge, UK; New York: Cambridge University Press, 1995.

Mills, Edwin Claude. *What is ASCAP?* New York: ASCAP, 1940.

Mordden, Ethan. *Make Believe: The Broadway Musical in the 1920s*. New York; Oxford, UK: Oxford University Press, 1997.

Mormenstein, Gary. *Hollywood Rhapsody: Movie Music and Its Makers, 1900 to 1975* New York: Schirmer, 1997.

Morton, David. *Off the Record: The Technology and Culture of Sound Recording in America*. New Brunswick, NJ: Rutgers University Press, 2000.

Muir, Peter. *Long Lost Blues: Popular Blues in America, 1850-1920*. Champaign, IL: University of Illinois Press.

Mulvey, Laura. "Visual Pleasure and Narrative Cinema," *Screen* 16.3 (Autumn 1975): 6–18.

Musser, Charles. "Rethinking Early Cinema: Attractions and Narrativity," *Yale Journal of Criticism* 7:2 (Fall 1994): 203–232.

Newcomer, Walter W. *Song Requirements of Talking Pictures*. New York: Walter W. Newcomer, 1928.

Noam, Eli M. *Media Ownership and Concentration in America*. New York: Oxford University Press, 2009.

Nolan, Frederick. *The Sound of Their Music: The Story of Rodgers & Hammerstein*. New York: Applause Theatre & Cinema Books.

O'Brien, Charles. *Cinema's Conversion to Sound: Technology and Film Style in France and the U.S.* Bloomington, IN: Indiana University Press, 2005.

Palmer, Christopher. *The Composer in Hollywood*. London: Marion Boyars, 1990.

Peterson, Richard A. *Creating Country Music: Fabricating Authenticity*. Chicago: University of Chicago Press, 1997.

Physioc, Lewis W. "Pictures Problems," *International Photographer* 1.8 (September 1929), 7–8, 10, 12.

Pitts, Michael R., and Frank W. Hoffman. *The Rise of the Crooners: Gene Austin, Russ Columbo, Bing Crosby, Nick Lucas, Johnny Marvin, and Rudy Vallee*. Lanham, MD: Scarecrow, 2001.

Prendergast, Roy. *Film Music: A Neglected Art*, 2nd ed. New York: W. W. Norton, 1992.

Propper, Irving. "American 'Popular' Music and the Copyright Law." In *Third Copyright Law Symposium*, 191–192. New York: ASCAP, 1940.

Read, Oliver, and Walter L. Welch. *From Tinfoil to Stereo: Evolution of the Phonograph*. Indianapolis, IN: H. W. Sams, 1976.

Reay, Pauline. *Music in Film: Soundtracks and Synergy*. London: Wallflower, 2004.

Rubin, Martin. "Busby Berkeley and the Backstage Musical." In *Hollywood Musicals: The Film Reader*, ed. Steven Cohan, 53–61. London; New York: Routledge, 2002.

Rudel, Anthony. *Hello, Everybody!: The Dawn of American Radio*. Boston: Houghton Mifflin Harcourt, 2008.

Rust, Brian. *The Columbia Master Book Discography, Volume III: Principal U.S. Matrix Series, 1924-1934*. Westport, CT: Greenwood, 1999.

———. *The Victor Master Book, Vol. 2 (1925-1936)*. Stanhope, NJ: Walter C. Allen, 1970.

Sadie, Stanley, ed. *The New Grove Dictionary of Music and Musicians*, 2nd ed. London: Macmillan, 2001.

Sanjek, Russell, and David Sanjek. *The American Popular Music Business in the 20th Century*. New York: Oxford University Press, 1991.

Sanjek, Russell. *Pennies from Heaven: The American Popular Music Business in the Twentieth Century*, revised and updated by David Sanjek. New York: Da Capo, 1996.

Saunders, Richard Drake, ed. *Music and Dance in California and the West*. Hollywood: Bureau of Musical Research, 1948.

Scheurer, Timothy E., ed. *American Popular Music: Readings from the Popular Press, Volume I: The Nineteenth Century and Tin Pan Alley*. Bowling Green, OH: Bowling Green State University Press, 1989.

Schindler, Colin. *Hollywood in Crisis: Cinema and American Society, 1929-1939.* New York: Routledge, 1996.

Schultz, Lucia S. "Performing-Right Societies in the United States," *Notes*, 2nd ser., 35:3 (March 1979): 511–536.

Schwab, Laurence, and B. G. DeSylva. *Good News: A Musical Comedy in Two Acts.* New York: Samuel French, 1932.

Segrave, Kerry. *Payola in the Music Industry: A History, 1880-1991.* Jefferson, NC: McFarland, 1994.

Shapiro, Nat, ed. *Popular Music: An Annotated Index of American Popular Songs, 1920-1969.* New York: Adrian, 1973.

Shepherd, John, David Horn, et al., eds. *Continuum Encyclopedia of Popular Music of the World.* London; New York: Continuum, 2003.

Shilkret, Nathaniel. *Sixty Years in the Music Business*, eds. Niel Shell and Barbara Shilkret. Lanham, MD: Scarecrow, 2005.

Silverman, Kaja. *The Subject of Semiotics.* New York; Oxford, UK: Oxford University Press, 1983.

Smith, Jeff. *The Sounds of Commerce: Marketing Popular Film Music.* New York: Columbia University Press, 1998.

———. "'It Does Something to a Girl. I Don't Know What': The Problem of Female Sexuality in *Applause*," *Cinema Journal* 30:2 (Winter 1991): 47–60.

Smith, Murray. "The Sound of Sentiment: Popular Music, Film, and Emotion," *16:9* 4.19 (November 2006), available online at http://www.16-9.dk/2006-11/side11_inenglish.htm [January 15, 2011].

Smulyan, Susan. *Selling Radio: The Commercialization of American Broadcasting, 1920-1934.* Washington, DC: Smithsonian Institution Press, 1994.

Spadoni, Robert. *Uncanny Bodies: The Coming of Sound Film and the Origins of the Horror Genre.* Berkeley, CA: University of California, 2007.

Spaeth, Sigmund. *A History of Popular Music in America.* New York: Random House, 1948.

Spring, Katherine. "'To Sustain Illusion is All That is Necessary': The Authenticity of Song Performance in Early American Sound Cinema," *Beyond Vitaphone: The Early Sound Short*, spec. issue of *Film History: An International Journal* 23.3 (2011): 285–299.

———. "Pop Go the Warner Bros., et al.: Marketing Film Songs during the Coming of Sound," *Cinema Journal* 48.1 (Fall 2008): 68–89.

Stanfield, Peter. "'Extremely Dangerous Material': Hollywood and the Ballad of Frankie and Johnny." In *Classic Hollywood, Classic Whiteness*, ed. Daniel Bernardi, 442–465. Minneapolis: University of Minnesota Press, 2001.

———. "An Excursion into the Lower Depths: Hollywood, Urban Primitivism, and 'St. Louis Blues,' 1929-1937," *Cinema Journal* 41:2 (Winter 2002): 84–108.

———. *Body and Soul: Jazz and Blues in American Film, 1927-63.* Chicago: University of Illinois Press, 2005.

Starr, Larry, and Christopher Waterman. *American Popular Music: From Minstrelsy to MTV.* Oxford, UK: Oxford University Press, 2003.

Steffen, David J. *From Edison to Marconi: The First Thirty Years of Recorded Music.* Jefferson, NC: McFarland, 2005.

Steiner, Max. "Scoring the Film." In *We Make the Movies*, ed. Nancy Naumberg, 216–238. New York: W. W. Norton, 1937.

Sterling, Christopher H., and John Michael Kittross. *Stay Tuned: A History of American Broadcasting*, 3rd ed. New York: Routledge, 2001.

Strauven, Wanda, ed. *Cinema of Attractions Reloaded*. Amsterdam: University of Amsterdam Press, 2006.

Suisman, David. *Selling Sounds: The Commercial Revolution in American Music*. Cambridge, MA: Harvard University Press, 2009.

Susman, Warren. *Culture of History: The Transformation of American Society in the Twentieth Century*. New York: Pantheon, 1984.

Tawa, Nicholas E. *Sweet Songs for Gentle Americans: The Parlor Song in America, 1790-1860*. Bowling Green, OH: Bowling Green State University Popular Press, 1980.

——. *The Way to Tin Pan Alley: American Popular Song, 1866-1910*. New York: Schirmer, 1990.

Taylor, John Russell. *Strangers in Paradise: The Hollywood Émigrés, 1933-1950*. New York: Holt, Reinhart and Winston, 1983.

Taylor, Timothy D. *The Sounds of Capitalism: Advertising, Music, and the Conquest of Culture*. Chicago: University of Chicago Press, 2012.

Thomas, Tony. *Film Score: The Art & Craft of Movie Music*. Burbank, CA: Riverwood, 1991.

Tinee, Mae. "Surprise Key to this Movie, 'Glad Rag Doll': Recalling 'Things Are Seldom What They Seem,'" *Chicago Daily Tribune*, May 7, 1929, 41.

Tucker, Sophie. *Some of These Days: The Autobiography of Sophie Tucker*. Garden City, NY: Doubleday, Doran, 1945.

Tyler, Linda J. "Commerce and Poetry Hand in Hand: Music in American Department Stores, 1880-1930)," *Journal of the American Musicological Society* 45:1 (Spring 1992): 75–120.

U.S. Dept. of Commerce and Labor, *Statistical Abstract of the United States, 1933* Washington, DC: U.S. Government Printing Office, 1933.

Vancour, Shawn Gary. "The Sounds of 'Radio': Aesthetic Formations of 1920s American Broadcasting," Ph.D. diss., University of Wisconsin-Madison, 2008.

Villamil, Victoria Etnier. *From Johnson's Kids to Lemonade Opera: The American Classical Singer Comes of Age*. Boston: Northeastern University Press, 2004.

Walker, Alexander. *The Shattered Silents: How the Talkies Came to Stay*. London: Elm Tree, 1978.

Warner, Jack L., with Dean Jennings. *My First Hundred Years in Hollywood*. New York: Random House, 1964.

Whitburn, Joel. *Joel Whitburn's Pop Memories 1890-1954: The History of American Popular Music*. Menomonee Falls, WI: Record Research, 1986.

White, Lee C. "Musical Copyrights v. The Anti-trust Laws," *Nebraska Law Review* 30: 1 (November 1950): 50–67.

Whiteman, Paul, with Mary Margaret McBride. *Jazz, Popular Culture in America 1800-1925*. New York: Arno, 1974 [1926].

Wickes, Edward M. *Writing the Popular Song*. Springfield, MA: Home Correspondence School, 1916.

Wierzbicki, James. *Film Music: A History*. New York: Routledge, 2009.

Wilder, Alec. *American Popular Song: The Great Innovators, 1900-1950*, ed. James T. Maher. New York: Oxford University Press, 1972.

Williams, Christopher. "After the Classic, the Classical and Ideology: The Differences of Realism," *Screen* 35.3 (Autumn 1994): 275–292.

Witmark, Isidore, and Isaac Goldberg. *Story of the House of Witmark: From Ragtime to Swingtime.* New York: L. Furman, 1939.

Wolfe, Charles. "Vitaphone Shorts and *The Jazz Singer*," Wide Angle 22:3 (July 1990): 58–78.

Wurtzler, Steve J. *Electric Sounds: Technological Change and the Rise of Corporate Mass Media.* New York: Columbia University Press, 2007.

SELECTED TRADES, NEWSPAPERS, AND MAGAZINES

Billboard
Exhibitors Herald-World
Film Daily
Film Daily Yearbook
Hollywood Filmograph
The Los Angeles Times
Motion Picture Almanac
Motion Picture News
Moving Picture World
Music Trade Review
The New York Times
Photoplay
Talking Screen
Time
Vanity Fair
Variety
The Wireless Age

LEGAL CASES

General Talking Pictures Corporation et al. v. American Telephone and Telegraph Co. et al., 18 F. Supp. 650, 1937.

Harms v. Cohen, 279 Fed. 276 D.C.E.D. Pa., 1922.

Herbert v. Shanley Co., 242 U.S. 591, 1917.

M. Witmark & Sons v. Calloway, 22 F.2d 412 D.C.E.D. Tenn., 1927.

M. Witmark & Sons v. L. Bamberger & Co., 291 Fed. 776. D.C., 1923.

M. Witmark & Sons v. Pastime Amusement Co., 298 Fed. 470. E.D.S.C., 1924; aff'd 2 F.2d 1020, C.C.A. 4th, 1924.

Remick & Co. v. American Automobile Accessories Co., 5 Fed. 2d 411 C.C.A. 6th, 1925.

Remick & Co. v. General Electric 16 F.2d 829 S.D.N.Y., 1926.

SELECTED ARCHIVAL MATERIAL

Cinema Press Books (Microfilm), Margaret Herrick Library, Academy of Motion Picture Arts and Sciences.

Colleen Moore Papers, Special Collections, Margaret Herrick Library, Academy of Motion Picture Arts and Sciences.

Mack Sennett Papers, Special Collections, Margaret Herrick Library, Academy of Motion Picture Arts and Sciences.

Paramount Pictures Pressbooks Collection, Special Collections, Margaret Herrick Library, Academy of Motion Picture Arts and Sciences.

Richard Barthelmess Scrapbooks, Special Collections, Margaret Herrick Library, Academy of Motion Picture Arts and Sciences, Los Angeles.

Stills, Posters and Paper Collections, Motion Picture Department, George Eastman House, Rochester, New York.

United Artists Corporation Records, Wisconsin Center for Film and Theater Research, Madison, Wisconsin.

Warner Bros. Archives, University of Southern California, Los Angeles.

INDEX

Boswell Sisters, 138

Bow, Clara, 77

"The Bowery" (song), 136

"Boyfriend Blues" (song), 85

The Boys and Betty (play), 26, 74

Bradford, James C., 37–38, 179n102

Bradley, Edwin M., 121, 168n7

Brady, William A., 21

Breil, Joseph Carl, 35–36

Broadway Babies (film), 6–7

The Broadway Melody (film), 7–8, 55–56

"Broken Melody" (song), 82

Brooks, Louise, 191n76

Brooks, Shelton, 25, 139

Broones, Martin, 127

Brown, Johnny Mack, 102–3

Brown, Lew, 56, 73, 127, 184n57. *See also* DeSylva, Brown & Henderson (DBH)

Brown, Nacio Herb, 55–56, 63, 127

Brown, Royal S., 35–36

Brunswick-Balke-Collender Co., 126

Brunswick Hour (radio program), 27

Brunswick Records

"How Long Will It Last?" and, 118

"Loose Ankles" and, 190n65

"My Tonia" and, 198n77

"Pagan Moon" and, 198n84

star-song identification and, 26–27

Warner Bros. and, 126

"Weary River" and, 92

Bryan, Alfred, 63, 138

Buffalo Times (newspaper), 105

Burgess, Dorothy, 131, 134–37, *134*

Burke, Joe, 63, 89, 138, 197n67

Burke, Johnny, 185n78

Burrows, James, 56

"The Caballero's Way" (Henry), 130, 198n78. See also *In Old Arizona* (film)

Caesar, Irving, 16

Cahill, Marie, 26, 74

"California, Here I Come" (song), 129

"California and You" (song), 26

Calloway, Cab, 138

Campbell, Connelly & Co., 58

"Camptown Races" (song), 35

"Can't Help Lovin' Dat Man" (song), 86

Cantor, Eddie, 23, 26, 73, 75

Carl Fenton Orchestra, 198n84

Carl Fischer, Inc., 59

Carol, Sue, 108–9

Carus, Emma, 74

CBS Radio Network

Crosby and, 198n84

formation of, 20

Viacom and, 169n15

WABC and, 28

"Weary River" and, 91–92

The Champion Spark Plug Hour (radio program), 21

Chandler, Helen, 85

Chaplin, Charlie, 69–70

Chappell & Company, 36, 55

Chappell-Harms, Inc., 58

Chappell Music, 169n15

"Charmaine" (song), 38, 41, 49, 180n108

Check and Double Check (film), 104, 106–12, *107*, *110*, 147

Chicago Daily Tribune (newspaper), 102

Chopin, Frédéric, 32

The Christian Science Monitor (newspaper), 191n2

Christina (film), 61

"Christina" (song), 61

"The Church Around the Corner" (song), 188n22

Churchill, Frank, 92

Civilization (film), 36

Clark, Helen (Emma Johnson), 189n55

Clarke, Grant

"Am I Blue?" and, 33–34, *33*, *34*, 189n58

The Squall and, 189n58

Warner Bros. and, 63

Weary River and, 90

The Classical Hollywood Cinema (Bordwell), 167n3

classical music

popular songs and, 16, 32

radio broadcasts and, 20

in silent cinema, 35

as tax-free music, 48

The Clicquot Club Eskimos (radio program), 21, *22*, 174n36

Close Harmony (film), 7

The Cocoanuts (film), 183n44

Cohen, Harvey G., 108

Collins, Lottie, 132–33

Colman, Ronald, 143